TITLE II-A

Robert Hogan ❧ AFTER THE IRISH

RENAISSANCE ❧ A Critical History

of the Irish Drama since THE PLOUGH AND

THE STARS

THE UNIVERSITY OF MINNESOTA PRESS   MINNEAPOLIS

Library of Congress Catalog Card Number: 67-20595

Preface

THIS book is an informal critical account of Irish dramatic writing since about 1926 when Sean O'Casey cried with savagery and sadness, "Inishfallen, Fare Thee Well," and followed Shaw and Joyce and so many other Wild Geese into exile. Modern Irish writing before 1926 has been thoroughly documented by many people — by W. B. Yeats, George Moore, Lady Gregory, Lennox Robinson, Oliver Gogarty, and a host of scholars, critics, and biographers. Those early years, so aptly called the Irish Renaissance, saw a great flowering of literary activity. In 1898, Yeats, Moore, and Edward Martyn formed the Irish Literary Theatre which was in a few years to grow into the Abbey Theatre. In 1926, a group of patriotic ladies incited an Abbey audience to riot in protest against Sean O'Casey's play *The Plough and the Stars*, and very shortly afterwards the author left Ireland hardly ever to return. Between these two dates, the greatest poet, the greatest playwright, and the greatest novelist in the English-speaking world were all involved in the Irish Renaissance. Shaw the playwright did only touch the movement at longish intervals, and Joyce the novelist only stood half-sneering on its periphery, but Yeats the poet was in its very center. A Renaissance, however, is not one man, one Shakespeare, one towering mountain in the middle of a vast plain; and Yeats was surrounded by a host of men of genius and talent — by the prolific and fascinating George Moore, by the indomitable Lady Gregory, by the diffident genius John Synge and the even more diffident genius George Fitzmaurice, by those men of inimitable talent Padraic Colum, James Stephens, Seamus O'Kelly, Lennox Robinson, George Russell, T. C. Murray, Rutherford Mayne, St. John Ervine, and Lord Dunsany, by the masterly O'Casey, and by so many others that this preface would be inordinately longer if I merely listed them.

A few of these men, like Fitzmaurice and O'Kelly, have still not received their due, but in general the major writers and writings of the Irish Renaissance have made their impact upon the modern world. In view of how much has been written about Irish writing before 1926, it is all the more startling to discover how relatively little has been written about it since. Some new people, particularly the writers of fiction, have made themselves heard. Liam O'Flaherty, Sean O'Faolain, Frank O'Connor, Elizabeth Bowen, Flann O'Brien, Bryan MacMahon, and Brian Moore have all made reputations for themselves outside of Ireland. The poets, however, have been less fortunate. Patrick Kavanagh and Austin Clarke are still fairly obscure names outside of Ireland, and the better young poets, such as Thomas Kinsella, John Montague, and Richard Murphy, are only beginning to be heard. Only three dramatists, in the forty years since *The Plough and the Stars*, have really caused much stir outside of Ireland. The earliest, Paul Vincent Carroll, is now sunk into a kind of semi-obscurity; of the two more recent ones, Samuel Beckett rarely visits Ireland and is rarely concerned with it in his plays, and Brendan Behan, who died much too soon, wrote only two full-length plays.

Perhaps now, when the second generation of modern Irish writers is growing old, writing memoirs, and dying, we can get enough perspective to pose the question of "What happened to the Irish Renaissance?" I can think of three answers, all mutually contradictory.

The obvious answer is that the Irish Renaissance is with Yeats in his grave. The view that Yeats was the impelling force in modern Irish letters, that he was a kind of cultural yeast, and that he was, as O'Casey called him, "The Great Organizer," has been developed by many critics and has much to recommend it. Peter Kavanagh, in discussing Yeats's purely theatrical activities in his book *The Story of the Abbey Theatre*, credits the death of Yeats as being the main cause of the Abbey's alleged disintegration as a vital artistic force.

The second view is that the Irish Renaissance as a school with a coherent aesthetic never really existed anyhow. In this view, if Yeats was a leader, he was one like Robert Emmet whose small army melted away

behind him as he marched toward war. Certainly the three main founders of the Irish Literary Theatre — Yeats, Martyn, and Moore — had the
most disparate artistic views, and the early years of the theatre are mainly the story of various defections. William Boyle dropped out for moral
and personal reasons, and Padraic Colum dropped out for patriotic ones.
James Joyce wandered off to Europe, James Stephens to London, and
Lord Dunsany to Fairyland, while Francis Ledwidge was killed in the
war, and Pearse, Plunkett and MacDonagh were shot for inciting a revolution. AE was mainly interested in agricultural reform and a personal
mysticism, Douglas Hyde in the Gaelic League, and Padraic Ó Conaire
in rambling and drinking. In the sense of a homogeneous school, the Irish
Renaissance might be said never to have existed at all.

The third view, and the one that I most believe in, is that the Irish
Renaissance never really stopped, but has continued, in poetry, fiction
and particularly the drama, to pour out a dazzling succession of brilliant
works. There has been no one particular figure to don the mantle of
Yeats, of course. O'Casey remained in exile, the effective coalition of
O'Connor and O'Faolain broke up long ago, O'Flaherty became pretty
much of a recluse, Kavanagh is rather eccentric, and everybody else is
either teaching in an American college or denigrating his colleagues over
a glass of stout.

Of course, modern Irish writing has always been composed of a host
of implacable individuals each going his own individual way and each
constantly talking about, although not always to, the others. If the period
since 1926 has produced no new Yeats, Shaw, or Joyce, it has, however,
produced for such a small country an astonishing number of first-rate,
second-rate, and third-rate writers. Second- and third-rate hardly sound
like eulogistic terms, but I mean them in no pejorative sense. If Shakespeare and Sophocles are the overwhelming masters, and Ben Jonson and
Molière scarcely less fine, then we must have some terms to describe the
best work of writers like Congreve and Wilde, as well as the best work
of writers like Maugham and Priestley.

The Irish drama since 1926 has been lustily criticized by Irishmen as
a barren period, but it seems to me an excitingly rich one. How else but
rich could one describe a time in which flourished such playwrights as
Lennox Robinson, T. C. Murray, Brinsley MacNamara, George Shiels,
Louis D'Alton, Paul Vincent Carroll, Denis Johnston, Mary Manning,
Micheál Mac Liammóir, Michael Molloy, Walter Macken, Seamus
Byrne, John O'Donovan, Bryan MacMahon, Lady Longford, Brendan

Behan, Hugh Leonard, James Douglas, John B. Keane, and Brian Friel? This is hardly an exhaustive list of Irish dramatic talent, but many of the names on it remain little known outside of Ireland. The reason is not, I think, any lack of talent. For instance, just the last four names on the list — Leonard, Douglas, Keane, and Friel — can easily hold their own with any quartet of current playwrights one could mention from England, France, or America. The reason for the obscurity of Irish playwriting has really to do with the economics of the principal commercial stages of the world, in London, Paris, and New York. Even in this day of violent advertising, a play never really becomes known until it has been staged with some commercial success in one of these theatrical capitals. Only then will it usually reach print; only then will it be staged by the university and civic theatre groups; only then will it be anthologized by professors and canonized as a reputable part of modern literature.

Commercial theatre is primarily a business. Occasionally it is capable of producing vast profits, but more often it loses heartbreaking amounts of money. It is one of the riskiest businesses in the world. And now especially, when production costs have rocketed and when more and more theatres have disappeared, the commercial stage has become quite cautious. For the most part, it tries to reproduce its own successes, either in the form of downright imitation or in a musical version of a previously successful straight play. With such conditions, it has become ever more difficult for the individual, the original, the experimental, or the foreign to get a hearing. Such facts account, I think, for modern Irish playwriting being little known.

This book, then, is a critical introduction to about thirty or forty valuable playwrights who have worked in Ireland in the past forty years. I am not so sanguine as to think that my judgments of several hundred plays can be always accurate or adequate. But I do hope that the book may introduce to a broader audience the superb work of many fine writers and also may suggest that the brilliance of the Irish Renaissance has continued almost undimmed down to our own time.

⌘

This book has some omissions of which I am painfully conscious. I have been able to see on the stage only a small proportion of the plays discussed here, for some of them have not been recently revived. Also, I have not been able to read all of the plays by all of the writers I discuss.

One reason is that plays are not always published, and it often requires detective work to track down a manuscript. In most instances, my ignorance remains despite vigorous attempts to dispel it, but there are still a few writers whose work I shamefacedly admit that I know only by reputation. I should have talked about Maura Laverty and Elizabeth Connor. I should have talked about Robert Farren and Francis Stuart, about Lord Dunsany's late plays, about Myles na gCopaleen's *Faustus Kelly*, about — well, at any rate, to them and to all of those others whose work I have scanted or omitted or been stupid about, I can only plead the largeness of the task and promise some day to make amends.

To some extent, the emphasis in this book may seem curious. It might seem that Yeats, O'Casey, and Samuel Beckett should loom as more commanding figures than I have allowed them to. I have given O'Casey only a chapter, Yeats a small part of a chapter, and Beckett nothing at all. I might plead that several books and many articles have already been devoted to each man, but my real reason is that I wanted to give a picture of the recent Irish drama that would place the writers in a perspective appropriate to their importance and influence. Beckett's plays are not really Irish in subject matter, many of them were originally written in French, and their influence on Irish plays is, except for a few instances, tenuous or negligible. The later plays of Yeats are seldom performed, and the Abbey, in the era of Ernest Blythe, shows little influence of Yeats at all. Yeats's later plays have certainly aroused intense admiration recently in academic circles. However, this book intends a theatrical rather than a literary or an academic criticism, and so I have given Yeats what seems to me, perhaps heretically, his theatrical due. O'Casey's early plays are often performed and quite influential. Indeed, one can cite almost dozens of plays consciously or unconsciously indebted to *Juno and the Paycock*. But I have not discussed the plays of O'Casey's early or middle periods, for they have been frequently and fully discussed elsewhere. I have rather concentrated on the best plays of O'Casey's last period, even though they were either not produced in Ireland or were influential only in arousing a storm of invective and abuse. My reason is that these plays seem potentially O'Casey's most influential as they are certainly so far his least discussed. I have not considered the relation of O'Casey's politics to his plays, for it seems to me a minor issue. I have not discussed the important issue of O'Casey's later dialogue, for it would take a lengthy essay to do the subject justice. I have discussed what seemed to me the major issue — the basic nature of the plays themselves.

In writing this book, I have become pleasantly indebted to many people for many favors — for information, opinions, gossip, and fascinating conversation, for lending me manuscripts to produce or to publish or merely to read, for letting me sit in on rehearsals and productions, and for bed, food and drink — much drink. I should especially like to thank Rivers Carew of *The Dublin Magazine*, Hilton Edwards of the Gate Theatre, Andrew Flynn of Progress House publications, Dermot Guinan of the Author's Guild of Ireland, Seamus Kelly of the *Irish Times*, Shiela Lemon of the Peter Crouch Agency, Liam Miller of the Dolmen Press, Micheál Ó h Aodha of Radio Éireann, John and Dorothy Robbie of Greystones, Mrs. Mary F. Thompson of Belfast, Hubert Wilmot of the Belfast Arts Theatre, and the firm of Bernard Campbell, solicitors, of Belfast.

My thanks must go again to Ronald Ayling, one of the most knowledgeable commentators on O'Casey, for reading, judiciously criticizing, and not hugely liking much of the manuscript. And also to Sven Eric Molin for taking time off from his own labors on T. H. White to chase around Dublin for me, asking questions, running errands, and buying books. And particularly to my editor, Marcia Strout, at the University of Minnesota Press: go raibh céad maith agat!

And, of course, my chief debt is to the following group of greatly talented men, the playwrights who have given me so generously of their time, their assistance, their criticism, their manuscripts, and, I hope, their friendship: Seamus Byrne, Paul Vincent Carroll, Padraic Colum, Tom Coffey, Cyril Cusack, Seamus de Burca, James Douglas, Conor Farrington, Brian Friel, G. P. Gallivan, Denis Johnston, John B. Keane, Hugh Leonard, Lady Longford, Donagh MacDonagh, Walter Macken, Bryan MacMahon, Mary Manning, Michael J. Molloy, John O'Donovan, and Joseph Tomelty.

Portions of this book have appeared in somewhat different form in *Players Magazine*, *The Dublin Magazine*, *Drama Survey*, and *The Educational Theatre Journal*.

Finally, I am indebted to the University of California for a summer research fellowship which allowed me to spend another summer in Ireland and to my wife for the same reason.

ROBERT HOGAN

Davis, California
January, 1967

Table of Contents

Illustrations between pages 4 and 5

I THE REALISTIC DRAMA OF THE ABBEY

I

The Abbey
Shadow or Substance of a Theatre?

THE old, fire-gutted building in Abbey Street has been at last razed. A handsome, splendidly equipped new theatre has been constructed on the site, and the Abbey, after its fifteen year exile at the Queen's Theatre in Pearse Street, has finally returned home. Although some Abbey apologists have compared this activity to the phoenix rising from its ashes, it has seemed to many Dublin playgoers more like the ashes rising from a rather burnt-out phoenix. As Paul Vincent Carroll remarked, "I am not surprised the Abbey, Dublin, disappointed — it has degenerated, more or less, into an undistinguished repertory of sorts." [1] Or, as Sean O'Casey remarked, "It is nothing now to have a play on in the Abbey; to be among the things with far less life in them than the poor ghost of Petroushka." [2] And an English commentator reviewing the company's most recent visit to London said, "Whatever its past glories the Abbey is now no more than an indifferently talented provincial repertory theatre. It no longer deserves a place in the world's spotlight." [3]

Although this book is a criticism of modern Irish playwriting and not a history of the modern Dublin stage, it is impossible to avoid discussing the Abbey. No matter what its artistic merits, it is the national theatre and has still enormous influence on Irish playwriting. Certainly this influence has been somewhat pernicious, but the modern Irish drama has largely been written either by or in heated opposition to Abbey standards. To understand that drama, we must first understand the Abbey.

⚜

A theatre may probably be gauged in three ways — by the range and depth of the actors, by the imaginative level and technical skill of producer, designer, and technicians, and by the quality and variety of its plays. By two of these standards, the Abbey today is a pale carbon of what it once was.

At various times Abbey acting set a high standard. The fact is apparent in the distinguished roster of players who graduated to London, New York, and Hollywood. Among them — Dudley Digges, W. G. Fay, Sara Allgood, Maire O'Neill, Arthur Sinclair, J. M. Kerrigan, Barry Fitzgerald, Cyril Cusack, and Siobhan McKenna. Still, it is difficult to believe that such a disparate group graduated from a school of acting, or that there ever really was an Abbey school, in the same way that a theory and a school emerged from the Moscow Art Theatre.

As this legend about the Abbey school of acting persists so tenaciously, it might help us to understand Abbey acting today if we briefly examined Abbey acting of yesterday. This legend of a school arose when the group, then known as the Irish National Theatre Society, appeared in London in 1903, playing Yeats's *The Hour Glass, Kathleen Ni Houlihan*, and *The Pot of Broth*, Lady Gregory's *Twenty-Five*, and Fred Ryan's *The Laying of the Foundations*. Both plays and actors made considerable impact. Arthur Walkley described the acting in the *Times Literary Supplement* in this fashion: "As a rule they stand stockstill. The speaker of the moment is the only one who is allowed a little gesture. . . . When they do move it is without premeditation, at hap-hazard, even with a little natural clumsiness, as of people who are not conscious of being stared at in public." [4] The second notable characteristic of the early acting was the emphasis on diction. Both Yeats and Frank Fay had devoted much thought to stage speech, particularly to the speaking of verse. Yeats's theories tended to be impractical and a little weird, although he was a brilliant, if erratic, lecturer and reader of verse. Fay developed into an excellent verse speaker [5] and a very competent voice coach. The crux of his theory was the development of a purity and clarity of enunciation. In a fine article on Abbey acting, Andrew J. Stewart described this early diction:

4

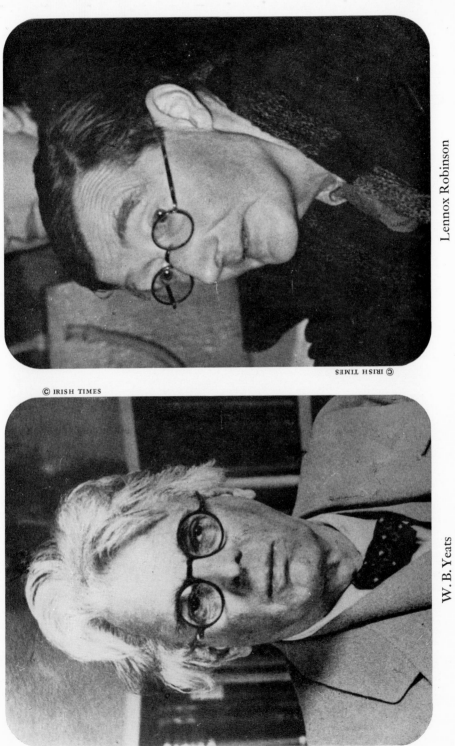

Lennox Robinson

W. B. Yeats

Lord Longford

Denis Johnston

Paul Vincent Carroll

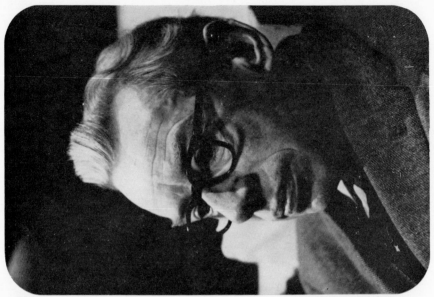

Donagh MacDonagh

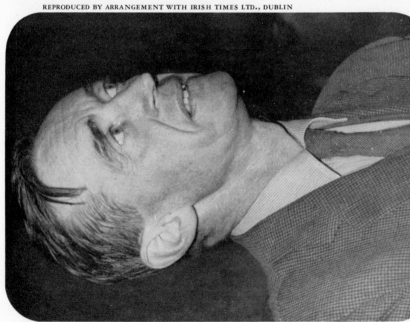

Michael J. Molloy

Joseph Tomelty

IRIS RADIO EIREANN — TELEFIS EIREANN

John O'Donovan

Bryan MacMahon

PHOTOGRAPHIC SERVICE, UNIVERSITY OF IOWA

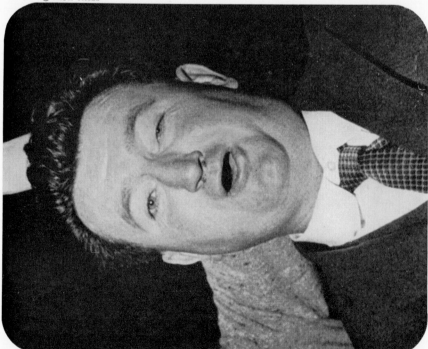

Brendan Behan

John B. Keane

Brian Friel

James Douglas

Tom Coffey

This past summer I saw Sara Allgood of the original company at the Rotunda in Dublin, in *The Cherry Orchard*. Her voice is deep, rich, flexible, and astonishingly beautiful. As she had studied under Frank Fay, the first voice teacher at the Abbey, I asked her after the play what he stressed when teaching voice production. "Frank Fay emphasized clearness of speech, strength without loudness, and particularly the greatest possible tone variety." U. Wright, who has been with the Abbey company since 1902, gave me additional information about Fay's methods. "He would make us sing A's and O's for hours, raising and lowering the key. He insisted on distinct final D's and T's. The ends of our sentences had to be well out. Sharp! He saw to it that we took breathing exercises." [6]

Simplicity of movement and clarity of diction, then, were what impressed the London critics in 1903 and what initiated the legend of an Abbey school. Two qualities may constitute a manner but hardly a school. A school is a complete approach to acting, a full and complex body of knowledge requiring for its mastery time and arduous application. These early actors were talented and well drilled in their parts, but they impressed chiefly by their novelty. The main Irish character the British stage had seen since Sir Lucius O'Trigger was the broth-of-a-bhoy stage Irishman of Boucicault. Also, Henry Irving and the other famous actor-managers were still at the height of their popularity, and these men represented the culmination of a complex tradition of acting which had been developing on British stages for two hundred years. This was a style which we would now call "theatrical"; by contrast the artless simplicity and patent sincerity of the Irish players was a refreshing shock. They had neither the technique nor the experience of the great players of the day, and the jaded critics were not comparing them with professional actors. From such a beginning, however, this story of an Abbey school has been built up.

The acting of the present company does not actually descend from that of the 1903 company. That simple style was singularly appropriate for the theatre's early plays, but a different type of play soon appeared. Most of the first plays, even when written in prose, sprang from a poetic impulse and were lyric in tone and diction. These plays soon became outweighed in the repertoire by realistic prose plays like Padraic Colum's *Broken Soil*, Lady Gregory's *Spreading the News*, and William Boyle's *The Building Fund*. These plays required the actor to hold the mirror up to nature, and portrayals were admired for being recognizable, even photographic, representations of Irish types.

5

Over the years, the bulk of Abbey plays has followed the realistic lead of Boyle and Lady Gregory. Some of these plays were superb, but in time many of them grew, like Boyle's own later plays, exaggerated, and this change caused changes in the acting. The realistic playing of comedy degenerated into a broadly farcical style, with nothing indigenously Irish about it except a brogue. As style, it is neither as broad nor as slick as that of a Brian Rix Whitehall farce, but like the Whitehall farce this "school" can hold only a rudimentary interest for the serious student.

For example, the chief comic actor at the Abbey after the departure of W. G. Fay was the inimitable Arthur Sinclair, and this is how Andrew E. Malone described his acting:

The company of which Arthur Sinclair was the dominating figure made the Abbey Theatre popular, but Sinclair, excellent though his acting very often was, reduced everything to the level of farce. How the audience laughed at Sinclair even in such plays as *The Shadow of the Glen* or *The Playboy of the Western World*! It has been said that Mrs. Patrick Campbell made of Yeats' *Deirdre* a *Second Mrs. Conchubhar*. With greater reason and justice it might be said that Arthur Sinclair made of the greatest tragedy the occasion of a laugh. That Sinclair could be a great tragic actor when he chose, his acting as Carden Tyrrel in *The Heather Field* stands as testimony, but he usually preferred to get a laugh. To Arthur Sinclair, perhaps more than to any other single individual, might be traced the decline of the Irish drama during the second decade of the Abbey Theatre's existence.[7]

When the theatre toured America in 1937, George Jean Nathan remarked that "lovely and musical speech aside, the present Abbey Theatre company has put the dub in Dublin. Not so long ago one of the finest acting organizations in the world, it is now a caricature of its former self." The main fault was over-playing, and the main offender was the theatre's chief comic actress. As Nathan said: "the Abbey company is obviously unable to control its fundamentally talented but personally over-cocky actress, Maureen Delany, and to prevent her from indulging in an outrageous overplaying, winking, snorting, and mugging that wreck any serious play she is in."[8] About the same time, Sean O'Faolain's *She Had To Do Something* was produced, and he described the production like this:

During rehearsal the producer worked like a nigger to tone down the exuberance of a body of actors accustomed to gutsy, uppercut, slash-and-bang, and even slightly vulgar drama, especially that kind of comedy. He succeeded admirably in holding them to a quiet key, and in rehearsals the play danced along nicely and lightly. Lo and behold, when the first night I beheld to my horror my *jeu d'esprit*, as I thought it, my frothy little piece of gaiety, turning minute by minute more and more into an Abbey farce, pointed plain as a signpost at every line to topical satire. Interested, I asked one of the actors why he had suddenly begun to play his part in that way, and his reply was illuminating: "It didn't seem to be going across," he said. "So I had to . . ." I forget his words but they amounted to — "I had to force the pace." Or, "I had to underline it" . . . By the third night gags had crept in. By the second week I could not even remember what kind of play I had tried to write.[9]

Another example of this degeneration may be traced in the career of the popular veteran actress Eileen Crowe, the widow of the great F. J. McCormick. In 1925, Holloway could describe her as: "the most promising of all the young actresses who trod the boards of the famous little theatre for many years past, and in many of her parts the spark of genius flashed in no uncertain way through her work. Despite the handicap of a rather hard and not very flexible voice, and at times, somewhat angular movements of body and arms, she surmounted her limitations in marvellous way."[10] He then remarked the wide range of roles she had played, both for the Abbey and the Dublin Drama League. In recent years, however, her acting has stayed pretty much within the range of the stock Abbey farce. Her current popularity does not stem from realizing the individuality of a role, but from repeating certain well-executed comic mannerisms. These mannerisms are not subtle, imaginative, or new, but the traditional ones of the farceur — the exaggerated double-take, the facial expression which stops just this side of mugging, and the over-all broadness of playing which stops just this side of slapstick. For example, consider her police sergeant's wife in John Ford's film *The Rising of the Moon*. There she spoke her lines with a broad stage Irishness and at the same time a sort of tongue-in-cheek wryness that indicated her awareness of the staginess. She acted in much the way that Maurice Evans acts Shaw — with an exaggerated artificiality coupled with an owlish gleam in the eye. Such playing has the actor both inside and outside of his part, and is a sophisticated matter requiring both technical accomplishment and no judgment in how that accomplishment should be used. In her less studied roles on the Abbey stage, Miss Crowe does the same thing, although reducing the owlishness and broadening her part to play for every easy laugh. Such acting really reduces to a game what should be raised to an art.

I am not suggesting that Abbey acting is invariably bad. On the contrary, the theatre at practically every point in its history has been blessed with good players and sometimes with great ones. Sara Allgood, F. J. McCormick, and Barry Fitzgerald, for instance, were three of the great players of our time. And certainly today there are fine actors in the company; but it is still true that many of the best recent actors leave. Cusack, McKenna, Macken, Marie Kean, and Ray McAnally are all cases in point. And the reason for their departure, as Cusack once remarked in the *Irish Times*, was not merely monetary, but artistic.

It is difficult for great acting to flourish in this atmosphere of playing for the easy laugh. Certain gestures, certain types of reactions, and certain inflections of the voice have by long practice proven trustworthy in evoking this "brainless, bovine laughter," as one critic called it, and the Abbey players have honed the craft of laugh-getting to — well, curiously enough, they have not honed it to perfection, despite all their practice.

For instance, on July 13, 1965, the theatre first played a farce called *The Pilgrim's Mother* by the Belfast writer Arnold Hill. This was a competent and thoroughly unremarkable fists-across-the-sea piece whose main merit was that it might attract some summer transpontine tourists. Its thinness requires a driving pace and a great deal of farcical "business," the slickly accomplished kind of playing that Brian Rix's company does in London. The Abbey players were decidedly spotty. The two female American roles were poorly played, and in the case of Kathleen Barrington, whose voice wavered from pseudo-deep-South to pseudo-New-Yorkese, just atrociously so. The good actor Philip O'Flynn could manage a Stubby Kaye New Yorkish type with only occasional lapses into Irish brogue, but Angela Newman in her caricature of the woman from the Big House seems rapidly to be displacing Eileen Crowe as the most mannered Abbey actress. Patrick Layde did a nice Colonel Blimp, but the revealing moment of the evening came when Harry Brogan in the perfectly straight role of the village priest made his entrance and was greeted by a ripple of expectant laughter before he had said a word. It will be hard for a director to undo the expectation of caricature that a couple of decades of broad playing has established.

The most damning charge against the theatre is that there is now a typical Abbey play. I think this charge is exaggerated, but Denis Donoghue put it well when he said:

For many years now the Abbey has been living and partly living upon a dishonest stock of Abbey "characters," Abbey gestures, Abbey idioms, Abbey coat-trailing: the dramatists currently sponsored do not try to write plays, they try to write Abbey plays; they fabricate scenes and situations capable of being processed into the famous Abbey "style." The actor who sums up these procedures most revealingly is Harry Brogan, to whom every character is Joxer. The most cunning Abbey dramatist is John McCann.[11]

John McCann, who recently served a term as Lord Mayor of Dublin, is one of the most prolific and popular of recent Abbey dramatists. Despite two quite good plays,[12] the bulk of his work is about on the literary level of the television *Peyton Place* or its Irish equivalent *The Riordans*. His various sagas of the Kelly family well illustrate his unvarying formula. Plays like *Twenty Years A-Wooing, Blood Is Thicker Than Water, Give Me a Bed of Roses, It Can't Go On Forever, Put a Beggar on Horseback*, and *A Jew Called Sammy* are all cut from the same cloth. They present a recognizable picture of lower-middle-class Dublin families, stock comic characterization, topical allusions, a plot revolving usually around money, a happy ending, and a platitudinous theme. Really, McCann might be called the George Lillo of the Irish drama, for he is a staunch supporter of such bourgeois verities as Honesty Is the Best Policy, Love Conquers All, and Business Is Business. In *A Jew Called Sammy*, for instance, he makes the points that virtue is rewarded, that cooperation in business (you pat my back, and I'll pat yours) is the essence of morality, that college students are basically good citizens but must be persuaded to shave off their beards, and that Jews are nice fellows, especially if they will confine their attentions to offstage characters named Rachel. McCann is no doubt on the side of the gods, but very naive gods they are.

One reason for the rise of such formula plays sprang, according to Dorothy Macardle, from the dangers of the repertory system:

In order to change their programme every week the company resorted to frequent revivals at short intervals and to the revival of those plays which they could perform with most facility. Their range became restricted; their excursions from the cottage interior rarely led them farther than to a tenement room, a lodging-house bedroom or a "parlour" in "the suburban grove," and the dramatists followed suit. For years we have seen plays performed which, quite obviously, have been written, not only for the Abbey Theatre, but for the Abbey players — for this actor's lift of an eyebrow and that actress's toss of the chin — and even for the Abbey property-room. I have heard the property man, in a tone of indignant protest, rebuking a new author who had made a demand considered exorbitant — "a mug with a black pig on it" was the direction in the script. The author was categorically instructed as to what was and what was not in the property-room, "So that another time you won't write ad-lib." [13]

When the theatre was initiated there was no single formula for Abbey drama, but several quite different impulses. This fact made for some hectic disagreement, but exciting theatre. Such healthy eclecticism did not last long after it became clear that the largest audiences appeared for the realistic plays of Padraic Colum, Lady Gregory, and William Boyle.

Colum, before he seceded from the theatre with a group of other young patriots, wrote for it three realistic plays, and the last, *Thomas Muskerry*, was a masterpiece. Not long after his break, Colum moved to America and has not been closely connected with a theatre since. The plays he has subsequently written — *Mogu of the Desert, The Grasshopper, Balloon*, and *Moytura* — tend to be poetic and mildly experimental. And, of course, only one has been done by the Abbey.

Lady Gregory has been overshadowed by Synge and Yeats, and is usually pigeonholed as a writer of simple peasant comedies. She also wrote, though, one brilliant short tragedy, several highly theatrical fantasies, and some effective histories and pantomimes as well as translations and adaptations. Despite this surprising range in an elderly lady, it was the comedies, like *Spreading the News* and *Hyacinth Halvey*, that drew people to the theatre in the early days. Less ostentatiously written than the plays of Yeats, Synge, or O'Casey, her plays are still impelled by a similar lyrical impulse of speech. They were not, however, at first greatly valued for their dialogue, which was actually thought a bit eccentric, but for the humor of their stories and the realism of their characterization. These two qualities in her work are a bridge to what has been called the Abbey play.

William Boyle is forgotten today and was never much known outside of Ireland. But of the hundreds of plays the Abbey has produced, the spiritual ancestor of most was not Yeats or Synge or O'Casey but Boyle. He wrote five comedies for the Abbey: *The Building Fund*, his best, produced in 1905; *The Eloquent Dempsy*, his most popular, and *The Mineral Workers*, both produced in 1906; *Family Failing*, produced in 1912; and *Nic*, produced in 1916. The first three were very successful, and their constant revival was a mainstay of the Abbey repertoire in the early years. In 1907, the *Playboy* riots seriously damaged the theatre's attendance — much of that damage caused by Boyle's withdrawing his plays in protest against *The Playboy*. Finally, Yeats and Lady Gregory lured him back into the fold, and for years afterward, almost up to the time of O'Casey, a Boyle play was revived each season.

Except for *The Building Fund*, Boyle's plays are negligible as literature, but they were effective theatre. His plots were moderately complicated, but clearly worked out. His humorous characters were more recognizable Irish types than Synge's. They were accurately, if not deeply observed; the comic politician of *The Eloquent Dempsy*, for example, is a twister who has not disappeared from Irish politics. Perhaps the key to Boyle's development might be suggested by the fact that his Jeremiah Dempsy became Arthur Sinclair's favorite role after that excellent actor had debased his talents in the pursuit of laughter. Somewhere in his huge diary, Joseph Holloway wrote that Sinclair judged the effectiveness of his performance of Dempsy by counting the laughs on successive nights. This same tendency to broadness grew more apparent in each of Boyle's subsequent plays. *The Building Fund* stood well within the boundaries of comedy, but each later play grew more and more farcical.

The popularity of Boyle over Yeats, Synge, and even Lady Gregory was the triumph of entertainment over art. Still, his realistic comedies and farces created an audience, whereas the lyric plays of Yeats and the grotesque comedies of Synge drove people away. In consequence, more plays like Boyle's were written and produced, which in turn began to deflect the theatre from experimentation and from poetry.

Although its apologists have always denied that the Abbey was becoming the House of Boyle, a continuing charge against the theatre, from its earliest years, has been that it produced much trivial work and rejected much that was excellent. Lennox Robinson, long one of the theatre's directors, believed there was little to this charge. Writing in 1951, he said, "In all these years the Directors had made surprisingly few mistakes in their choice of plays and players. The rejections of *John Bull's Other Island* and of Sean O'Casey's *The Silver Tassie* were doubtless errors of judgment, but in both cases subsequent productions made belated amends." [14] Ernest Blythe, the present managing director, writing in 1964, unequivocally agreed:

Obviously it could well happen that the Abbey might fail to see the worth of an outstanding script submitted to it. It is safe to say, however, that it has not done so as yet, though in two or three cases an important play, which was ultimately performed in the Abbey, was, for varying reasons, returned to its author when first submitted. . . . The only case in which the Abbey definitely failed to produced a play of high merit which had been submitted to it, was that of Denis Johnston's satirical fantasy, *The Old Lady Says "No!"* Actually the quality of the play was appreciated, but it required a style of production outside the range of the Abbey producer of the time. It was returned to the author; but the Abbey gave a subsidy to Messrs Edwards and Mac Liammóir to enable them to produce it in the Peacock Theatre in which their newly-founded Gate Theatre was then operating.[15]

Nevertheless, this apology is too sweeping, for there are many instances of the Abbey producing poor plays and rejecting good ones. Synge himself wrote that *The Tinker's Wedding* was not to be played, "as they say it is too immoral for Dublin." [16] And, indeed, the play was not done in Dublin until the 1950's, and then not by the Abbey. By common consent, one of the most brilliant writers ever staged at the Abbey was George Fitzmaurice, whose *The Country Dressmaker* of 1907 was frequently performed in the early days. Fitzmaurice the Abbey most definitely failed to encourage, and, as we shall see, some of his most masterly work is still unstaged.

Since 1926, there are numerous instances of the theatre rejecting or ignoring meritorious work. The most publicized case was O'Casey's *The Silver Tassie*, a play which Allardyce Nicoll thought by itself justified the movement of Expressionism. The Abbey did make "belated amends" by staging the play, but one of its directors, Brinsley MacNamara, resigned in protest. Other than the *Tassie*, the Abbey in all of the years following O'Casey's departure from Ireland staged only a couple of his one-acts. In 1957, before O'Casey banned professional productions of his plays in Ireland, the American critic Henry Hewes asked Ernest Blythe why the Abbey preferred to produce popular melodramas instead of O'Casey's unproduced recent work. He received this curious answer: "While O'Casey's later plays may be better than most of the ones we do, audiences here expect more from O'Casey and would be disappointed to find his later plays not as good as 'Juno and the Paycock' or 'The Plough and the Stars.' But they expect less from other writers." [17] In recent years, one director offered to stage O'Casey's entire canon if the author would withdraw his ban. Of course, in the 1960's, O'Casey's star had begun to shine again, and, although he made no reply to the offer, he might well have paraphrased Dr. Johnson's letter to Chesterfield: "Is not a Theatre Director, my lord, one who looks with unconcern on a man struggling for life in the water, and, when he has reached ground, encumbers him with help?"

In the 1920's and 1930's, the Gate Theatre was quite diligent in rescuing Abbey rejections. Their big coup was in securing the early work of Denis Johnston, but there were many similar instances. When T. C. Murray's *A Flutter of Wings* was rejected by the Abbey, Hilton Edwards was immediately on the telephone to ask for the play. The Gate staged Colum's *Mogu of the Desert* as well as Austin Clarke's first play *The Hunger Demon*. Two of the Gate's biggest successes were the Abbey rejections *Marrowbone Lane* by Dr. Robert Collis and *Juggernaut* by David Sears. Several of the more "daring" plays of the Abbey's Lennox Robinson were staged at the Gate, and it was the Gate who invited Walter Starkie to be on its board of directors after the Abbey had pushed Dr. Starkie off its own board.

The most significant Abbey discovery of the 1930's was Paul Vincent Carroll, who once in a curtain speech at the theatre promised to submit all of his future plays first to it. However, the theatre alienated Carroll by a tactless and foolish rejection of *The White Steed* which went on to win the New York Drama Critics Circle award for the best foreign play of 1939.

The Abbey's stock answer to the frequent criticisms of the poverty of its recent repertoire is that no good plays have been submitted. However, Seamus Kelly, the astringent drama critic of *The Irish Times*, has written: "Good plays are not scarce. In very recent times small theatre groups in Dublin have produced three which should have demanded production by the Abbey, and would, one feels confident, have got Abbey production in Yeats's time. They were *The Purple Path to the Poppy Fields* by Maurice Meldon; *The Quare Fellow* by Brendan Behan; and *Waiting for Godot* by the Dubliner Samuel Beckett. All three were successful."[18] The Abbey again made "belated amends," to Behan at least, by staging *The Quare Fellow*, but why did they not stage it in its first, Gaelic version? And why did they not stage it until it had become famous? *The Hostage*, because of its "daring," is in little danger of being performed at the Abbey, but some attempt might have been made to secure Behan's three charming one-acts which John Molloy excellently did at the Gate.

The theatre has rejected work of one of the best dramatists since Behan, John B. Keane. It made "belated amends" by staging *Hut 42*, but only after *Sive* had become one of the most produced plays in Ireland and after half a dozen other Keane plays had been staged throughout Ireland, as well as in England and the United States.

The fact is that belated amends are not enough and that some of Ireland's finest dramatists have been either discouraged or ignored by the Abbey. One could perhaps defend rejecting O'Casey or Carroll if one were constantly staging premieres of writers like Shaw. That defense is rather flimsy when one is staging John McCann.

Technically, the quality of Abbey productions is better now than it ever was. The early plays, produced in the ramshackle hall in Camden Street, the Antient Concert Rooms, the Molesworth Hall, or the Abbey itself, were done with great simplicity. W. G. Fay was a more than competent director, and good work was done by Norreys Connell and A. Patrick Wilson. Arthur Shields and Lennox Robinson were apparently somewhat erratic, but O'Casey had a high opinion of Robinson as a director. Synge and Lady Gregory were observed by Holloway to be unobtrusively effective in handling actors, and Yeats, although he must have been fascinating, was apparently hopelessly bad.

Until her recent retirement, Ria Mooney staged many of the latter-day plays. She was a woman of much experience and somewhat receptive to dramatic experiment. When I asked her, once, if her job at the Abbey was exciting, she replied, "No, there's nothing to do with those plays. One's just like another. You rack your mind trying to think of something new, but it boils down to last week you put the door over here, so now you'll put it over there." Still, Miss Mooney did not escape the Abbey atmosphere; every play I saw her put on was calculated to arouse as much broad laughter as possible. Her direction stressed the "Abbeyness" of plays rather than whatever originality they possessed. Ulick O'Connor, in a persuasive apologia for the Abbey, remarked:

. . . laxness on the resident producer's part has allowed the actors to play down to the audience. Sometimes they play for laughs like music hall comedians, buying guffaws cheaply from the all-too-willing gathering. Lack of attention to the mechanics of acting, especially vocal production, has led voices, so that in the hands of the present producer they are quite incapable of doing a verse play. There is plenty of talent in the present Abbey. But the producer has allowed performances to go forward that would disgrace a convent school.[19]

The Abbey was never notable for its staging, lighting, or costuming. The depthless stage of the old building was a great hindrance, as was the constant shortness of cash. Still, some steps were taken toward experiment. Yeats introduced the Gordon Craig screens, Robert Gregory made some early experiments with lighting, and even Miss Horniman was once drawn in to design costumes. In later years, Yeats founded a school of ballet at the Abbey, and his own later plays posed problems of staging not to be solved by the methods adequate for *Mountain Dew* and *Boyd's Shop*. The theatre's current staging of realistic plays is painstaking and precise; the drawing rooms and farm kitchens are admirably done. There have even been a few mildly stylized jobs.

The responsibility for what the theatre has become lies mainly with its board of directors. Yeats, Synge, and Lady Gregory — the early directors — certainly had critical faults and lapses, but they always put the artistic merit of a play first. However, in 1925 the theatre received a government subsidy, and the new board of directors included Yeats, Lady Gregory, Lennox Robinson, and the first government representative, George O'Brien. O'Brien was a conscientious man who disclaimed critical ability or knowledge of the stage. His attitude toward his job is shown by this conversation from Holloway's journal for October 12, 1925:

I was home with George O'Brien, the Director of the theatre appointed by the Directors to see that the grant is properly used. He has to read and approve of the theatre's new plays, and just got one of O'Casey's pieces to pass judgment upon and did so by deleting many mentions of Christ and bad words. He thinks it is a fine play and likely to be very popular. . . . Then he got Robinson's play, *The White Blackbird*, to pass judgment on, and though he saw the nasty undercurrent and the suggestion of incest, he didn't like to turn it down for fear it might be said that the government was interfering unduly with the liberty of the theatre — though in fear and trembling at what might be the result. He wouldn't like a row or for instance the Catholic Truth Society to march with banners up and down outside the theatre, or rows like *The Playboy*.[20]

O'Brien's timidity is also reflected in *Lady Gregory's Journals*, wherein she relates how strenuously he objected to much of the language of *The Plough and the Stars*, demanding and getting a number of excisions. Yeats staunchly defended O'Casey's language, but still the addition of a government representative to the theatre's board was the entering wedge for Philistinism. As Paul Smith put it:

This hankering after genteelness and political respectability was not the intention of the early directors of the Abbey. They wanted an art theatre, not a commercial theatre nor a political soapbox. It was their avowed determination to chase the "stage-Irish scarecrow" actor out of theatres everywhere. By the 1940s the Abbey did chase out the red-headed, beady-eyed, flat-nosed, freckled and crafty gombeen dressed in a tight-fitting, short-sleeved and trousered suit of large checks and twirling a shillelagh; but, alas! it replaced him with a bowler-hatted, whey-faced, crafty and provincial civil servant dressed in a tight-fitting, short-sleeved and trousered suit of black.[21]

Although the civil servant was now on the board of directors, there were some efforts to stem the tide. O'Brien was shortly replaced by Walter Starkie, a Trinity College don and author of, among many other things, a good book on Pirandello. In 1935, the board was further strengthened by the addition of F. R. Higgins the poet, Brinsley MacNamara the playwright, and Frank O'Connor the short-story writer. In the same year, however, Ernest Blythe, the politician who as minister of finance for the Free State had engineered the subsidy, was also appointed. MacNamara soon resigned in vehement protest against the staging of *The Silver Tassie*. In 1939, Yeats died, and then Starkie and O'Connor were maneuvered off the board. In the early 1940's, Higgins died, and Robinson alone remained of the old members. The recent additions to the board, men such as Robert Farren the poet and Gabriel Fallon the journalist, did little to stem the influence of the managing director, Blythe. The bowler-hatted civil servant had taken over with a vengeance, and the art theatre was nearly submerged. Donat O'Donnell put it well: "Ireland, like Germany and Russia, has always been much afflicted with people who were wildly interested in the idea of culture in general, as a sort of catalyst to nationalism, but quite indifferent to any particular play or poem. The personality and prestige of Yeats could keep these little folk in check, but now, since his death, they are all over the place." [22] For years Blythe maintained an impressive stolidity in the face of constant attacks on his policy. Knowing the value of dignified silence, he has ridden out storm after storm with massive imperturbability — or, as Seamus Kelly less reverently put it, "he's the cutest layer-low and sayer-nuffin since Brer Rabbit." And Blythe himself remarked on the Third Programme a few years ago, "I'm a politician, and I have a thick skin, so I don't give a damn what they say about me — not one damn!" [23]

However, as water can finally wear away even a granite pre-Celtic dolmen (to which he has also been compared), so criticism has finally worn away Mr. Blythe, at least to the extent that he has published a pamphlet called *The Abbey Theatre* which meets all of the important criticisms raised against his policy over the years. I myself am not an apologist for Blythe; I think his directorship is largely responsible for the theatre's deterioration. But some criticisms of his policy have been motivated by those typically Dublinish qualities of spleen and envy, and the pamphlet makes clear that there are points in his favor.

He did engineer the government subsidy, and he has helped to increase that subsidy until it is now ten times what it once was. He also kept the Abbey going in its long, commercially difficult exile in Pearse Street; when he talks of the commercial necessities of the theatre he knows more what he is talking about than do most of his critics. Under his directorship, the Abbey really has become an established national theatre; the new building in Abbey Street, besides being a hope for the Irish drama of the future, is also a memorial to Blythe's patience and tenacity.

To see what direction the theatre has taken since Yeats's death, one must know Blythe's conception of his task. In the first paragraph of his pamphlet, he writes:

If the strength and weakness, the achievements and shortcomings of the Abbey Theatre are to be correctly gauged, it is necessary to bear in mind the over-riding purpose of the movement which brought it into being. That purpose was not the establishment of a cosmopolitan Arts Theatre. Neither was it to bring to Dublin the works of outstanding foreign dramatists nor to exploit public interest in stage or screen celebrities. It was to preserve and strengthen Ireland's national individuality by fostering the growth, both in Irish and in English, of a distinctively Irish drama.[24]

As a general statement of policy, this would probably have been acceptable to Yeats and Lady Gregory, but Blythe means by it something which the founders would have thought too narrow. According to him, the theatre was born from "a great awakening of patriotic feeling which took place in Ireland towards the end of the nineteenth century" and by "the effect of the work for the preservation and restoration of the Irish language which had been done by the Gaelic League."[25] Though some of the early actors and writers were drawn into the movement mainly for patriotic reasons, Yeats, Synge, and the Fay brothers were hardly patriots first and artists second. And to assert, as does Blythe, that George Moore was "a strong Nationalist like the others," is tantamount to confessing total ignorance of George Moore. Yeats himself did not hesitate to reject Colum's patriotic play *The Saxon Shilling* when he thought it bad art, nor did he hesitate to keep *The Playboy* on the boards when the patriots were condemning it as a libel against Ireland. When a later group of patriots denounced *The Plough and the Stars*, it was Yeats who leapt to defend the play as a work of art. In 1934, the United Irish-American Societies of New York and Fianna Fail, Inc., of New York objected to the Abbey's intention of playing Synge and O'Casey on their impending American tour. Consequently, De Valera said in the Dail that he had "made representations to the Directors regarding the type of plays produced in the United States," and for several months pressure was kept up on the theatre both indirectly and in De Valera's *Irish Press*. Again, it was Yeats who stoutly resisted the government censorship. Yeats had his failures of judgment, but his main criteria were always aesthetic. Yeats emphasized the phrase "National Theatre" on the second word and Blythe emphasizes it on the first.

Strong evidence to support this point is Blythe's emphasis on plays in Irish. Yeats and Lady Gregory staged plays in Irish a few times, but they never considered the theatre as an adjunct of the language revival. When the company was playing in the Queen's, drama in Irish had to be confined to one-act plays which followed the main program and to a pantomime running for five or six weeks at Christmas. Even so, Irish was to be heard, Blythe estimates, "on about a hundred and twenty nights per annum." Through Blythe's efforts, the present company is, except for a few old stagers, bilingual. In answer to the charge that this policy has lost the theatre some good actors, Blythe replies that the Abbey has helped promising non-Irish-speaking actors "to spend a period in an Irish-speaking district."

Although Blythe does not quite say it, one gets the feeling that he is looking forward to a day when it will be possible to have a totally Irish-speaking theatre in a totally Irish-speaking country. Really, the Irish language is, in Ireland, a dead issue kept in a semblance of life by a handful of elderly political men. The language revival was concurrent with and connected to the political revival and the literary revival, but the language revival has essentially failed. Seventy years of intensive effort by devoted people have created no nation of Irish speakers. The native-speaking districts have continued to dwindle, and the children who must take Irish in the schools do not really learn it and almost never have to use it. In the almost seventy years since the production of Douglas

Hyde's *Casadh an tSúgáin*, there is still no repertoire of plays in Irish. Even Blythe has admitted that "The majority of the plays to be performed in Irish will have to be translations of European classics or of contemporary successes." [26]

Nevertheless, he believes "that the continued existence of the Irish nation, as a community with coherence and a character of its own, can be ensured only by saving the ancestral language and by thus giving the country the possibility of retaining a vigorous and distinctive living culture and making its unique individual contribution to world thought and progress." This seems shortsighted and unrealistic, for there is no question of the uniquely Irish character of *The Rising of the Moon*, *The Playboy*, or *The Plough and the Stars*. They are quite as Irish as *Casadh an tSúgáin* and considerably more so than any of the lowbrow Gaelic pantomimes.

Blythe really wants to use the Abbey for an untheatrical purpose. He remarks, "in what it can do for the Irish language in the years ahead the Abbey Theatre will have an opportunity of outdoing the influence it exerted in its early days." Basically, it is this attitude that keeps Blythe from being a good director for the theatre. When a theatre becomes anything other than a theatre, when it becomes a podium for propaganda, or a political football, or a weapon in a language revival, it then becomes something less than a theatre. It loses its artistic honesty. It loses its character.

There is a tendency when writing of the Abbey to fall into hyperbolic condemnation. Perhaps this is so because criticism is carried on in Ireland more like warfare than like reasoned discourse. Or perhaps it is that one expects so much from the Abbey. It is true that under Blythe's direction the theatre has become the right wing — and sometimes the reactionary right wing — of the Irish theatre. Yet it has turned up over the years a much larger number of fine plays than the world outside of Ireland knows. Most of those plays have been realistic, whereas much of what is vital in the Irish drama since 1926 has been written in opposition to Abbey realism. Still, the Abbey is by no means a dead force, and recently there have been some symptoms of a genuinely increased vitality.

Early in 1965, an impressive group of Irish intellectuals was given thirty shares each in the theatre and the function of advising the directors. What this advisory group may accomplish can hardly appear immediately; there has already been some criticism about their ineffectiveness. A couple of these men whom I have chatted with, however, are quite sanguine about what they may accomplish; one described the directors appearing at meetings as "five frightened men." To my mind, the addition of these advisers is eminently healthy. The leadership of the theatre has been too long a closed corporation. New minds, new ideas, and a freer atmosphere for debate may be what, in the long run, the Abbey needs for its total rejuvenation.

Probably at no time in the last forty years has the future of the theatre looked brighter. The Abbey is home again. It has an excellent building tailored to its needs. It has a government subsidy which, although not large enough, would have dazzled Yeats and Lady Gregory. It has a company which, despite faults of style, is experienced, competent, and in one or two cases almost brilliant. It has, as we shall see, a reservoir of writing talent in Ireland equal to any anywhere. If its leadership were bold, independent, and adventurous (and the theatre is, as one dramatist recently remarked, becoming deStalinized), nothing could keep it from surpassing its own past and from becoming again one of the first theatres of the world.[27]

2

The Abbey Dramatists: 1926–1945

THE first twenty years after O'Casey's departure are usually considered barren ones for the Abbey; a favorite amusement of the Dublin literati has been to revile the poverty of the company's repertoire. The witty savagery of this continuing onslaught may have risen partly from the Irish climate which seems conducive to spleen, partly from the theatre's occasional improbable standards of excellence, and partly from a bored irritation with plays which, despite their frequent merit, often resembled each other.

Actually, that resemblance was sometimes more apparent than real. It seemed real because of the actors' unvaryingly broad manner of playing. A sophisticated comedy by Lennox Robinson and a dour drama by George Shiels were both likely to come across the footlights as broad farce. When Valentin Iremonger and Roger McHugh protested from the audience in November, 1947, they were protesting the playing rather than the plays. If there were no new plays to generate riots in the theatre, there were plenty of good, sound, new plays. These years saw some of the strongest work of Yeats, Robinson, MacNamara, T. C. Murray, Rutherford Mayne, and St. John Ervine. George Shiels poured forth a steady flow of increasingly wry plays that grew ever farther away from the broad buffooneries that had made his reputation. Some fascinating new talents appeared: Paul Vincent Carroll, Teresa Deevy, Jack B. Yeats, Frank O'Connor, Sean O'Faolain, and Louis D'Alton, to mention only the best. Among them, these worthy writers gave about seventy-five new plays to the Abbey, which would have made an enviable reputation for a less famous theatre.

꿥

Lennox Robinson's first play, *The Clancy Name*, was produced by the Abbey on October 8, 1908, when Robinson was in his early twenties. Between that October day and the other October day on which he died fifty years later his association with the theatre was almost unbroken. He was its manager, one of its best directors, a member of its board, and one of its most prolific writers. The number of his plays and the frequency of their revival probably put him on a par with George Shiels in his influence on the style of the modern Abbey drama.

Yet Robinson's work is not all of a piece, and he cannot be pigeonholed as a prototypical Abbey dramatist. He could turn out a genial comedy or a thoughtful drama, each an unexceptionably conventional piece of Abbey realism, differing from dozens of others only by greater facility of technique. But Robinson was a civilized and urbane man whose vision stretched beyond the Abbey and beyond Ireland. Impressed by the technical innovations and probing psychology of Strindberg and Pirandello and O'Neill, he was not always content with stage morality or conventional realism.

In general, it can be said that Robinson wrote four kinds of plays: conventional popular comedies, thoughtful realistic dramas, excursions into experiment and satire, and excursions into psychology and morals. The first two categories contain most of his popular, better-known plays, but not his most interesting ones.

His most popular and still very adroit comedy is *The Whiteheaded Boy*, written early in his career in 1916. The notable later comedies are *The Far Off Hills* (first presented on October 22, 1928), *Is Life Worth Living?* (first performed under the title of *Drama at Inish* on February 6, 1933), and *The Lucky Finger* (first presented at Bowling Green University and then on August 23, 1948, at the Abbey). *The Far Off Hills* was quite popular, but both it and *The Lucky Finger* were only traditional, lightweight comedies which would pleasantly amuse without ruffling anyone's composure. *Is Life Worth Living?* is set at Inish, a small seaside resort which Robinson used as the locale for three later plays. A group of third-rate actors, the Hector De La Mare Repertory Company, has been hired to stimulate the summer tourist trade, but the company performs only somber, brooding tragedies by Strindberg, Ibsen, and Tolstoy. The effect on the townspeople is remarkable: they lose their comfortable placidity and become intense and gloomy. There are attempted suicides and murders, a case of arson, and the alarming instance of a mousy politician who speaks up in the Dail for the first time to cast a deciding vote that forces the government to go to the country. He has been impressed by *An Enemy of the People*.

The dialogue arises believably from the absurdity of the situation, but often attains such delicious insanities as this:

MICHAEL: . . . did you hear the terrible thing that's after happening to Jim Clancy?
ANNIE: No, what is it?
MICHAEL: Threw himself off the end of the pier. . . .
ANNIE: Was he drowned dead?
MICHAEL: No, ma'am. Bruised. The tide was out.

Robinson avoids easy buffoonery, however, by some realistic restraint. His actors, Hector and Constance Constantia, must have been a temptation to draw broadly. By treating them as people, however, he gains two charmingly convincing character studies of aging, down-at-the-heel troupers. One almost has to look back to *Trelawney of the Wells* to find something as good.

Robinson's main conventional serious dramas in our period were *The Big House* (performed on September 6, 1926), *Killycreggs in Twilight* (April 19, 1937), and *Bird's Nest* (September 12, 1938). *The Big House*, which has none of the comic exaggeration often associated with the Abbey, has a theme with an enduring pertinence for Ireland. His Ascendancy family has a divided allegiance to England and to Ireland. Two sons die in the First World War, and despite years of public service the father and daughter remain subtly apart from the Catholic Irish. Both have tried to lessen this distance, but their house is still burnt by Republicans as a political reprisal, and the old people remove to England. Kate, however, decides to rebuild, having been finally convinced that Ireland is her country just as much as that of the Catholic Irish. In the post-Treaty days when the Anglo-Irish were losing much of their influence, this point needed to be vigorously made. Probably it needs to be repeated today.

Michael J. O'Neill, in his useful book on Robinson, remarks that the play slips into melodrama. Apparently he is criticizing the ghost of Ulick

Alcock, the dead brother who loves Ballydonal House. The theatre, however, demands theatrical measures; on that ground the ghost seems effective in consolidating the theme and also a pleasant divergence from total realism. Actually, the period between 1918 and 1923 might have called forth much more melodrama than Robinson wrote in. If one compares *The Big House* with Lord Longford's ghostless but much more melodramatic *Ascendancy*, one may see how thoughtful and civilized Robinson's play is.

Killycreggs in Twilight is also a conventional problem play, but its theme interestingly reverses that of *The Big House*. The heroine, Judith de Lury, is what Kate Alcock might have become after twenty years of scrimping and toiling to preserve the Big House. Indeed, Judith says: "There's no room in Ireland now for places like Killycreggs, for de Lurys and their like lounging and fishing and shooting. I wish we'd been burned out in the Troubles; I wish all our sort had been burned out. I wouldn't have behaved like that fool-girl in the play, *The Big House*. I would never have rebuilt Killycreggs, I'd have thanked God to be quit of it." In the earlier play, Robinson stressed the need for the Anglo-Irish to preserve their immiscible identity. Here, Judith marries below her class, and Robinson is saying that the old distinctions are meaningless and are quickly being extinguished. He spends much of the play attacking the Anglo-Irish culture which he personifies by "the de Lury charm," an enervating quality that keeps a man from accomplishment and makes him fribble away his time in the feckless occupations of a leisured class. In this play, the businessman beats the aristocrat, a theme quite acceptable at the new Abbey.

The play is finely characterized and beautifully built. None of the characters is skimped, and Judith is superbly drawn. In this play, Robinson looks back to Ibsen rather than to Strindberg, for he gives a full background rather than an isolated study in neurosis. It is an accomplished job, one of Robinson's best.

By contrast, *Bird's Nest* is, despite moments of effective pathos, a thin and dull domestic drama. It is Robinson's second Inish play; its theme contradicts the theme of *Is Life Worth Living?* There, Robinson said that attempts to bring art to this small town were absurd; here, he says that such attempts are singularly important. Other than that contradiction, the piece is of little interest.

Robinson's excursions into a more probing psychology and a more sophisticated morality were not well received at the Abbey; most of them were not produced there. Of such plays as *The White Blackbird* of 1925, *Give a Dog –* of 1929, *All's Over Then?* of 1932, *When Lovely Woman* of 1936, *Roly Poly* of 1940, and *The Demon Lover* of 1954, only two were performed at the Abbey. *Give a Dog –* was first produced in London and then in Dublin by the Dublin Drama League, while *When Lovely Woman, Roly Poly*, and *The Demon Lover* were all produced by the more tolerant Gate.

These plays are not Robinson's most successful, but in them he was trying to probe more deeply into character and to tap starker emotions than he did in his conventional Abbey work. *Give a Dog –*, for instance, is hardly risqué, but its scene in which the hero and his married friend entertain two chorus girls at supper was a bit much for the Abbey. Still, it is a well worked out piece of realistic theatre, important for its idea that creative genius is often hampered by convention. *All's Over Then?*, which the Abbey did produce, is less successful but still interesting. It is a somber, rather Strindbergian, psychological study of a woman twenty years older than her husband, who so jealously loves him that she attempts to kill her own daughter whom she sees as a rival. Robinson concentrates so fully on character that the play remains merely a case history, absorbing but not widely applicable. He spends little time building up a realistic background; there is little sense of a surrounding society. Like *The Father* or *Miss Julie*, this play has its characters working out their story in an almost societyless vacuum.

When Lovely Woman took a more urbane view of sex than the Abbey could approve, and *The Demon Lover* was a Strindbergian study in infidelity. Both appeared at the Gate, as did the modernization of Maupassant's "Boule de Suif" which Robinson retitled *Roly Poly*. The play, performed during the war, so irritated the French and German legations that it was forced to close and Robinson was challenged to a duel. Besides the beautifully drawn character of the prostitute, the whole play is a streamlined, wry, fierce job. It was probably the best adaptation done by an Irish dramatist until Hugh Leonard dramatized Joyce's *Portrait of the Artist* twenty years later.

Robinson's excursions into satire were not popular, but at least they were put on by the Abbey. *Ever the Twain*, produced on October 8, 1929, was one of the theatre's rare deviations from realism. The play has a touch of Expressionism in Act III when some dancers in a speakeasy dance in puppet-like fashion, and rather more than a touch in the satirical ending of Act II which utilized actual puppets. This lack of parochialism in technique was paralleled in the casting when Meriel Moore and Micheál Mac Liammóir of the Gate took prominent roles. Holloway and other typical Abbey patrons criticized Robinson's ingratitude to the United States in writing of it so caustically. But, although Robinson makes some telling hits at the expense of the ladies' tea club circuit, he also punctures the cultural pretensions of his European lecturers and shows how essentially in quest of the dollar they are.

Even less successful and more satiric was the adaptation of Sheridan's *The Critic*, which was produced on January 6, 1931. This local and topical updating of Sheridan's play has unfortunately not been revived or published.

Church Street, produced on May 21, 1934, is a long one-act, technically more striking than any other play Robinson wrote. It tells of an Irish playwright who writes unpopular plays about London society and who returns briefly to the Irish village of his birth. He is repelled by its dullness, but his aunt accuses him of being dull and suggests that the villagers embody more dramatic stories than he realizes. His imagination thus stimulated, he considers the villagers more closely, staging for himself and his aunt their real stories. The crux of the play is the nature of playwriting, and it makes two points: first, one should write about what he knows; second, art demands selection and arrangement. The first point is made by the contrast between the guests' original entrance and Hugh's imaginary restaging of it. In the beginning, only hints of their real stories appeared; in Hugh's version, the real stories are brought to the surface. The second point, about arrangement, is dramatized by Hugh's selective restaging of the originally higgledy-piggledy entrance. At first, "All come in awkwardly, in a bunch, and having got in don't quite know what to do with themselves. . . . the audience should say to each other, 'What bad acting, what rotten production.'" In Hugh's version, each guest is introduced singly, playing out his characterizing scene before the next guest is brought on.

Curtis Canfield and Michael O'Neill have complained that the imagined scenes are too short to suggest a character's full personality. My feeling is that they are theatrically sufficient; if they were longer they would swamp the point of the play. After all, the play is not about half a dozen individual stories, interesting though they are; the play is about the nature of art, the stories are only illustrations. One of them, about two impoverished elderly ladies wrestling with pride and poverty, seems to me both full and poignant. In technique and in content, this is one of

26

Robinson's most accomplished plays. What it says is engrossing; what it dramatizes is moving.

In our period, Robinson gave eleven plays to the Abbey and had several rejected ones produced elsewhere. His successful Abbey plays are slickly done realistic pieces with conventional themes. Those of his plays that diverge from conventional realism or morality were either not staged at the Abbey or had little influence. Robinson was no bold experimenter like O'Casey or Johnston, but he was not inextricably wedded to conventional theatre. He deserves as much honor for *Church Street* and *Give a Dog* — as he does for such popular successes as *The Whiteheaded Boy* and *The Far Off Hills*.

A more entrenched realist than Robinson was T. C. Murray, who was first represented at the Abbey on October 27, 1910, with his somber short tragedy, *Birthright*. A Corkman like Robinson, Murray was born on January 17, 1873, in Macroom. A schoolteacher, he was for the seventeen years preceding his retirement in 1932 headmaster of the Inchicore Model Schools near Dublin. He was not so prolific a dramatist as Robinson, and as a schoolmaster he was naturally less involved with the practical theatre. His other plays include *Maurice Harte* of 1912, *Sovereign Love* of 1913, *The Briery Gap* of 1917, *Spring* of 1918, *Aftermath* of 1922, *Autumn Fire* of 1924, which was well received in London also, *The Pipe in the Fields* of 1927, *The Blind Wolf* of 1928, *A Flutter of Wings* of 1929, *Michaelmas Eve* of 1932, *A Stag at Bay* of 1934, *A Spot in the Sun* of 1938, *Illumination* of 1939, and *The Green Branch* of 1943. All of these but the last were produced; all but *Illumination* were published. Another play, *The Serf*, was produced at the Abbey in 1920 under the pseudonym of Stephen Morgan; Murray never publicly acknowledged it and it was never published. He died at the age of 85.

Unlike Robinson, who was equally adept in comedy and in serious drama, Murray's forte was realistic tragedy. The good Murray play was a solidly constructed and closely observed piece of realism. Sometimes one feels it was too solidly constructed and too closely observed, for his beginnings and middles are painstakingly slow and sometimes dull. All of his careful preparations usually pay off, though, in the husbanded strength which bursts forth finally to sweep the play with a fierce impetus to a gutting conclusion. Murray was perhaps a timid man; still, his

plays honestly and powerfully investigate such themes as spoiled voca-
tions, clerical interference in education, and even incest.

His most typical play in the period covered in this book is *Michaelmas
Eve*, a story of how greed for land and money pushes people into made
marriages rather than love matches, and of how their lives are embittered. The arrangement of the plot is somewhat unMurrayish, for the
play's incidents are spread throughout rather than artificially restrained
until they burst forth in one tremendous climax. Murray's fine structural
control builds up a tense theatrical suspense, however, until the last moment when he pulls his punch and settles for pathos rather than the tragedy which would rise more logically out of the action. He should have
punished the servant Hugh Kearns who threw over his real love, the
servant girl Moll Garvey, to marry a rich lady farmer. After the marriage, when Hugh has become a little disillusioned with his wife, Moll
attempts to make love to him and he repulses her violently. She then in
a rage poisons his tea, and Murray actually allows Hugh to lift the cup
to his lips a couple of times before Moll breaks down, confesses, and
leaves the house broken in spirit. To make his theme meaningful and his
main plot parallel to a more meaningful subplot, Murray should have
punished Hugh rather than Moll. The major fault is Hugh's, and so
should the tragic suffering be. For some reason, perhaps conventional
morality, Murray veered away from this aesthetic necessity. Often he
was tripped up by his Catholic, middle-class society, but often the artist
in him pushed him on anyway. Just as technically his plays suggest a
struggle between high passion trying to escape from phlegmatic realism,
so thematically do they suggest the lawless artist trying to escape from
lawful authority. Sometimes he succeeded; in this play of 1932 he did
not quite make it.

Murray's other notable work in the period covered here consists of
three not very successful attempts to broaden his range: *The Pipe in the
Fields*, a one-act produced at the Abbey on October 3, 1927; *The Karavoes*, first performed at the Abbey on April 30, 1928, under the title of
The Blind Wolf; and *A Flutter of Wings*, first staged by the Gate in
1929. *The Pipe in the Fields* attempts to escape from realism into something more lyrical. It tells of a country boy who buys a fife from a passing stranger and who sees visions when he plays it. The pace in the early
stages is funereal; the play could profitably have ten pages and one character dropped. It is reminiscent of the early plays of Yeats, and there may
be some influence of the later Yeats in the symbolic dancer who is seen

only by the boy. Despite dialogue which is too talky and explicit, Murray achieves a few moments of lyric exaltation, but the play is far from an unqualified success.

The Karavoes is a traditional story about a destitute peasant family on the verge of starvation. When a rich traveler begs for a night's lodging, the old father is driven by anguish and greed to murder him. The next morning the family learns that the traveler was their long-lost son who had returned to surprise them. Stricken beyond words, the old father and mother take poison. The story certainly has the essentials of tragedy, and Murray brought to it all that fine structuring and purity of language can do. The problem, however, is that tragedy requires a richness of texture which *The Karavoes* lacks. If the author's caution had not led him to put his explosive fable in faraway Hungary, if he had set it in the peasant Ireland that he knew, and if he had written it in the rich peasant idiom that he could fluently command, then he might have written a tragedy instead of only a very actable melodrama.

A Flutter of Wings caused a flutter of surprise among Murray's friends, for it was his first Abbey rejection after twenty years of writing for the theatre. Although snapped up by the Gate, the comedy is quite bad and the Abbey's rejection was sound. The first two acts plod along with little resembling wit or humor. Then the last act brings a great rush of plot, a super-pure morality, and a quite improbable change in the heroine. Earlier she had been a pert and independent young miss, but in the last act she becomes a total prude and collapses from shock when an attractive young man kisses her. We then get such stilted dialogue as: "Have you no decency — no shred of honor left? . . . I was a weak fool. . . . You smash into atoms a woman's faith in human decency. . . . Your — affections — are they engaged? . . . I'll fight you to the bitter end!" We could be back in the world of *East Lynne* and *Lady Audley's Secret*.

Murray's other late work is unimportant. *A Stag at Bay* and *A Spot in the Sun* are routine exercises in one-act tragedy; *Illumination* is a two-act religious play with little appeal for a non-Catholic audience. Murray did not write his best work in our period, and he had a limited range. But his strong tragedies played a large part in fixing realism as the dominant Abbey manner; they also acted as a brake on the theatre's ever-present tendency to brainless farce.

St. John Ervine is one of the most distinguished men of Irish letters, but his important plays were also staged well before the beginning of our story. In 1911, his *Mixed Marriage* was performed at the Abbey, to be followed by several one-acts. In the fall of 1915, after he was appointed manager of the theatre, he staged his masterpiece *John Ferguson*. An Ulsterman, his strong Northern sentiments put him out of sympathy with many of the players; on May 29, 1916, the players greeted patrons coming to the theatre with a handbill announcing their refusal to play under Ervine any longer. The actors then dispersed. Some, under the leadership of Arthur Sinclair, formed a successful touring company. In September, a new manager, J. Augustus Keogh, was brought in to form a new company.

In the meantime, Ervine's own interests turned away from Ireland. He fought in the war and lost a leg. He became an important drama critic for *The Observer*, and later spent a year as an astringent guest critic on a New York paper. His *John Ferguson* and *Jane Clegg* were the financial saving of the New York Theatre Guild. In more recent years he has written a number of comedies for the British stage somewhat in the style of Somerset Maugham. He also published some novels, as well as highly opinionated biographies of Parnell, General William Booth, Craigavon, Wilde, and Shaw.

His first post-O'Casey comedy at the Abbey was *Boyd's Shop*, produced on February 24, 1936, and later filmed with the Abbey players. A middle-class comedy set in an Ulster village, this play's realism is quite authentic. It has no theatrical exaggerations, no Ulster versions of Joxer, and no big moments like the wooing scene in *The Whiteheaded Boy*. It has, however, an honest effectiveness: the chorus of middle-aged gossips is delightful, and Boyd, the grocer, is a solid portrait of an upright man.

His next Abbey play was *William John Mawhinney*, an unpublished comedy produced on March 23, 1940.

His last Abbey play, *Friends and Relations*, was first performed on June 30, 1941. It tells of how the friends and relations of a millionaire react to his will. Much of the play's value lies in its well-considered, two-pronged theme. Ervine raises the questions of the use to which a very large sum of money should be put and of how self-sufficient and divorced from society a man ought to be. Although he avoids a direct answer to either, he also avoids a platitudinous conclusion and creates an absorbing story with well-drawn parts.

Ervine's wittier and more sophisticated plays have not been performed at the Abbey, but his Abbey work has an honesty of observation, a restraint, and a commendable intelligence. In their quiet way, his plays are consummately done.

⚜

Rutherford Mayne was also an Ulsterman. His early work, such as *The Drone*, was written for the Ulster Theatre in Belfast which he helped to found in 1904. The brother of Helen Waddell who is known for her book *The Wandering Scholars*, his real name was Samuel J. Waddell. He was an accomplished amateur actor who made a considerable impression in O'Neill's *The Emperor Jones* when that play was produced by the Dublin Drama League and the Abbey in the middle twenties. Earlier, in 1909, he joined the Irish Land Commission and eventually became land law commissioner in the Free State.

His first Abbey play since O'Casey was a minor comedy, *Peter*, staged on January 28, 1930. Despite the baldly drawn travesty of an American woman ("Gee, I say kid, you suits me just cruel"), there are some good broad parts in the play, including a grunting Nero Wolfish Inspector of Hotels, a nice stock British colonel named Tiger Blake, and an engaging portrait of an Irish Babbitt. There are also some beautifully absurd exchanges of dialogue. Here, for instance, is a droll bit between Colonel Blake and Mr. McCleery, an Ulster poet:

MR. MCCLEERY: "Away where the curlews cry on the bog
There sounds the faint wild bark of the dog,
And oh! to be there
When the canavan fair
Billows and sways in the evening air."

COLONEL (*delightedly*): Right! I say, jolly good! Bog – dog. Damn fine! Love bogs and dogs. On you go. Another verse.

MR. MCCLEERY: I'm just working at the next one. I – well – I – I haven't quite got the idea for the next one.

COLONEL (*enthusiastically*): Well. Extraordinary. Yes. Jolly good idea. Now let me see. We're out in the bog. Yes. I have it! Next verse. Grouse. Drive. Butts. Grouse coming over you with a following wind. 90 miles an hour. Grand! Next verse. Get into the butts. Describe the grouse coming over with the wind. H'up! Over they go! Bang! Bang! Right and left barrel. H'up! Got 'em! Good dog! Fetch 'em!

Mayne's last Abbey play, *Bridge Head*, was performed first on June 18, 1934. The story would seem an intractable one for the drama, as it de-

31

picts the efforts of the Irish Land Commission to reapportion land more equitably. However, the story might nevertheless work even outside Ireland, for in its most general sense it is about an unheroic dedication to public service, and such social selflessness is so rare in practice and yet so engrained in Western morality, that the play is a pertinent reminder of semi-forgotten ideals. The theme is made even more persuasive by the muted key of the play. It has no heroics, no fine speeches, no grand scenes of renunciation. Instead, there is a quietly established sense of reality that is cumulatively most moving. Such soberly effective plays about untheatrical problems testify to the value of realism at its best.

꩜

Brinsley MacNamara was also a pseudonym. Its owner John Weldon was born in County Westmeath in 1891, one of seven children of the local schoolmaster. He came to Dublin when he was seventeen, acted for a time with the Abbey, and in 1918 published his first good novel, *The Valley of the Squinting Windows*, which was so outspoken a portrayal of provincial life that it provoked a boycott of his father's school. He produced a long series of stories, novels, and Abbey plays. His first play was *The Rebellion in Ballycullen* produced in March, 1919. This was followed in November, 1920, by *The Land for the People*; in November, 1923, by *The Glorious Uncertainty*, a racing drama which may owe something to Boucicault's *Flying Scud*; and by *Look at the Heffernans!* produced in April, 1926. *The Master* appeared in March, 1928; *Margaret Gillan* in July, 1933; *The Grand House in the City* in February, 1936; *The Three Thimbles* in November, 1941; and in August, 1945, a sequel to *Look at the Heffernans!* called *Marks and Mabel*. In 1950 he published a pamphlet commemorating the first fifty years of the Abbey and containing a not very accurate list of productions.

He was made a director of the Abbey in 1935. Later in the year, however, the theatre produced O'Casey's previously rejected *The Silver Tassie*, which caused immediate outraged protests from religious and patriotic groups. But the loudest, most outraged voice was MacNamara's. In two columns of invective in the *Irish Independent*, he denounced his fellow directors for producing the play and the Abbey audience for their "wholly uncritical, and I might say, almost insane admiration for the vulgar and worthless plays of Mr. O'Casey." His co-directors asked for his resignation and he gave it. He was thereafter for several years the drama critic of the *Irish Times*; he died February 4, 1963, in Dublin.

He was a moody, perhaps egotistic figure, but a playwright of craft and strength. His plays are about evenly divided between fluent, light-weight comedies and stark, grim tragedies. Though the comedies are smoothly good-natured without being exactly witty, the tragedies seem written in moods of unrelieved depression. His comedies of domestic intrigue were popular and no worse than John McCann's later sagas of the Kelly family, but they probably accelerated the deterioration of the Abbey standard of realism.

Margaret Gillan, however, is a strange, strong play about domestic intrigue, marriage, and money. What distinguishes it from many similar plays is the superb title character and the intensity of tone. Margaret is a full and demanding role that would require a virtuoso performance to overcome the pervasively overwrought tone of the whole. The play is packed with fiercely angry confrontations, and if power and vehemence were enough to make a tragedy, MacNamara would have written a resounding one. There is no rest, however, no pause, and perhaps even no wisdom in the play. Everything is turmoil, passion, and violence; it would take accomplished playing to keep the play from slipping over into screaming melodrama. Probably the piece is more embarrassing than cathartic. The fault, though, is not a matter of technical control; if anything, the play's structure is overcontrolled. The real flaw is the unnatural vehemence, the mad exacerbation, the raw attack upon the human state in Ireland, and the lack of any humanizing alleviation. Nevertheless, it is a remarkable play that reminds one of the frenetic blood tragedies of the Jacobeans — powerful, savage, and unhealthy.

George Shiels, more than any other playwright including Lennox Robinson, wrote the typical Abbey play of the 1930's and 1940's. Almost totally realistic, his plays ranged from asinine farce to adroit and wryly thoughtful dramas. He rivaled O'Casey in popularity; his *The Rugged Path* of 1940 was the Abbey's first long run, packing the theatre for twelve weeks.

Shiels was born in 1886, in Ballymoney, County Antrim. As a youth he emigrated to Canada, but after seven years there he met with an accident while working for a railroad company. Permanently disabled, he returned to Ballymoney and wrote short stories and articles for local papers before turning to the writing of plays. His early plays were done for the Ulster theatre, but after the Abbey accepted *Bedmates* of 1921 he wrote mainly for the Dublin theatre. His second Abbey production was *Insurance Money*, produced late in 1921; followed by *Paul Twyning* on October 3, 1922; by *First Aid* on December 26, 1923; by *The Retrievers* on May 12, 1924; by *Professor Tim* on September 14, 1925; by *Cartney and Kevney* on November 29, 1927; by *Mountain Dew* on March 5, 1929; by his very popular comedy *The New Gossoon* on April 19, 1930; by *Grogan and the Ferret* on November 13, 1933; by *The Passing Day* on April 13, 1936; by *The Jailbird* on October 12, 1936; by *Quin's Secret* on March 29, 1937; by a revision of *Cartney and Kevney* on November 8, 1937; by *Neal Maquade* on January 17, 1938; by *Give Him a House* on October 30, 1939; by his long running *The Rugged Path* on August 5, 1940; by its sequel *The Summit* on February 10, 1941; by *The Fort Field* on April 13, 1942; by *The New Regime* on March 6, 1944; by *Tenants at Will* on September 10, 1945; by *The Old Broom* on March 25, 1946; and by *The Caretakers* on February 16, 1948. There were a few other plays performed in Ulster, such as *The Tame Drudge*, *Tully's Experts*, *Border Wine*, and *Moodie in Manitoba*, and he left several unperformed plays in manuscript, the best of which is the superb *Slave Drivers*. Shiels saw only one of his plays, an Abbey performance in Belfast of *Professor Tim* which he witnessed from the wings. After several years in Ballymoney, he was able to buy a house near the sea at Carlough, where he died on September 19, 1949. He was not greatly known outside of Ireland, but his influence on the Abbey repertoire was immense.

Of his post-O'Casey work, *The Jailbird* is muddled and superficial, whereas *Cartney and Kevney*, *Mountain Dew*, *Grogan and the Ferret*, and *Neal Maquade* (later revised as *Macook's Corner*) are simply slight, pleasant entertainments. *The New Gossoon*, however, is one of his best comedies, with little of the inanity that spoiled some of his earlier work. It has a real theme, the clash between the old and new generations. Luke Carey, the new gossoon, is a wild scamp who has bought a rattletrap motorcycle and tears around the countryside to dances. He has secretly sold some of his mother's sheep to pay for the cycle, and he is in trouble with a neighbor called Mad Henly for bringing Henly's daughter home at three in the morning. Luke is a type which had rarely appeared before in Abbey plays; Robinson's ne'er-do-well in *The Whiteheaded Boy* would seem his closest ancestor. Luke stands for the generation which appeared after the Civil War, a generation more influenced by the modern world than by the past of Ireland. In recent years, the films and television have created a yet newer breed of gossoon, and a recent play like James McKenna's *The Scatterin'*, about Dublin Teddy boys, really only depicts the Luke Careys of today.

Luke's widowed mother has for twenty years refused to marry her handyman Ned Shay because of a foolish promise extracted by her husband on his deathbed. But at the end of the play Luke is not only settled down with a neighbor girl who can take him in hand, but Ellen is finally to be married to Ned. The rambunctiousness of the younger generation is criticized as much as the stolidity of the older.

The characters are shrewdly drawn except for the farcical mad Henly, and he is very funny in the theatre. The best role — indeed, one of the best character parts in recent Abbey drama — is that of Rabit Hamil, a shiftless, scheming, and hypocritical poacher. Acted first by F. J. McCormick and later by Harry Brogan, this character is nearly as fine as O'Casey's Joxer Daly. The play has some needless overcomplexity of plotting toward the end, but still its point, humor, and honest observation must probably rank it with Robinson's *The Whiteheaded Boy* as one of the best conventional comedies the Abbey has produced.

The Passing Day is notable for the mild experimentation of its flashback scenes and for almost the first indication of Shiels's growing wryness. The main character is an amazingly miserly shopkeeper, and there is hardly a character who is not thoroughly selfish and repellent. The play may be an attack on the businessman's mentality which is corroding civil life in Ireland, but it is hard to be certain, for Shiels unfolds his story without comment.

Quin's Secret also examines chicanery in business, though its real interest lies in the characterization of the honest young clerk, the drunken manager, and the rascally foreman. Such characters sound as if they had emerged from some latter-day version of *The London Merchant*, but each is convincingly real. Crilly, the foreman, is one of the Abbey's best twisters since the Eloquent Dempsy; Dolman, the manager, is an accurate study of weakness; and even the straight part of Quin the clerk seems tailor-made for the quiet style of an actor like Cyril Cusack, who portrayed him. The play does not sufficiently suggest that its story is a crucial sympton rather than an isolated instance, but it is a craftsmanlike job.

35

Give Him a House is Shiels's most tough-minded play up to this time — perhaps a bit too sardonic for the theatre. It depicts a morality as actually practiced by men of no more than ordinary good will, rather than the morality we have become accustomed to from pulpits, editorials, and conventional plays. In the beginning, Pat Hooey is a Communist because he has no property. At the end, when he is a man of property and a public official, he rationalizes his about-face from his former ideals. His story is repeated in the actions of most of the other characters, who are also, while not actually dishonest, always willing to sacrifice a principle to attain a profit. This not implausible view of human nature is quite opposed to the platitudinous morality of most plays. Still, Shiels does make his case fairly and without overstatement. Predictably, the piece has not been popular.

The Rugged Path was a milestone for the Abbey. Considering Dublin's size, its twelve-week run would be the equivalent of a smash hit in London or New York. The discovery of how profitable a long run could be helped to form the theatre's present policy of keeping plays on as long as they draw. Peter Kavanagh comments about the matter: "The audience, not the poet, was in control now, and it demanded to be flattered. The theatre was packed every night with people demanding, and receiving, soft sentiment and superficialities. Even the standard of acting had to be lowered to suit the tastes of the public." [1] Unquestionably, the acting of *The Rugged Path* grew ever broader during its run, but the acting was hardly Shiels's fault, for neither *The Rugged Path* nor its sequel *The Summit* was a brainless farce. Both plays are worthily realistic portraits of rural Ireland. They both form one continuous story, on which Shiels never loses his grip. The story's significant theme contrasts the older Irish tolerance for lawlessness and contempt for the informer with the new responsibility that must necessarily, if painfully, be accepted by citizens of a free nation.

The first play shows how the Dolis family from the mountains has terrorized the neighboring farmers. When young Peter Dolis kills an old man for £2, the Tanseys, a family of law-abiding farmers, are afraid to accuse him partly because of their fear of retribution and partly because of the old prejudice against informing. When the son finally persuades the father to give evidence, this would have been an easy place to end the play. Shiels does not settle for the easy solution, however. He has the jury fail to convict Dolis, ending the play on the sinister note of a shot crashing through the window of the Tanseys' house.

The action of *The Summit* takes up immediately where *The Rugged Path* left off. Peter Dolis has triumphantly returned, but his arrogance teaches the community that the old lawlessness is an anachronism that must be replaced by reason, cooperation, and respect for authority. An old political enemy of Tansey forgets past quarrels and comes to his aid. Banded together, the farmers can enforce lawfulness, exile Peter Dolis, and make the rest of the Dolis clan return to their mountain and keep the peace. Even though the play offers a solution, Shiels avoids a tritely happy ending by a final wry indictment of the Irish character, in these closing lines about the old man who was murdered:

> CASSIDY: There's one thing we must do, Michael; we must put up a bit of a headstone to John Perrie.
> MICHAEL: It's a sorry monument!
> CASSIDY: And we must carve on it this inscription: "John Perrie, aged 74, was murdered by a neighbour for two pounds."
> SEAN: And an Irish jury found him Not Guilty.

There is not an overdrawn character in either play. The lawless, ingrown, vicious Dolis family comes across with persuasive restraint, as do also a frightened, time-serving neighbor woman and an engaging hypocrite of a traveling man. The Tanseys and the police sergeant are straight parts, but not flat ones. They have a quiet credibility. Without being masterpieces, *The Rugged Path* and *The Summit* represent the best kind of work the Abbey has produced in recent years — the solid, conventional, realistic play that makes a pertinent comment upon modern Ireland.

The Fort Field is an anti-fantasy with satirical overtones. Set in Ulster during World War II, its theme is again Ireland's coming of age. The adolescent past is symbolized by the fort field which has in it a fairy ring regarded by the townspeople with superstitious awe. When an engineer son of one of them returns home to plow the fort field up for an airfield, he meets strenuous resistance from the people, who fear the retribution of the fairies and grogans. In a subplot, two Dublin students on a walking tour appear, and one wants to write a popular book on Ireland. But he too is still viewing the country through mists of Celtic twilight. Ultimately, the student is reduced to practicality; the natives end up by pitching into the field themselves, accepting the army bulldozers with equanimity and the influx of English money with glee. One might wish that Shiels had replaced romance with something other than bourgeois money-grubbing. Still, it is a continuously engrossing play that faithfully reflects what has happened to the country; a commonplace practicality, a businessman's mentality, has emerged more and more as the dominant note in Irish life.

Tenants at Will in its original version, which was rejected by the Abbey, is reported to have been a broadly panoramic play. The revision, which the theatre produced, is a too simple, too optimistic view of the plight of the small farmer a few years before the Great Famine. Gerard Healy treated the same material more honestly in *The Black Stranger*.

The Old Broom, first produced in 1944 by the Group Theatre in Belfast, is another play about a grasping Irish family, full of hypocrisy, *nouveau riche* snobbishness, and lust for money. It has some fine darkly comic scenes — in particular, one in which old Broom draws out the young solicitor who wants to marry his middle-aged daughter into ever more damaging admissions of conscious hypocrisy. As in some of Shiels's other plays, there is an uncomfortable tolerance for the end justifying the means. Certainly this play has a dry force, but this thoroughgoing recital of ignoble motives and this sour collection of shrews, reformed drunkards, and ruthless businessmen may be a bit more actuality than a drama, without compensating excellences, can take.

Shiels's last produced play, *The Caretakers*, is also about money squabbles and a will. But, although most of the characters are mean, grasping, and ruthless, this play remains a curiously broad and almost bright comedy. The reason is that many of the characters are such fine humors that it is difficult to take the plot as seriously as its savage motivations demand; instead, one is seduced into enjoying its twists, reversals, and counterturns for their own complexity. Curiously, though, Shiels again solves his plot in a way which flouts the morality of the theatre. He cuts a couple of moral corners in winding up his plot, and paints again a world in which the end justifies the means. Not only does he paint such a world, but also he makes no criticism of it. However appropriate a view this is in reality, it is distinctly disconcerting to find it in a work of art.

Shiels's unpublished and unproduced last play, *Slave Drivers*, is one of his harshest in theme and smoothest in style. It depicts a family of Ulster landlords who own a slave plantation on the eve of the American Civil War. The closest way to suggest its flavor is to call it an Irish *Little Foxes*, and it by no means shrivels in comparison with Lillian Hellman's rasping melodrama. Miss Bess, the landowner, cheats her nephew William out of his property. Robert, her brother, cheats her out of hers. William, while professing a drunken anguish about slavery in America, coolly seduces and then deserts a worthy young girl. The family's agent, their attorney, and most of their servants are as venal and selfish as the family; and Miss Bess is a violent, shouting, cuffing, memorable old termagant who gallops her horse to exhaustion and drinks herself into insensibility every night.

Most remarks about Shiels's work reflect either the broad writing he was doing in the 1920's or the broad treatment his work received in the Abbey in the 1930's and 1940's. Actually, his later work has more merit than its interpretation at the Abbey would suggest. The best of his later plays are tightly knit, convincingly realistic diagnoses of his country's morality. These tart, dour pieces are far from the buffooneries and kitchen comedies usually associated with him. They might have been written by a quizzically amused pragmatist, and in their quiet way they are almost as disturbing a reflection of modern Ireland as the gaudy invectives of O'Casey. It took Shiels a lifetime of writing, but what a distance he came: he began as a clown and ended as an artist.

In the first twenty years after O'Casey's departure, the Abbey discovered no new writers of his stature, though it did uncover some fine new talents. Coming into prominence at the same time as Paul Vincent Carroll was Teresa Deevy, a devout Catholic lady of a much smaller but quite definite talent. Miss Deevy was born in Waterford, had become totally deaf in her teens, and had depended ever since on lip-reading. Her first play at the Abbey was *The Reapers*, which was produced on March 18, 1930, and followed by the one-act comedy *A Disciple*, produced on August 24, 1931. Also in 1931, she and Carroll jointly won an Abbey play competition, and her play, *Temporal Powers*, was produced on September 12, 1932. Her one-act *The King of Spain's Daughter* was done on April 29, 1935; her best known play, *Katie Roche*, was performed on March 16, 1936; *The Wild Goose* was done on November 9, 1936; and her last Abbey production was the one-act *Light Falling*, put on at the Experimental Theatre on October 25, 1948. In addition to these Abbey productions, her *Wife to James Whelan*, which Michael J. Molloy thought better than *Katie Roche*, was done at Madame Bannard Cogley's Studio Theatre Club on October 4, 1956, and later broadcast over Radio Éireann and the B.B.C. Her *Supreme Dominion* (also called *Luke Wadding*) was broadcast over Radio Éireann in 1957, and later briefly staged for the Franciscan Fathers of Merchant's Quay. In his appreciation in the press on the event of her death in January, 1963, the young playwright James Cheasty wrote of her kindness, simplicity, humility, and helpfulness to young writers, and also complained that "the neglect by the Abbey Theatre of the work of Teresa Deevy is a sad reflection on that institution."

On the basis of four or five of her at least fifteen plays, Miss Deevy has been definitely pigeonholed. As J. D. Riley put it:

Her plays for the most part are of rural or provincial Ireland and her heroines young girls on the verge of womanhood. She deals with that tragi-comic period in her heroine's lives — a period heightened dramatically to an instant — when they put aside a portion of their happiness, freedom, ideals and their very personality in order, inevitably, to gain greater and deeper happiness in the world of responsibility and all-too-common sense.[2]

Her range was a bit wider than this otherwise accurate description suggests, but *The King of Spain's Daughter* does have as its main merit the revelation of a young girl's personality. Annie Kinsella is an incurable romantic, young, fresh, volatile, alive. Even when forced into a dull marriage, she transforms it into a magical adventure. She opens her prosaic fiancé's notebook, sees how he has solidly and phlegmatically saved a shilling each week in order to be married, and says:

ANNIE: February, March, April . . . June, July, August . . . October — and I was black out with him then — November, December, April, June, August —

MRS. MARKS: A good sensible boy.

ANNIE: Boy! (*She laughs exultantly*) I think he is a man might cut your throat!

MRS. MARKS: God save us all!

ANNIE: He put by two shillin's every week for two hundred weeks. I think he is a man that — supposin' he was jealous — might cut your throat.

And on that note of triumphant romanticism, the little piece ends. It is a play that could have been written by a T. C. Murray made drunk with exhilaration; it is that rare.

The heroine of *Katie Roche* is Annie Kinsella more fully rendered. Like Annie, Katie is drawn into marriage with an older man. Like Annie, she is young, flighty, romantic, and unable to stop flirting with her old beau. Although no King of Spain's daughter, Katie is the illegitimate child of one of the neighboring Big Houses, which seems to her grand and romantic. She is brought down to earth when her husband carries her off to a prosaic life in Dublin, but like Annie she has a final twist of exultation when she realizes that there is a kind of romance in facing her new life bravely.

Despite the slightness of *The King of Spain's Daughter, Katie Roche* is even less successful. Katie is much fuller and more complex than Annie — possibly too full and complex for the naive art of the stage. Even the "people" who appear so convincingly in Ibsen's front parlors are not far from simple Jonsonian humours. In Katie, Miss Deevy tried to portray an illogical character in a flux of contradictions; such a portrait is much more difficult than a permanently fixed character like Ibsen's Engstrand or a logically developing one like Ibsen's Nora.

Miss Deevy tries to reflect Katie's constantly changing moods by a peculiar quality of the dialogue. The speeches break off halfway through a topic and abruptly switch to a new topic or adopt a new tone. Fiction can more easily handle such quick shifts, for dramatic dialogue must be obvious enough to be caught on the wing. Three or four contradictory tones in the same speech are probably too dazzling. Here, for instance, is the passage when Katie is deciding whether to marry Stan:

KATIE: Oh — (*in turmoil*) — who knows what they wish! (*Clasps her hands. — then, seeking strength*) "One false step and you're over the precipice, one bad link and the chain goes snap, one wrong act and a life is ruined, one small . . . one small . . . one . . . one" (*trying to concentrate*) — ach! — (*turns to run from the room, meets Stan coming in. He opens his arms, takes her.*) Oh-h . . . Oh-h . . . (*in ecstasy*).

STAN: I couldn't wait. (*Kisses her.*)

KATIE: Oh! (*Overcome. Then frees herself; stands back from him.*) Yes, I'll give you my hand.

STAN: That's right. That's a good girl. Now don't be nervy. Don't be upset. It's only the strain. (*Pats her shoulder reassuringly. Katie stiffens.*) Why — even I felt it. We'll be sensible. We'll get married very soon. My sister will live with us — if you don't mind. She'll go away sometimes. (*Katie looks at him now with the anger of a child at a clumsy companion.*)

In the couple of minutes which this short sequence takes, the actress must convey her confusion, her attempt to overcome it, her inability to overcome it, her despair and flight, her shock, her "ecstacy," her control, nervousness, aversion, and finally her anger — a sequence which runs from hysteria to coolness, from love to hate. Each point must be made clearly and instantaneously. Few actresses could do it, and few audiences could take it in. For this reason, the play is not quite a success, but at least it fails by trying to be too good.

The volatility of Annie and Katie is also apparent in Martin Shea, the hero of *The Wild Goose*. Martin is a young man at the end of the seventeenth century who is fluctuating between three desires — to become a priest, to marry Eileen, to fight England by enlisting in the French army. In most plays, the hero merely has a dilemma, two simple alternatives. Miss Deevy again poses a more complex problem, and again she does not clearly suggest how she wants her audience to feel. Again, she is portraying the immature mind trying to come to grips with the world, and so again there are some abrupt changes of topic and tone. Martin is often of two minds rather than one, and often lashes out at something he will later espouse. The psychological rightness of this picture of immature indecision cannot be denied, but how much comes over clearly on the stage is debatable.

Nor does the audience get as close to Martin as it did to Katie. Katie has opportunities to explain herself, but Martin is seen mainly from the outside, by means of the observation and comments of others. When he speaks, it is always decisively, even though a few minutes later he may be quite as decisive in an opposite direction. The actor playing Martin has the difficult problem of portraying a mental chaos that is never overtly revealed by the dialogue.

The plot reflects Martin's indecision well, but that is probably its main fault. Necessarily, it does not seem to progress. Martin dashes from alternative to alternative. Because he does not grow from immaturity to maturity, we do not have the usual satisfactions of a well-made progressive plot. The plot does exactly what Miss Deevy wants it to, but it may well be too unconventional to work successfully on the contemporary stage.

Other than the admired *Wife to James Whelan* which I have not read, Miss Deevy's best remaining play is *Going Beyond Alma's Glory* of 1951, a radio play with two excellent characterizations. One is Edmund Spillane, a former journalist who has spoiled his prospects by drinking, betting, and embezzling. The other is Mona Pewitt, his wife, a fine study of an actress whose egotism loses her jobs. The plot concerns the pathetic attempts of these middle-aged, disillusioned, and battered people to fight back to each other, and shows how they fail. The play is outside of what is usually considered Miss Deevy's range; it is not about callow and romantic young people, but callow old ones for whom the vision of romance has faded. Though designed for radio, it has one simple set and could be easily staged.

Miss Deevy had a quiet, subtle talent, and within the realistic mode she made intriguing experiments with structure and dialogue. Her talent never developed as much as it should, and perhaps the reason was the lack of a stage. Certainly, short plays for radio and long ones for religious orders did not give her pen enough exercise.

꽃

Jack B. Yeats, the distinguished painter brother of the poet, had one play, *La La Noo*, presented at the Abbey proper, and two others performed at the Abbey's experimental theatre, the Peacock. The unpublished *Harlequin's Positions* was done on June 5, 1939, *La La Noo* on May 3, 1942, and *In Sand* on April 19, 1949. The two published plays suggest that Yeats was a sensitive and cultivated amateur of talent, with a nice eye for detail and a good ear for dialogue. Still, he never took playwriting seriously enough to learn its necessities and limitations. Quite as much as his poet brother, Yeats used the drama as a personal rather than a public statement.

The point, for instance, of *La La Noo* is so lightly woven into the leisurely action that it is almost invisible. And the action itself is less a plot than a situation leading up to an accidental and illustrative death and then dropped. A stranger walks into an isolated pub in the West, chats with the publican about the state of the world, and then seven women come in to escape from the rain. They leave to catch their bus, are driven back again by the rain, leave once more, and are driven back drenched. The stranger and the publican dry their clothes for them. Then, while starting a lorry to help them catch the bus, the stranger is accidentally killed. The women react with a cold unconcern and, as the rain has stopped, leave. The theme is that the modern world with its machines, cars, roads, airplanes, and submarines is changing people's nature. The silent, solitary people, like the stranger and the publican, are still courteous and humane, but the modern ladies are barely civil. Because the play has an illustrative situation rather than a conventional story, its audience may well become irked, wondering when something significant is finally going to happen. What Yeats needed in this play was a collaborator like Murray who had a fine sense of structure, or like Lady Gregory who knew the value of compression.

In Sand is the story of a sentence. On his deathbed, Tony Larcson leaves a legacy to some little girl if she will write in the sand of the beach the sentence, "Tony, we have the good thought for you still." The rest is a loosely told story spread over many years and miles which illustrates how people halfway around the world have written this legend in sand. The theme, as Jack MacGowran correctly remarked, is that "Monuments and bells, and other forms of remembrance may be reminders of a man's worth for many years, but more lasting still is that which remains in the minds of men to be passed on in their turn." [8] There are fine things in this quiet, sadly moving play, but there are also passages whose meaning, while not obscure, has only a puzzling relevance. Act III, Scene 1 is virtually a fifteen-page monologue of reminiscence by an old sailor. Although fine on the page, the passage is narrative rather than dramatic and would require masterly acting to hold its audience.

Indeed, the length of Yeats's plays is probably the most revealing symptom of his amateur status. Had their simple themes been compressed into one act, the plays would have seemed less puzzling; however, it was a sign of health that the Abbey was still willing to do puzzling plays.

⚐

In 1935, Yeats added the young short story writer Frank O'Connor to the Abbey board to fill the vacancy left by MacNamara's resignation. O'Connor approached the job enthusiastically and wrote four plays, three in collaboration with the theatre's producer Hugh Hunt and one on his own. His plays with Hunt were *In the Train*, taken from one of his stories and produced on May 31, 1937; *The Invincibles*, produced on October 18, 1937; and *Moses' Rock*, produced on February 28, 1938. Alone he wrote *Time's Pocket*, produced on December 26, 1938. One can say little about these plays, for only the ingenious one-act *In the Train* has been published. None was received with great enthusiasm, and *Time's Pocket* was hotly attacked. O'Connor has later mildly disparaged his plays, but he made a spirited defense of *Time's Pocket* at the time. After Yeats's death, Ernest Blythe maneuvered O'Connor off the Abbey board, as Walter Starkie was also maneuvered, and the loss I am inclined to think was a major one.

During his tenure, however, O'Connor persuaded several other young men to write plays, and probably the most notable results were *The Dear*

44

Queen by Andrew Ganly, a Dublin dentist (produced on April 4, 1938), and *She Had to Do Something* by the distinguished short story writer Sean O'Faolain (produced on December 27, 1937). The central situation of O'Faolain's play — Mrs. Arnold's attempt to bring culture to a small Irish town — is the same as Robinson's *Is Life Worth Living?* and Lady Longford's *The Hill of Quirke.* The characters come close to being Jonsonian humours, and the dialogue, without ever being artificial, carries the piece blithely along in a vein of high comedy. There are some droll plays on words. For instance, when the daughter says, "Mother, it's the canon, the canon, the canon at every hand's turn. Can't we live our own lives in peace and quietness?" — the mother then replies, "But that is not the way people live in this country. There are canons to the right of you and canons to the left of you." The minor character Dr. Beasley is also addicted to puns, most of them awful and all of them endearing. In the first scene, the characters are about to practice a trio, but Mrs. Arnold has to meet the Russian dancers at the quay, whereupon Beasley remarks, "It's half-past eleven. The steamer is in at twelve. I'll run you down to the quay. The quay of B Sharp, eh?" This is a most quotable play; the playfulness of its dialogue might be summed up in Petroff's remark, "What a lovely language English is!"

<p>

Louis D'Alton was one of the most complete men of the theatre to write for the Abbey, and, although little known outside of Ireland, he came close to being a dramatist of the first rank. He was born in Hardwicke Street, Dublin, in 1900, the son of Frank D'Alton, an Irish actor of the old school who had played with Barry Sullivan and toured with Charles Dillon. Young D'Alton was educated in London and entered the civil service in Dublin in 1916. He left two years later to study art, and in the early 1920's worked in Dublin as a cartoonist. He gave that up to join Victor O'Donovan Power's Irish Players, with whom he toured the Irish provinces. Then, after a season at the Queen's where his father was producer, he formed his own touring company.

His first play, *The Man in the Cloak,* was produced at the Abbey on September 27, 1937, with Cyril Cusack in the role of James Clarence Mangan. Then he wrote, produced, and played the lead in the Abbey production of *To-morrow Never Comes,* which was first done on March 13, 1939. On January 29, 1940, the Abbey produced his *The Spanish*

Soldier; it later played in New York. *The Money Doesn't Matter*, produced on March 10, 1941, had one of the longest runs in Abbey history, and on October 20 the theatre did *Lovers Meeting*. On February 18, 1947, *They Got What They Wanted* was performed; it was later filmed by an English company. D'Alton also published two novels before he died in London on June 15, 1951. He had been associated in various capacities with the Abbey for eighteen years, and after his death the theatre did three more of his plays: *The Devil a Saint Would Be* in September, 1951; *This Other Eden*, probably his best play, in June, 1953; and *Cafflin' Johnny* in March, 1958.

The Man in the Cloak is also one of D'Alton's best. The first and third acts show Mangan the poet toward the end of his life — seedy, shabby, poor, and delirious. The second act is an opium dream in which salient scenes of Mangan's life appear to him. The part of Mangan is effectively understated rather than romanticized. This Mangan is a weak-willed sponger who knows the limitations of his talent, and who in one anguished moment cries out: "I would teach men wisdom and I am known for my folly. I ambitioned praise and admiration. . . . I excite ridicule, pity, contempt. I would sing great songs, but most often I can make nothing but trifling jingles. I have had moments of genius in years of mediocrity. Why was that little seed, that germinates for brief moments, planted within me to destroy me?" This is a fine play for actors with half a dozen excellently drawn roles in addition to Mangan. Perhaps this rancid tirade from Mangan's father might illustrate the excellence of the characterization and the justness of the dialogue:

JAMES MANGAN: Well, you're a fine lot, indeed, aren't you. Why doesn't anyone speak? Am I some kind of a monster with seven heads? (*Pause*) That must be it. I'm a pariah. (*Pause*) Well then, why don't you all get out of the house and leave me in peace? But of course, I'd quite forgotten, I've no right to tell anyone to get out. None at all. I'm a failure; I am not a successful bourgeois. Well, it can't be helped, it's not my nature; that's all. And you're all disappointed in me. It is too bad. (*Looks round with a sneer*) You should have provided yourself with a different kind of father.

MANGAN: We didn't —

JAMES (*Mocking*): No, no, of course you didn't. You couldn't, could you; you cannot choose what sort of a father you'll have? No. It is most unfortunate. Well, for that matter a father can't choose the sort of children he'll have. I suppose we are all disappointed. Life is disappointing.

This promising beginning was followed by two weaker plays: *The Mousetrap*, an overwrought, *Juno*-like family tragedy, and *The Spanish Soldier*, an unfocused study of religious fanaticism. His next, *The Money Doesn't Matter*, was quite clearly focused on two major middle-class pre-occupations in Ireland, money and snobbishness. Tom Mannion, a businessman in a Midlands town, is a proud, driving, self-made man who rose out of the slums to own half the town and to marry an upper-class girl. When the play opens, his wife is dead and his children are not turning out the way he wanted. Francis, the oldest son, became a priest and died in the foreign missions. Refusing to marry a rich boob Tom has picked for her, Norah goes off to a convent. Harvey dies by racing his automobile. Phillip is a drunken sponger; Veronica has married a wastrel. The play ends with Phillip and Veronica managing to creep back into the house, and with Mannion becoming still more obsessed with money and status.

The play is engrossing although D'Alton pays more attention to his plot than to his characters. As stage roles, the parts are adequate; those of the drunkard Phillip and of Michael Harney, the horseriding block-head, are done with a nice touch of satire. The intriguing among the minor characters keeps Mannion off the stage, however, for considerable lengths of time. And Mannion, although wrong, needs some of the strength of, say, Ibsen's Borkman. D'Alton gives us merely a stage type, the Irish equivalent of Rice's Counsellor-at-law or Schulberg's Sammy Glick. This is a significant type, more pertinent now than when D'Alton wrote, but he has only sketched in its outlines. For that reason and despite its taut plot, the play seems like Ibsen and water.

Lovers Meeting is a domestic tragedy about that perennial theme of Irish drama, the made marriage. D'Alton makes his point through the story of three sisters and the daughter of one of them. Frances Linehan accepted a made marriage for security. Her husband is a heavy drinker, and, although they manage to exist without quarreling, they spend most of their time ignoring each other. Hannie Martin, her sister, married for love, but her husband abandoned her. She is now a pitiful, half-cracked, middle-aged woman who haunts the post office hoping for a letter from America. The third sister, Jane Sheridan, entered a made marriage also, but she once reneged on her bargain, and her daughter Mary is the child of her old beau, Mick Hession. This slip has made her fanatically insistent that Mary shall not repeat her mistakes: Mary must choose between a solid middle-aged farmer whom her mother insists she marry and Joe

47

Hession who she does not know is her half-brother. Joe, faced with Jane's opposition, is driven to murder his uncle to gain land and money and thereby become presentable as a husband. When he is caught, Mary is forced into an engagement with the farmer; on her wedding day she hangs herself.

There is an Ibsenian patness to the plot which the characterization helps to camouflage. Tom Sheridan, though not drawn with depth, is convincing, and Jane is a meaty woman's role. The minor characters are fresh and playable types, though in the most recent Abbey revival they were played so broadly as to be reduced to cartoons: Angela Newman as Frances enters wearing a hat that would not be out of place in a Christmas panto, and Ria Mooney's Hannie is so full of grimaces and twitches that it makes one want to scratch. Played appropriately, *Lovers Meeting* should stand up as one of the Abbey's sounder realistic plays.

They Got What They Wanted is a minor but genial family comedy about money and matchmaking. As in *Juno*, the impelling movement of the plot is an inheritance which does not materialize. The character drawing is fine, particularly in the main role of Bartley Murnaghan, the father whose inability to hold a job has dampened neither his nor his children's spirits. Bartley embraces poverty with a happy equanimity, continuing to delight his children with a ceaseless flow of buoyant Shakespearean quotation and ebullient verbiage of his own — such as his fine self-description: "A flower of culture rising from a dunghill of primordial fecklessness."

For as Catholic a nation as Ireland, religious plays are rare, and comedies about religion rarer still. The best comedies are probably Carroll's *The Wayward Saint*, Molloy's *Daughter from over the Water*, and D'Alton's *The Devil a Saint Would Be*. In D'Alton's play, an elderly lady from Kerry has conversations with an Irish saint who counsels her to do good works and give up her worldly possessions. She does, but her actions cause only evil: she gives her store to her niece's husband who promptly becomes a skinflint; she gives ten pounds to a tinker to buy a horse, and all the tinkers in the vicinity get roaring drunk. Everyone decides she is mad, and to cap it all her saint was really a devil in disguise who had come to tempt her with the pride of saintliness. After she allows herself to be sent to the madhouse, the true saint appears, but she will not believe him until he stoops to the devil's tactics of trickery to win her. The play ends with the old woman and the saint appearing at St. Peter's gate to persuade him to let them in.

The play says more than Molloy's and is funnier than Carroll's. D'Alton preserves a light touch throughout; toward the end there is a moment or two of wonder. D'Alton has sometimes been called a second-rate Shaw; certainly if this play had been Shaw's it would have been thought a minor work. Minor Shaw, however, can be major fun.

This Other Eden is even more Shavian and has been called, with typical Dublin snideness, a poor man's *John Bull's Other Island*. Using the discussion technique, the play is certainly a witty modern consideration of the issues Shaw had discussed. Like *John Bull's Other Island* and O'Casey's *Purple Dust*, D'Alton's play characterizes Ireland and the Irish character by opposing to it England and the English character. D'Alton's representative of England is Roger Crispin, who has not yet taken to wearing kilts like Behan's Monsewer, but who is well on his way to becoming more Irish than the Irish.

Crispin has come to Ballymorgan to buy an estate, and finds the town in the throes of a patriotic celebration. A memorial hall is to be dedicated to the memory of Commandant Carberry who was killed in a skirmish with the Black and Tans. Carberry's real character has been glossed over in the general hero worship, but one of his faults, which everyone knows save the person most concerned, is that he sired a child out of wedlock; this situation allows various aspects of Irish hypocrisy to come under a wittily scathing fire. To make his points and uphold the most typical Irish views, D'Alton gives us not only an Englishman who is violently apologetic for England's past oppression and who sees in Ireland a sort of truer England, but also a disillusioned idealist, a delightfully rabid patriot, a nonentity of a backbencher, a canny old tyrant of a parish priest, and a Garda sergeant intent above all on preserving the appearance of order and decorum.

Although the play is an extended debate, D'Alton is Shavianly canny about holding the attention of the audience. He gives the play more than enough plot and such noisy incidents as the blowing up of the memorial hall and a village riot. Like Shaw, he embodies his opinions in showy Jonsonian humours, giving the play a pervasive overtone of farce. I had thought to convey the flavor by extracting a passage, but the dialogue moves so fluently that it is difficult to bring any quotation to a close. Suffice it, then, to say that in this play D'Alton plays the Shavian game almost as well as the old master.

Cafflin' Johnny is a three-act entertainment with none of the serious point of the two previous plays. A caffler is a trickster and high-liver,

and Johnny Fortune, before he left home in youth, had an almost legendary reputation for caffling. The plot is impelled by Johnny's return as a
middle-aged man from his wanderings, and the first half of the play is as
clever in plot as it is deft in dialogue. In the last half, D'Alton seems to
take both plot and Johnny more seriously, for the play becomes a probing of the character of a failure who leaves home for the last time, content at least in having made more of a success out of his reputation than
he has out of his life. This second half is quietly poignant, but we had
been led by the first half to expect more fun of a high order.

D'Alton's best scenes depend on situation rather than on verbal decoration or wit. A delightful scene like the one between the incognito Johnny and his caffling nephew Nicky depends on the audience's seeing ironies at the expense of both Johnny and Nicky, who see none.

> JOHNNY: . . . Oh, a wonderful man, Cafflin' Johnny. (*Dispassionate-
> ly*) He'd great style. . . . a touch of genius. You missed something
> not knowing him.
> NICKY: Och, I'm as well off, maybe.
> JOHNNY: You might be better off. For d'ye know he'd take what you
> had in your pocket out of it and leave you under a compliment to
> him.
> NICKY: I suppose he often left you achin'?
> JOHNNY (*Fervently*): You never said a truer word. If you had known
> him. . . .
> NICKY: I don't want to know him.
> JOHNNY: I can see that, mind you. (*Very reasonably again and quite
> sincerely*) Of course, Johnny had terrible faults, I won't deny. . . .
> Oh, *terrible* faults. He was too generous, too forgiving, too open
> handed, too modest, too unsuspecting, too. . . . as I say he had
> terrible faults.
> NICKY (*Ironically*): After a litany o' faults like that it'd be hard to see
> what virtues he could have. But you didn't mention his worst fault.
> JOHNNY: Being too modest you mean.
> NICKY: No, then. But they say he was an outlandish liar.
> JOHNNY (*Shocked*): Who said that?
> NICKY: Everyone without exception. They say you couldn't believe
> the Lord's prayer out of him. They say the truth used to go bad on
> his tongue. They say you'd actually see the lies comin' out of his
> mouth.
> JOHNNY (*Thoughtfully*): I suppose he was a little fanciful at times.
> NICKY: The way I heard it he was a heedyous liar! ! !
> JOHNNY (*Indignantly*): He was not a hideous liar. He was an inspired
> liar; he was a unique liar; he was an imaginative liar.

NICKY (*Shortly*): He was a liar anyway.
JOHNNY (*Not heeding him*): Above all he was a truthful liar.

With such playable scenes as this, with an excellent dying fall, and especially with its fine main role, *Cafflin' Johnny* is one of the more charming minor works of the recent Irish drama and a fitting capstone to an accomplished career.

3

Paul Vincent Carroll
The Rebel as Prodigal Son

I'M AS Irish as a terrier and with as sharp a bite," Paul Vincent Carroll once wrote, and that is a fair description of the best known and most personally dynamic Irish playwright to appear between O'Casey and Behan. Still, it is not the whole description; it needs to be paired with a statement like "I am not trying to teach anybody anything. I have finished with such presumptions. I have learned humility — the greatest asset in the equipment of any creative writer." [1] Only with these extremes in mind can the contradictory career of Carroll be explained.

Carroll is a flamboyant individual, and yet that individuality rarely appears in his plays. Unlike Yeats, Lady Gregory, Synge, Dunsany, O'Casey, or Behan, he developed no really settled point of view, but tried without much success to weld divergent views together. From one play to the next, his themes contradict each other. He has been by turns an astringent critic and an abashed conformist. He has been a satirist attracted to mysticism and a realist attracted to fantasy. He has been an outspoken critic of photographic realism whose best known plays have been realistic and whose unrealistic experiments have been halfhearted. He has a lyric impulse which he has half smothered by reading the Augustans, and a penchant for comic chaos which he has tempered by studying the painstaking plot structure of Ibsen and T. C. Murray. He has been one of the best known and most successful of modern Irish dramatists, but he has lived outside Ireland for years and has done some of his best work for the theatre of Scotland. Despite his great accomplishment, he is one of the great failures of Irish letters: after a brilliant beginning he floundered rather than developed.

✤

Carroll was born on July 10, 1900, in the outskirts of Dundalk in County Louth, son of a country schoolmaster who educated the boy until he was fourteen. Then, as Carroll says, "I . . . escaped to Dublin in 1914, where I entered training as a teacher, learned to drink a bottle of Guinness without spluttering and haunted the pit of the Abbey Theatre, to which I owe everything dramatic that I have." [2] He witnessed the 1916 Rising, and when he returned in 1920 to Dundalk he saw the town with new eyes. He was an idealist who had seen in the Abbey "the spiritual rebirth of the Irish race"; that rebirth took for him a practical form in the Rising. Back in Dundalk, by contrast he saw only clerical domination, philistinism, and middle-class complacency and greed. [3] On his father's advice, he emigrated to Glasgow, where from 1921 to 1937 he taught in state schools. He continued to look back on Ireland with a caustically critical eye, however, and the faults he saw he attacked in his early plays.

It was not until 1930 that he achieved an experimental production in the Abbey's Peacock Theatre with a little unpublished one-act called *The Watched Pot*. In 1931, to combat the shortage of good new plays, the Abbey offered a prize competition which was won jointly by Carroll and Teresa Deevy. Carroll's play was called *The Bed of Procrustes*, although he later changed the title to *Things That Are Caesar's*.

The play is an angry indictment of narrow clericalism. Father Duffy, the priest in the play, advises the heroine to accept a loveless marriage arranged by an avaricious parent. Eilish, the heroine, endures the marriage for a year, but then she walks out, taking off her wedding ring and saying to the priest, "On the word of a self-seeking woman, you took that in your hand and called it holy. But it too belongs to Caesar. . . . Take it then, Sacred Heart, and bury it in the hell you made for wicked things." The play is really an Irish *Doll's House*; when Eilish walks out the effect is as cutting a criticism of modern Irish morality as Nora's slamming of the door was of European middle-class morality of the nine-teenth century.

Although Carroll was angrily painting in blacks and whites, his priest is no total villain, but a man with a rational, persuasive, and, as Carroll later decided, admirable view of life. When Eilish charges the priest with caring nothing for her personal happiness, he replies, "You are nothing. I am nothing. But this thing we are part of, is everything." Though Father Duffy is represented with some fairness, he is not a fully drawn or an excellent character study of a priest. That character did not come until Carroll wrote *Shadow and Substance*.

Before he wrote it, however, he tinkered with a play about Robert Emmet, and then wrote a play about Jonathan Swift. The early version of this play, *Farewell to Greatness!*, was thought rather poor, but in the 1950's a revision was successfully presented on B.B.C. television with Micheál Mac Liammóir as the Dean. The play is not major Carroll. Despite a strong ending, it is a bit dull in its early stages. There is probably, though, no other play of Carroll so personally revealing. The agonies of Carroll's Swift, who fluctuates between platonic love for Stella and sensual passion for Vanessa, seem to some extent Carroll's own agonies. Certainly, Swift's savage indignation at human folly was a quality that at an earlier stage of his career Carroll must have felt considerable empathy with.

The Swift play arose from Carroll's close study of English literature of the Augustan Age, and from it sprang *Shadow and Substance*, his most successful play. Of it, he wrote:

I decided one day to resurrect Dean Swift, make him not only a Catholic, but a learned interpreter of Catholicism, and throw him into the modern mental turmoil in Ireland, which could be complicated by contact. From him came the character of the Canon. . . . The rebel schoolmaster and the Canon represent the conflicting forces that crush Brigid (the spirit of the nation) between them. But, then, you Americans don't believe in symbolism.[4]

Carroll's "symbolism" fits, but is hardly woven discernibly into the play. The real reason for the play's international fame is that its theme has an obvious, moving, human relevance.

The play's Canon Skerritt is one of the best roles in the modern Irish drama. A proud, austere, unconsciously selfish, and highly civilized man, the Canon is an actor's dream. It is actually his relish for good wine, good food, good pictures, and good conversation that makes him selfish. His comparison of the civilized amenities with the roughness of life in rural Ireland makes him sardonic, autocratic, semi-oblivious of his duty, and wistfully longing for his early life in a romanticized, civilized Spain that never was.

Against the Canon, Carroll opposes a rich collection of middle-class hypocrites and fools; the audience is in thorough sympathy with the Canon as he deflates these characters or uses them for his own purposes. But Brigid, his servant, a sweet and simple young girl, is another matter: although her almost simple-minded innocence has endeared her to the Canon, he really uses her in quite the same way that he uses the others.

The main action shows how the Canon reacts when the girl tells him that she talks to St. Brigid. Carroll is not, however, mainly interested in whether there was a miraculous appearance, but in the Canon failing Brigid, just as Father Duffy earlier failed Eilish, through a lack of human sympathy. Partly, this lack springs from the Canon's personality, though his attitude is the one prescribed by the Church. He does not regard the "miracle" with the easy credulity of his curates, but with a healthy skepticism. And, as he is the most articulate spokesman for religion, his failure must, in the play's terms, be regarded as the failure of religion itself.

The morality of *Shadow and Substance* is less black and white than that of *Things That Are Caesar's*. In O'Flingsley, the fiery schoolmaster, Carroll draws a humanitarian critic. O'Flingsley has pseudonymously published a book critical of the Church, and his values stand opposed to those of the Canon. However, Carroll arranges his plot to stress that the teacher also fails Brigid. Carroll's refusal to put all the blame on the Church and none on the humanitarian makes the play more persuasive than the simple condemnations in *Things That Are Caesar's*, but it boded no good for Carroll's future development. It is dramatically valuable that the Canon is not all bad nor the teacher all good, but Carroll's ability to see good in the Church and chinks in his own armor is a quality that grew in him and hurt his subsequent plays. In later plays, his tolerance for the Church grew and his personal rebellion diminished. He recently remarked to me that he did not believe in taking sides in a play, but merely in putting oppositions together. But he has also said, "And in case you think I'm a heretic and an infidel, I'm a good Catholic, even if I have little time for the army of little boyish Irish curates who believe in the shamrock and the harp." [5]

Carroll's next play, *The White Steed*, was foolishly rejected by the Abbey. Carroll charged that the rejection was not made by the ailing

Yeats who, he said, had approved of the play, but by the new directorate dominated by Frank O'Connor, F. R. Higgins, and Ernest Blythe. There may have been some justice to this charge, for the directors ignored Carroll's dare to make public a letter from Yeats about the play. At any rate, this incomprehensible rejection was to begin Carroll's alienation from the Abbey; once again the theatre was driving away its strongest writer. Carroll was pleasantly vindicated when the play ran successfully in New York and, like the previous year's *Shadow and Substance*, won the New York Drama Critics Circle Award for the best foreign play of the year.

The play is notable for two points: it shows that Carroll was growing closer to the Church, and it brought upon him the cliché that he had only one subject. As Peter Kavanagh put it: "He had said everything in *Things That Are Caesar's*, and each subsequent play was but a repetition. The brilliance of his technique was not enough to disguise the superficiality of his thinking. . . . Even Carroll's characters never varied from play to play, and those who were unable to recognize the sterility of thought did at least tire of looking at his Canon." [6] This play is again set in County Louth at the foot of the Mourne Mountains, and we do again have a canon, a schoolmaster, and a prime collection of fools and bigots. The criticism is still unjust, for the theme is new though the characters are familiar. Ibsen, to whom Carroll owes much of his ability in constructing a plot, often did the same thing. One might subtitle *Hedda Gabler* "Variations on *A Doll's House*." Both plays have as the central character a wife who secretly manipulates the destiny of some other character, and both have the husband, the gloomy and corrupted family friend, the helpful woman friend, and the seedy man with the shady past. Ibsen, like Carroll, has assigned somewhat different moral values to the figures, but the figures remain the same. In *The White Steed* we have a lovable canon instead of an autocratic one. We have a wishy-washy schoolmaster instead of a fiery one. We have a complex and determined heroine instead of a simple and determined one. As *Hedda* is no poorer than *A Doll's House* despite the similarity of technique, *The White Steed* is no poorer, for that reason, than *Shadow and Substance*.

The reason *The White Steed* is not quite so good is that its characterizations, although similar, are poorer. The main part, Canon Matt Lavelle, is an old parish priest whose legs have become paralyzed. His parish duties have been taken over by a ferociously religious curate who is forming the more time-serving parishioners into a kind of religious Gestapo. The old Canon is a benevolent man opposed to such hypermorality but powerless in his wheelchair to stop it. When the curate has pushed matters to an insupportable extreme, the Canon miraculously regains the use of his legs, steps in, and rights matters. Carroll meant his old priest to be an answer to the narrow religiosity he had earlier criticized. Canon Matt, Carroll's compromise between human sympathy and moral authority, is a wise, tolerant, easygoing old man who likes his dinner and likes to hear the sports results on the wireless. He even takes a tolerant attitude toward the touchy subject of mixed marriage. Still, despite Carroll's good intentions, Canon Matt is little more than a stage priest with a few lovable crotchets and a heart of gold. Played by Barry Fitzgerald — as, in fact, the part was — the Canon would take on an effective stage reality, but the character is evidence that the less critical Carroll grew, the less of an artist he grew.

That point may appear clearer if we skip ahead a few plays to *The Strings, My Lord, Are False* of 1942, in which a priest is again the main character. This play's Canon Courteney is the least convincing figure in Carroll's gallery of clerics, and this play is his least critical and most eulogistic of religion. An account of how the citizens of Glasgow behaved during a bombing raid in the war, it is a patriotic paean as well as a fervent indictment of human suffering. While one must sympathize with the theme, even a sympathetic reading cannot allow that Carroll has translated it into art. Canon Courteney is utterly self-sacrificing, courageous, and devoted — so much so that he seems hardly human. Like other eulogistic literature, the play remains a tract and not a testament.

Looking back over these four plays, one notices how Carroll's attitude toward religion has mellowed, and how his themes and characters have grown more conventional. *The Strings, My Lord, Are False* is an almost complete reversal of the attitude of *Things That Are Caesar's*. I am not so foolishly bigoted as to suggest that superb plays cannot be written from a Roman Catholic standpoint, but it seems incontrovertible that Paul Vincent Carroll could not write them.

⚜

Carroll has called himself "an enemy of photographic realism," but his enmity resembles his enmity toward the Church. He has never really cut the apron strings of Papa Ibsen,[7] and he seems to realize that fact: he once wrote, "All my life I have had in me two irreconcilable crazes — my rigid insistence on the inviolability of the fourth wall, and on the other hand my almost overwhelming longing to cross the stage with the tabs in my hand, opening them as I go and say to the audience, 'Sit up now, folks, we're ready.'" [8] Unfortunately, he never did allow himself such freedom; his deviations from realism have been only tentative excursions into fantasy, mysticism, and satire.

There had been hints of mysticism in *Shadow and Substance* and in *The White Steed*, and Carroll turned to fantasy in the alternately sad and funny one-act *Coggerers* (later retitled *The Conspirators*). This fine tragi-fantasy is set in the entrance hall of a Dublin library on Monday morning of Easter Week, 1916. In the hall are busts of Irish patriots — Mitchel, Lord Edward, Wolfe Tone, Emmet, and Parnell — and the busts speak as characters in the play, acting as a chorus for the big drama outside and for its microcosm inside, the death of the charwoman's son. Few plays in such a short space arouse such a moving and various body of emotions as this thoroughly successful little piece does.

Coggerers, despite Carroll's irritation with the theatre, was performed at the Abbey on November 22, 1937, as was his next long play, *Kindred*, which appeared on September 25, 1939. *Kindred* contained some elements of fantasy which were so unsuccessful that Carroll removed them on the second night. Still, the play failed in both Dublin and New York, where it was slated by some of Carroll's warmest admirers. It was his last play at the Abbey, and it has not been published.

The Old Foolishness, produced on May 7, 1943, at the Arts Theatre, London, is unlike those usually associated with Carroll, and might well be compared to O'Casey's late plays. Like them, it celebrates life, vigor, and beauty. Its realism is softened by a more romantic tone than can be found elsewhere in Carroll; even the comic speeches have an O'Caseyan lilting exaggeration. For instance:

> DAN: . . . And did ye hear her tellin' Peter her mouth was for kissin'? Man, I dream of a fine lovely woman sayin' that to me! "Dan, me hero, take your face out of me scented hair, and crush me mouth."
> . . .
> TIM: . . . You were born too far west, Dan.
> DAN: So I was. Fastin', prayin' and bein' respectable, and the oul' foolishness buried in pagan ground. It must have been grand in the oul' days when ye lay back and said to your woman, "Dance, yous lovely divils, dance, or I'll chop your heads off."

By his Old Foolishness, Carroll meant that same vigorous pastoral past that O'Casey used as a touchstone of the good life. And against the Old

Foolishness, Carroll pits some of the same adversaries — the narrow, life-quenching morality of the Church, the stony ideals of embittered patriotism, the dull safety of an arranged and loveless marriage.

The character who arouses the Old Foolishness in the men is Maeve McHugh, another of Carroll's women on a pedestal and his best girl's part since Brigid. In Brigid, he conveyed saintliness and simplicity; here he tries, pretty successfully, for romance. However, as in O'Casey's later versions of pastoral, the idyl is shattered by the modern world. The neighbors and the inevitable canon disapprove of the carryings-on, and the last scene is a dying fall that movingly makes Carroll's point — which is that the Old Foolishness must be caught on the wing, for it has no place in modern Ireland. The play's greatest fault is its length. If about ten pages could be judiciously cut, there would be little to criticize in this sadly humorous play. It is a pity Carroll did not explore this vein further.

Instead, the bombing of Glasgow deflected him into *The Strings, My Lord, Are False*, which was followed by a piece of grimly serious realism, *The Wise Have Not Spoken* of 1944. In the savagery of its theme, this play harks back to *Things That Are Caesar's*. Intending the play as a cutting criticism of Ireland, Carroll mentions the heavy hand of the Church, grasping politicians, emigration, and even the Rising and the Troubles. This time the good priest is a silenced priest, an outcast. The home of the MacElroys, the scene of the play, is an embryo Ireland from which much of the love and all of the beauty have fled. Though Carroll's points are fairly taken, some of the characters are so exaggerated, and the story is so intensely melodramatic, that the theme seems overstated. It is a black play whose theme might be summed up in Father Tiffney's speech:

Laws, laws, laws. The modern Deity, the stop-gap of idiotic men. Christ made only one law — to love one another. It's not laws we want in this country, nor taboos, nor censorship — it's love, knowledge, dignity, an understanding of each other, a supernatural meeting-point as old as time, not a tower of Babel where fools, puritans, and scoundrels shout each other down. . . . Just look at this place — a warping, killing crookening rat-trap where the human mind and spirit are driven mad.

"— a warping, killing crookening rat-trap where the human mind and spirit are driven mad" is as savage an indictment as one might find outside of Swift, and this whole play seems impelled by a raw irascibility. The serious characters, Francis and Catherine MacElroy, both seem livid cries of pain. Francis, representing idealism reduced to violence, spends his time cleaning his gun and crying moodily for blood. Catherine has some strongly plausible moments toward the end, but mainly she is a thin symbol of sexual starvation and guilt. Though strong characters, both are exaggerations; the play is too bleak and black to be either good theatre or convincing statement. Still, it does give an insight into Carroll as a man neither completely housebroken by conventional morality nor ever completely emancipated from it.

Carroll's Glasgow years brought close ties with the emerging Scottish theatre. During the 1930's, he wrote plays for the Curtain Theatre of Glasgow, and when it was closed by the war he became, in 1939, the "resident" playwright of the Rutherglen Theatre near Glasgow. In *James Bridie and His Theatre*, Winifred Bannister remarks that this theatre's main actors were taken into the Glasgow Citizens Theatre. When that theatre was founded by Bridie in 1942, Carroll was made one of the founding directors,[9] writing for it some notable plays. One, *The Strings, My Lord, Are False*, we have discussed. Another, originally titled *Weep for To-morrow* and first presented by the Glasgow Citizens Theatre in the 1947–1948 season, was roundly slated. "The foyer was full of angry, embarrassed people," and one critic described the character of Femina as "the most objectionable female he had ever encountered in fact or fiction."[10] Carroll gave me a later version of this unpublished script, entitled *Goodbye to the Summer*; it is a rather good play with some awful things in it. Femina, for instance, is a caricature of a Communist, but the old dominie and his drunken gardener crony are quite believable and lovingly drawn. The play is as neat a piece of plot-building as Carroll has ever done. The specific problem of the vanishing Scottish village and the good human qualities such a life fosters might not be convincing outside Scotland, but there is enough merit in the play, despite Femina, to warrant its production.

Carroll's 1950 play, *The Chuckeyhead Story*, was read in manuscript by George Jean Nathan who enthusiastically approved of it. It has more exaggeration than any previous play, but the exaggeration works better, perhaps because it springs from high spirits rather than fierce indignation. Carroll calls the play, which in its revised and published version was retitled *The Devil Came from Dublin*, "A Satirical Extravaganza." What distinguishes it from the usual farce is that the stereotypes are new and fresh, and that the language has an exuberant playfulness rare for this simple genre.

The action takes place during the Second World War in the village of Chuckeyhead near the Ulster border. As the food shortage in Ulster is serious, everyone in Chuckeyhead, even the priest, is engaged in smuggling. A District Justice arrives from Dublin to catch the smugglers, and this delightful pomposity is the devil of the title because he stands for the Ireland that attempts to repress the vigor and vitality of living. The main virtue of the play is probably its main fault. Act I is too long, and throughout Carroll gives his audience a bit too much of a good thing — a fact he is aware of, for he wrote me that in directing the play the drinking should be played down. With pruning and stronger curtains, this would be one of the liveliest Irish farces.

Carroll's finest Scottish play is the two-act *Green Cars Go East*, which was published in 1947 and produced in 1951. Set in a tenement district in the East End of Glasgow in the 1930's, it has a couple of Irish characters, but is basically Scottish, with a Scottish theme. It is worth noting, in passing, that Carroll's three Scottish plays help disprove the cliché that he is a writer with one subject.

Until an ending which is too contrivedly optimistic, *Green Cars* is an absorbing, strong, and honest job that comes close to being for the slums of Glasgow what *Juno and the Paycock* was for the slums of Dublin. The Lewis family, like O'Casey's Boyle family, is almost on the rocks. The father, Ted Lewis, is a loafer like Captain Boyle, but Mrs. Lewis is no Juno. She is an ignorant, easygoing, slatternly, foolish woman, and her family is held together by the daughter Mary, a teacher in a slum school. Mary scrimps to put the older boy Bill through the university, and she persuades the younger boy Charlie to take an honest job before he winds up in jail. She remains fiercely devoted to her family, although it means putting off her marriage to a teacher from a middle-class family, and perhaps even losing him. Through much of the play, it seems as if the slums will drag Mary down. I do not question Carroll's view that an indomitable person can lift himself up by the bootstraps; his Mary is a moving presentation of suffering, endurance, and, surprisingly, gaiety. But the ending shows her rescuing the whole family and even getting back the fiancé whom she had apparently lost: through three fourths of the play, Carroll had drawn such a convincing picture of a brutal, sordid, and degrading atmosphere that wholesale happiness at the end is too sweeping to be convincing. The first three fourths, however, is as fine as anything Carroll ever wrote.

The best known of Carroll's recent plays is *The Wayward Saint* of 1955. In it, he returns to the Mourne Mountains and the Paul Vincent Carroll stock company. His Canon Daniel McCooey is a simple, gullible priest who like St. Francis talks to birds and animals, and who is a kind of male counterpart to Brigid of *Shadow and Substance*. However, the girl's part was played straight, whereas the Canon's is permeated by a charmingly humanizing faultiness. The devil, in the form of Baron Nicholas de Balbus, is able to play on the Canon's pride and to give him a droll self-importance about being a saint — a fact which suggests the influence of D'Alton's *The Devil a Saint Would Be*. Also, the Canon's saintliness is humanized by his willingness to trick his bishop, his housekeeper, and his grocer in ways not far distant from outright lies.

The play is nicely of a piece, and its pleasant humor never deserts it. Its main fault lies in the quality of Carroll's inventiveness. The Canon's miracles — stopping clocks, making lights blink, raising chairs — are pleasant theatrical devices, but not particularly fresh or striking. The play, even when compared with O'Casey's *Cock-a-Doodle Dandy*, seems imaginative, but the imagination does not seem first-rate. The piece is mildly charming, but never quite delightful, and Carroll's own wild mind seems muted in it. This restraint is evident in his remarks about the play:

When I was a young playwright, I had a bee in my Irish bonnet about reforming people through the medium of the stage. I suppose I caught the bug from such dramatizing conversationalists as Bernard Shaw and Alexis Tolstoy, and ignored the warnings of true dramatists like J. M. Synge, who never wanted to reform anybody. . . .

Today I have no longer any desire to reform anyone but myself, and I am afraid I'm making a rather poor job even of that! Henrik Ibsen, that dour Norwegian reformer, apart from his constructional brilliance, to which I owe so much, bores me with his humorless strictures which continually remind me of that dour patron saint of mine, St. Paul. To make matters worse, the people I wanted to reform in my younger years have turned out to be much nicer people than myself, and that paradoxical slap on the jaw of life has taught my presumption a very salutary lesson. . . .

In *The Wayward Saint*, I have no axes to grind. I just want people to enjoy themselves and stop lifting the lids off the Carroll philosophical dustbins in search of alleged truth. I'll walk with you, whatever your creed or race. If you don't believe, as I do, that fundamental innocence and simplicity are the powerful bulwarks of a civilization moving frighteningly on to an unknown future, I'll still walk with you and not preach. Only one right I reserve in this rebel heart of mine — in any country where I live, either permanently or temporarily, I instinctively belong as a creative writer to the Opposition, and the chief function of the Opposition is to oppose.[11]

This strikes me as both a beautiful and a sad statement. It suggests that despite his "rebel heart," Carroll has always been brought up short by authority. His strictures on the Catholic Church have always been blunted by his ultimate belief in the Church, and his irritation with realism has always been foiled by his debt to it. Just as he always follows a criticism of the Church by a eulogy of it, so technically does he follow up a tentative diversion into experiment by an example of total realism. The upshot is that his great artistic promise has never been completely realized. He has not developed as a thinker, but wavered between two conflicting impulses. He has not developed as an experimental playwright, but only tried furtive forays away from realism. He is a rebel who has never truly rebelled.

That seems to me an enormous waste, for, make no mistake about it, Carroll has a talent rivaling O'Casey's. O'Casey's genius was strong enough to hammer out an inimitable style because he was not afraid to be the conscience of his race. Carroll could never quite do that.

Still, he has made a rare contribution to Irish drama, and a larger one than he has so far been credited with. He must be remembered not only for the superb realism of *Shadow and Substance* and *The White Steed*, but also for the equally fine realism of *Green Cars Go East*, and for the beautiful lyricism of *The Old Foolishness*, and for the wild hilarity of *The Devil Came from Dublin*. In these plays, he was writing at the top of his form, and that top was very high indeed.

4

The Abbey Dramatists: 1946–1965

JUDGING writers still in their prime or just reaching it is an uncertain task at best. It seems safe to say, however, that in its last twenty years the Abbey has encouraged four exceptional talents — Walter Macken, Bryan MacMahon, Seamus Byrne, and John O'Donovan. The theatre also produced the early work of some of the most promising younger men — Maurice Meldon, Hugh Leonard, John Murphy, and Tom Coffey. It even produced writers who originally made their reputations outside of the Abbey — notably Brendan Behan and John B. Keane.

This worthy record could have been worthier, and it must be balanced by many instances of insufficient encouragement. Although Walter Macken has recently served a few months as the Abbey's artistic director, his last production was by a commercial management during the Theatre Festival. Seamus Byrne's last play was done for the Festival after having been rejected by the Abbey. Bryan MacMahon appears to have turned away from the theatre altogether, and has rewritten his best play as a novel. John O'Donovan was so distraught by his last Abbey production that he refused to submit any more work to the theatre. Maurice Meldon's second play was accepted by the Abbey but never produced, and his best plays were done by the 37 Theatre Club. Most of the recent work of Hugh Leonard and Tom Coffey has been done by commercial managements at the Theatre Festival. John Murphy's second play was rejected, and he has left the country. The production of Behan's *The*

Quare Fellow only came after the author's repeated urging and after the play had been a London success, while the production of Keane's *Hut 42* was distinctly "belated amends" for previous rejections.

In the last twenty years, the Abbey has not avidly sought new talent, but it has produced twenty-five or thirty good plays by about ten interesting new writers. It was also producing new work by such established writers as D'Alton, Molloy, and Denis Johnston; it was constantly reviving some of the better plays from its earlier repertoire; and it was occasionally producing a notable foreign play like O'Neill's *Long Day's Journey into Night* and Brecht's *Galileo*. All this adds up to a more than respectable record.

⚜

Walter Macken is one of the most successful modern Irish writers, and one of the best . His plays are little known outside Ireland, but his fiction has found a fairly wide, Book-of-the-Month Club, upper-middle-brow audience. His critical reputation lies about halfway between that of a Frank O'Connor and that of a Maurice Walsh. Still, even though his stories lack the qualities likely to get them discussed in the *Hudson Review* or *Modern Fiction Studies*, they are fine work, and no less fine for being both traditional and easily readable.

Macken was born on May 3, 1915, in the city of Galway, and his novel *Sullivan* seems a fictional parallel to his own life. His father died when Macken was a boy, and he attended the Patrician Brothers primary and high schools in Galway. After school, he was a clerk on the county council for a short time, but when he was sixteen or seventeen, he became involved in the Gaelic Theatre, the Taibhdhearc, in Galway. He played there until he was twenty-one, when he eloped to London with the daughter of a local newspaper editor and thereafter sold insurance for two years. When Frank Dermody, the Taibhdhearc's director, went on to the Abbey, Macken returned and stayed nine years, acting, producing, and writing plays in Irish.

His first play in English was *Mungo's Mansion*, which was performed at the Abbey on February 11, 1946. His other published English plays are *Vacant Possession* which has been produced so far only by amateurs, *Home Is the Hero* in which he played both on Broadway and in the film, and *Twilight of a Warrior* which is possibly his best. His unpublished plays include *Look in the Looking Glass* which was done at the Abbey in March, 1958, *The Voices of Doolin* which was produced by Cyril Cusack during a recent Theatre Festival, and *The Last Gentlemen*. In recent years, after a two-year stint of acting at the Abbey and Broadway appearances in *Home Is the Hero* and Molloy's *The King of Friday's Men*, he has given most of his creative energy to fiction. Besides *Sullivan*, he has written two novels banned in Ireland, *Quench the Moon* and *The Bog Man*. His volumes of short stories include *The Green Hills and Other Stories* and *God Made Sunday*. His best work in fiction is his moving novel of Galway fishermen, *Rain on the Wind*, and his historical trilogy composed of *Seek the Fair Land*, which is set in Cromwell's time, *The Silent People* about the Famine, and *The Scorching Wind* about the Rising and the Civil War. He has written one other novel called *I Am Alone* and a children's story called *The Island of the Great Yellow Ox*.

Macken's early plays, with their broad characterization and heightened speech, suggest the early O'Casey. *Mungo's Mansion* is both a strong evocation of slum life and a strong condemnation of it. The main character is Mungo King, an old docker now crippled and confined to an upstairs room in his house in Buttermilk Lane. His eleven children are crammed into the house, with a couple of lodgers on the top floor. His elder children are eager to move from the slum that is slowly killing his youngest son, Tomeen. Still, Mungo, with the tenacious stubbornness of a domestic tyrant, refuses to move and lose the companionship of his cronies, Mowleogs Canavan and Winnie the Wild Ducks. Indeed, despite its condemnation of the Claddagh district of Galway, the play suggests that this was an exciting place to live. Consider, for instance, this casual dialogue between Winnie in an upstairs window and Maggie Badgers in the street:

> MAGGIE'S VOICE: It is me indeed, Winnie! God bless yeh up there, leanin' outa the winda yeh look like an advertisemint for a bath every Saturday night with Sunlight soap.
> (*She laughs shrilly at this sally.*)
> WINNIE: They's more than me that wants a bath indeed, if we have teh be personal, Maggie Badgers, an' if yeh took teh scrubbin' yerself oo a Saturday night the poor sinner like yeh might be more plazin' to the Lord in His Sight, goin' up teh holy communion with a snitch on yeh like the back ind a me boot, an' no more a the sanctity a the Lord in yer soul than a Turk, God bless the mark.
> MAGGIE'S VOICE (*slightly annoyed*): Oh, is that so, me lady, the one that's goin' around pretindin' teh be the Lord's anointed, doin' me good deeds, how are yeh, slippin' up teh the hock-shop every Monday mornin' if yeh don't mind, doin' good deeds an' robbin' the pin-

nies outa the mouths a orphans with yer little bitta commission, an'
thin butter wouldn't melt in yer mouth.

WINNIE (*annoyed*): Oh, indeed, sez the Queen a Claddy, airin' herself
like the Connemara cow she is, goin' round with her topin' dirty
black porter, an' her poor starvin' children at home pullin' their rags
around thim an' their mouths ever open like a pack a young skal-
tauns starvin' with the hunger, a nice one teh talk indeed!

The play has half a dozen such good roles and several moments of real
comedy and suspense — particularly in the broadcast of the horse race
and in Mungo's being trapped alone by the murderer. The worst fault
is the length. Macken develops many scenes beyond what was needed
and makes some points twice over. Despite that, it is an amusing, tensely
gripping play. Although Macken substitutes broad melodrama for tragedy and includes a happy ending, he was still doing for Galway's Claddagh what O'Casey had done for Dublin's Mountjoy Square.

Vacant Possession takes place in the Gantry, a deserted, decrepit old
house in Galway which is about to be knocked down. Into it come the
Delaney family and their friend Fixit Maloney. The Delaneys have been
dispossessed because Gunner, the father, has drunk up the rent money.
Tacked on to this tragedy is a story of a robbery done by Wee-Wee
Brady and a cultured old crook called Gabbler Blake. The effect of the
main story is a bit dissipated by the detective-story unraveling of this
minor plot, which takes up most of the space at the end. Still, this story
of seedy down-and-outs is fine theatre, and the last curtain — with the
Gantry being demolished and the gramophone playing, "Sure, a little
bit of Heaven fell from out the sky one day — — — They called it Ire–e–
e–e–land" — is as sardonic as the singing of "Keep the Home Fires Burning" at the end of *The Plough and the Stars*.

The dialogue can also stand comparison with the early O'Casey's. For
instance:

MAGGIE: There ain't nothin' Fixit can't do with an oul' hammer an'
nail.

GUNNER (*heavily sarcastic*): He'd a been a rale useful man to'v had
around at the Crucifixion.

Or this exchange between Fixit and his enemy Revenge Horgan:

FIXIT (*a little daunted*): Now lookit here, Jamesy Horgan, can't we
reach a quiet peaceful settlement? Can't we sit down nice an' quiet
like respectable dacent people an' hammer the thing out without
bloodshed?

REVENGE: We'll hammer it out all right, but they'll be plenty a bloodshed, an' it'll be your blood, d'ye hear? Yeh'll be pumpin' blood like a stuck pig whin I'm done with yeh, yeh lousy little jiltin' craw-thumpin' lump a scavenger mess.

In this least known of Macken's plays, the dialogue is again racier and the characterization larger than life, but that hardly seems a great fault when what emerges is so entertaining.

The O'Caseyan reminiscences are still evident in Macken's best known play, *Home Is the Hero*, though the characterization has become more restrained and truer to life than to the theatre. The play is set in a County Council house in Galway, its story a variation of a favorite Irish theme, the revelation that the hero is really a villain. The O'Reilly family, like the Boyle family in *Juno*, is composed of a false-hero father, a long-suffering mother, a son, and a daughter. The daughter is as headstrong as Mary Boyle, the son Willie maimed like Johnny Boyle. It is Willie, however, who holds the family together, rather than the mother Daylia, who likes her drop. Paddo, the father, is a brute of a man who five years earlier had killed a neighbor and is now returning home from prison. His cronies plan a great welcome, but his son and daughter greet him less enthusiastically. And before the evening is over, Paddo has beaten Josie, terrified Daylia, and knocked Dovetail downstairs. Then, faced with his children's revolt, he leaves home, and the play ends with the family happy as they were before.

This résumé makes Paddo appear a great brute, which apparently is what Macken wants. Yet there is an ambivalence about the character. Paddo has paid for his murder and suffered remorse, yet Macken seems to squelch sympathy for him. When Paddo apologizes to the wife of the murdered man, Macken presents the apology as wrong. Paddo is horrified at Willie's wanting to marry the daughter of the murdered man, at Rosie's flashy beau, at Daylia's drinking. In other words, the facts make a case for him, but Macken never allows the audience to feel as much sympathy as the facts would allow. The result is a curiously cold, almost ill-tempered play, although technically it is an adroit example of the best Abbey realism. It is tightly structured, and its characters, with the exception of the Joxerish Dovetail, are drawn with believable restraint.

Twilight of a Warrior must stand or fall by the strength of its main character — and Dacey Adam does not quite have the vigorous full-bloodedness that the story demands. He is a man of the people, a hero of the Troubles who has married the daughter of a manufacturer and taken over the business. He is meant to be a dominating personality, a fighter rigidly controlling the lives of all about him. And perhaps a fine actor, like Ray McAnally who first played the part, could convey the strength that Macken wanted, but that strength is not completely written into the part. We are told about it more than we see it. Macken was attempting the kind of character that Gorky succeeded superbly at in *Yegor Bulychov and the Others*, that Ibsen succeeded at in *John Gabriel Borkman*, and, for that matter, that Shakespeare succeeded at in *King Lear*. He was attempting to draw a patriarch whose world is crumbling, and the success of such a play depends on the writer's ability to create a giant. Sadly, Dacey Adam is not quite that giant, for Macken has much to say in this play to modern Ireland.

Broadly, Dacey is an example of the temper which led Ireland from 1916 through the Civil War. Macken seems to say that such ruthless and commanding figures have no place today. Although Dacey has taken an Anglo-Irish business concern and made it more profitable, he has also driven the humanity from it, a fact resented by his Anglo-Irish wife. He tries to order the life of his son, a poet who revolts against him. He tries to decide whom his daughter will marry. Obviously, Dacey stands for a great deal, and much of it is suggested in the story of Mary Ann. When Dacey was on the run, Mary Ann took him in and tended his wounds. She came to mean for him the worth of the common people of Ireland. Years later at a political meeting, Dacey saw her again, still poor and still indomitable. The wars of the gunmen and politicians had neither helped nor harmed her; she seemed to contain for Dacey all the guilt he felt for what he and his kind had made of Ireland.

Dacey's sister and brother suggest another view of what the politicians have made of the Rising. The sister Gubby piously tends the memory of Dacey's heroism; the brother Affey, who had been a hero in the First World War, reduced to being Dacey's yes man, has his own bravery ignored. The point seems to be the parochialism of Ireland.

Apparently Macken purposely gave Dacey the last name of Adam, the first man; one wonders if it is too subtle to note that "Dacey" is an anagram for "decay." At any rate, the young man who wants to marry Dacey's daughter is named Abel Martin, and in his kind seems to reside the hope for Ireland's future. Despite the story's heavy load of meaning, it never becomes merely allegorical. One is always interested in the story as story and in the characters as people. We might sum up the play by calling it a good tragedy without a great tragic hero, a *King Lear* with the main role filled by Arthur Miller's Joe Keller.

The Voices of Doolin was strongly criticized when it appeared at the 1960 Theatre Festival, but it is a good play. Like *Twilight of a Warrior* and his most recent play, *The Last Gentleman*, it shows that Macken has a growing interest in a thicker characterization than most plays usually attempt. Doolin is a confirmed alcoholic whose doll-making factory has gone on the rocks. Except for his teenage daughter, his family has turned against him. Impelled by the older daughter's fiancé, Morgan Cumisky, the family tries to persuade Doolin to sell the factory to a large concern which will make plastic dolls instead of the china ones Doolin had lovingly produced.

Doolin has just returned from an asylum where he has been taking the cure. What he has seen there has so frightened him he thinks that with help from his family he can fight his way back to normalcy. In some tautly dramatic scenes, however, his wife, elder daughter, son, and an old friend all refuse that help, and Cumisky gives him a bottle to tempt him to sign over the factory. Only when Doolin sees Cumisky making a pass at his younger daughter does he pull himself together a little and begin to fight. The audience's sympathy is quite with him, for none of his relatives is free from guilt, and Macken's theme seems to be that no man is so stainless that he can condemn another.

In some remarkable scenes Doolin, alone onstage, fights the voices that plague him, and the picture of this gutted and tormented man rising to a precariously held strength is never overdrawn or theatrical in a hypersimple sense. It is a challenging acting role, one of the most fully drawn in any Irish play of recent years. The minor characters are plausible; none is the larger-than-life cartoon Macken earlier relied on. In his six produced plays, one can see Macken's growth from theatrical simplicity to a complexity reflecting real life. His recent death has deprived the Irish theatre of one of its finest talents.

᭼

Bryan MacMahon is known outside of Ireland as a writer of fiction; his inclusion would be mandatory in any but the slimmest of anthologies. He has written only three serious plays, but two are so good that it is difficult to discuss them with a proper critical restraint.

MacMahon's home is Listowel in County Kerry, the little town that also gave birth to George Fitzmaurice, Maurice Walsh, and John B. Keane. MacMahon was born in 1909. His mother was a schoolteacher, and he received a good, cheap classical education at the local college. Since training at St. Patrick's College, Drumcondra, as a teacher, he has taught in the primary school at Listowel for thirty-five years. Indeed, he keeps coming back to teach in it despite jaunts to lecture at Harvard or the Iowa Writers Workshop. For ten years he ran a bookshop in Listowel, and he also founded the Listowel Drama Group. His early playwriting was conventional journeyman work done to give the company something to play; his three mature plays have been performed by the Abbey.

His first writing was a poem in *The Bell*, and his books include *The Lion Tamer and Other Stories* of 1949, *Children of the Rainbow* of 1952, *The Red Petticoat* of 1955, and a children's story, *Jack O'Moora and the King of Ireland's Son*. He knows a great deal about Irish folklore — knowledge reflected in his play the *Song of the Anvil*. He is well versed also in tinker lore, and this knowledge is reflected in his favorite play, *The Honey Spike*, which was published in novel form in 1967.

His first serious play, *The Bugle in the Blood*, produced at the Abbey in March, 1949, is a trifle dated, for it treats of the post-Treaty days, with the son of the Trimble family jailed for political activity and dying on a hunger strike. There is no great originality about the theme or experimentation in the technique, but the play is strong and effective. The basic family tragedy is here: Joe, the father, old, tired, and debilitated by a stroke; Maroya, the mother, a fire-breathing patriot; Evelyn, the daughter, like Mary Boyle, pregnant and deserted; Andy, the younger son, a scholarship boy turned to violence by his brother's death and, like Johnny Boyle, killed at the end of the play. The Joxer figure is cut in two — half Botany Connell, a cobbler neighbor, wise, dependable, and mildly humorous; half Circus Jack, a street strongman, a drunken braggart, and a showy part for an actor. There is a Maisie Madigan neighbor in Mrs. Monahan, a well-drawn caricature of a prying snoop.

Like O'Casey, MacMahon gets his effects from songs, from poems, and from the juxtaposition of comedy and tragedy. The end of Act II, in its veering back and forth between tragedy and comedy, is particularly fresh, unpredictable, and meaningfully incongruous. And the last scene of the play — with its somber funeral, the drunken antics of Circus, and the melodramatic fight between Andy and a sympathetic policeman — is even better. In its theme, its characters, and its manner, the play is imitative, but it imitates quality.

Song of the Anvil somewhat resembles Molloy's *The Visiting House*: its subject is the desire for a bit of fantasy and romance. The people of the isolated valley of Glensharoon in County Kerry demand a touch of poetry to make existence bearable, and the poetry comes from Ulick Madigan, who pretends to go into a trance and then comes up with some entrancing fable. He has a craze for coloring life. As he explains it himself:

To you this place is picturesque. To me it's daft and desolate. And it's dying fast. Once, out of the struggle for the land, came storytellers, dancers, poets, men who made fiddle-music fit to stir the stars. But they are all dead — all dead, I tell you, man. The young people — they have all gone across the sea. We were alone and moving towards our end. And then, when all seemed lost, one winter's night, we held a trial all night long until the crack of dawn to find who'd tell a flamin' variegated lie. . . . I won! And do you know what 'twas like? 'Twas like as if the Voice of God was roaring from my blood. Ever since then, for me, gannet and gull, lizard and eel, even the tongs and kettle on the hob, must speak and act like Christian men.

Ulick's story of the Golden People is based on his memory of a colony of ants; in his hands, however, it becomes translated into legendary stuff about a fabled people, and the people in the glen become a bit like Golden People.

There are four chief forces in the story — the classic storytelling of Ireland, exemplified by Ulick; the force of pagan superstition exemplified by Darby Jer O'Shea, a half-sinister old spell-casting wizard; the Christian force exemplified by the retired, weak, and drunken Father "O'Priest" McHugh; and the force of youth exemplified by the American girl Ellenrose Schneider. Through most of the play, the characters are in the grip of the traditional Irish past, and MacMahon means no fanciful Crock o' Gold whimsy of a past; his play is often grim and full of terror. At one point, the people learn that Ulick has betrayed their secret life to a reporter, and despite their affection for him they prepare to brand him with a hot iron. They are prevented only by luck and by Ellenrose, Father O'Priest, Darby Jer, and Ulick all working together in a kind of tangled cooperation.

MacMahon's meaning comes clear at the end of the fable when Ulick, now absolved of his priesthood, is about to wed Ellenrose, and when the people demand that Father O'Priest take Ulick's place and tell them a story. The story is about a man named Christy Love, a biblical story told in Irish idiom. In other words, when all of elements of the theme are pervaded by Christianity, there will be a truly Golden Folk in Ireland.

Although the story is heavy with meaning, it is far from allegory. Kit-

sy Carty, an aging spinster, and Mick-Twin and Paddy-Twin O'Donnell, the old boys who have courted her for years, are excellent parts;
there is hardly a character not subjected to pressure and forced by the
action to become more than a stock type. Indeed, the surprise at seeing
characters which in another play would be only lovable stage-Irishmen
suddenly become stonily inhuman is a strange and frightening experience. The plot itself veers from humor to fantasy to satire and finally to
a rousing melodramatic climax. The play also requires dancers, singers,
and musicians. It is as theatrical a play as the Abbey has staged in the last
forty years.

One of its few rivals is MacMahon's own *The Honey Spike*, which
was first produced on May 22, 1961. It is the story of Breda and Martin
Claffey, a young tinker and his wife, and of their race across the length
of Ireland to get Breda to the hospital she desires, the Honey Spike of the
title, before her baby comes. It is difficult to describe the richness of this
play. One could call it an Irish *Mother Courage*, except that it is more
thickly textured and more moving. One could call it an Irish *As I Lay
Dying*, except that it is a more public statement. As in all great journey
literature, this journey offers an objective correlative for man's state; it
is both quest and test, an allegory of life. But though it is as meaningful
as a *Pilgrim's Progress*, it is also as specific as a *Huckleberry Finn*. It is
grounded in the real life of Ireland. Its tinkers are adequate individuals
and significant types. It is not only Martin and Breda who come across
with force; the play is a cross-section of Ireland in space and in class.

It begins at the Giant's Causeway in the far north, then shifts to the
Border, to Lough Derg, and to Killorglin in Kerry on the Gathering Day
of Puck Fair. During the journey we see the types of people who make
up modern Ireland — I.R.A. raiders, a brace of farmers, a West-Britonish
major from the Big House, a Civic Guard, a priest. Also woven into the
play are riddles, ballads, the spectacle of Puck Fair, fights, and violence.
This is one of the few plays that successfully transfers the picaresque
form to the stage. It is funny, exciting, satiric, and, in its final juxtaposition of birth and death, tragic. At the end when the child lives and Breda
dies, Martin cries out in one of the great speeches of the Irish drama:

Breda! Breda Claffey! Breda, you lovely bitch that I love as man has
never loved a woman before. Breda! Come out and walk with me again.
Come out and swing your arms around my neck. You've no complaint
of me. I raced you from the Causeway in the Six. We made the bed of
honour 30, 40, 60 times, we did. Come out, let you! For you I raced my

cob. Through guns and hurleys lifted above my head I brought you to your honey spike. Come out, I tell you now. Come out! The two of us were grand. Only come out, let you, and then the pony-bells will rung for us again. Hey! Breda Claffey, listen now! Listen, I tell you! The world is thronged with things is lovely at the break o' day. Come out, you stubborn heedless strap! Come out, or else I'll drag you by your hair. I tell you that I'll drag you by your . . . lovely shining rippling hair.

The Honey Spike is impelled by much real observation and intimate knowledge; its realism is lifted by waves of lyricism and emotion and enchantment and song. It is one of the most masterly pieces of theatre that the Abbey has ever done.

⚘

Seamus Byrne is a slight, slim man who looks considerably less than his sixty-odd years. He was born in Dublin on December 27, 1904. He attended Blackrock College and then the National University where he received his LL.B. in 1927. He qualified as a solicitor and practiced for nine years in Leitrim before he became involved in politics and was jailed for his activities in the new I.R.A. in 1940. After a hunger strike of twenty-one days, he was released, having served nine months of his two-year term. In 1950, his play *Design for a Headstone* was produced at the Abbey and was initially attacked by both the left and the right, by the I.R.A. and by Maria Duce. The play ran, however, for six weeks. In November, 1951, his *Innocent Bystander*, a study of embezzling solicitors in a provincial town, was played at the Abbey. The script of his third play, *A Hawk in the Handsaw*, has been lost. A collaboration with the actress-producer Shelagh Richards, the play is the story of a review comedian's desire to play Hamlet. Byrne's last play, *Little City*, has been several times revised, but Byrne had to wait several years for a producer. The reason, in part, was probably the play's subject, abortion. However, Byrne submitted the piece to a learned Jesuit who called it "a first class study in the doctrine of grace." At present, Byrne is contemplating a new play on alcoholism.

Byrne is now a consultant for two law firms. He succeeded Gabriel Fallon as critic on the *Catholic Standard*, but has since given up dramatic criticism. In recent years, he has become disillusioned with politics, regarding everything that has happened politically in Ireland since 1916 as a disaster.

Design for a Headstone, first produced on April 8, 1950, is one of the

Abbey's strongest realistic plays since the war. On its sixth night, however, an ultra-right-wing Catholic organization staged a demonstration in the theatre: there were shouts of protest, an attempted assault on the author, and some young men rushing down the aisle to shout refutations of a line in the play. The next night the police were brought in, and the demonstration, which had no popular support, dwindled away.

The action of the play is Mountjoy Prison before 1950, well after the Civil War. Byrne is concerned with the second generation of Republicans who continued to fight after the country at large had settled down to peace. The strength of the play is in its theme — a discussion of how the Church is at odds with Republicanism. The political prisoners are about to lose their political status and to be treated as ordinary criminals. To defeat this move, the Republican leader, Conor Egan, goes on hunger strike. The prison priest opposes the strike as a sin, and just before Egan's death refuses him absolution and breaks him down. The conflict is not hedged; the priest is not treated with kid gloves, but even roundly abused by one of the prisoners. Byrne really offers no solution, though he states a central problem of modern Ireland with rare strength and clarity. His final insight is more than a superficial comment about the Church's being on the side of established government; it is rather a revelation of how Jesuitically opportunistic the Church is in its primary interest of saving souls.

Much of the later action is taken up with the old-fashioned device of a letter, and some of this plot manipulation seems artificial, although that fault may be less apparent in the excitement of production. The ending also shows how a jailbreak is foiled, how the I.R.A. in its reprisals kills the wrong men, and how many of its own valuable men are killed. Though this effective point may partly obscure the main theme, at the end another Republican is planning a hunger strike, and it is not at all clear that he too will be broken by the priest. The final feeling is that a dilemma is unresolved — and that there has been a vast human waste.

The play has a large cast, over twenty big parts and many walk-ons. Naturally, some roles are skimped, but many are vivid. In particular the old lag Jakey is a full, vital part, and the role of Ructions McGowan, played originally by Walter Macken, has some biting lines. The characters have none of the frowsy flavor of those in Behan's *The Quare Fellow*,[1] nor is the play permeated by the author's personality. Its real strength lies in the passion of what is said. Here, for instance, is Ructions's outburst to the priest:

More subtleties! More snares! Church and State, moving, hand in hand, to crush the soul of a single man — because he rose up from his knees — because he struggled to his feet, and dared to raise his eyes to the light! And this, you call your sacred, bounden duty. Towards whom, towards what? Towards God or man? Is this the tribute due to Caesar by Holy Mother Church — or the Scarlet Whore of Babylon giving the beast his money's worth?

Byrne's revolutionaries come across as men of passionate sincerity. Neither they nor their beliefs are treated with a false romanticism, and the play squarely attacks a controversial issue. That is a rare quality at any time and in any country; it is especially rare in Ireland.

Little City, produced by Phyllis Ryan at the 1964 Theatre Festival, is set in a shabby third-rate hotel in the Dublin suburbs. It has, at first sight, three unconnected strands of plot, one major and two minor. On reflection, however, one sees that each strand reinforces Byrne's theme. The main strand concerns the housemaid of the hotel, pregnant by the proprietress's son, who has skipped off to England. This plot shows how both the girl's friends and her enemies push her toward an abortion which she does not want. One minor plot shows several lodgers deciding to demonstrate against a "Communist" play; most have neither read nor seen it, and are responding entirely to hearsay. The protest finally develops into a drunken brawl in which one protester brains another with a lead pipe. The other minor plot concerns a shady smalltime wheeler-dealer who plans to branch out from receiving stolen goods into the illegal production of drugs and nostrums.

Each action suggests that nearly everyone in the play, save the housemaid Clare and the retired chemist Canning, is eaten up with greed or selfishness. Byrne gives us enough incidents to suggest that these people are no isolated individuals, but symptoms of a whole society's failings. The characters are not monsters, but disconcertingly believable, a fact that makes the play even more savage. Even the sympathetic boots who tries to help Clare is a canny chancer who fully intends to make money out of her abortion. But, on the other hand, even the venomous proprietress has moments of selfless love and anguish over her wretched son, while the coldest and most practical villain, the abortionist Graham, is effectively underplayed as a cold pragmatist. *Little City* is not so rich a play as *Design for a Headstone*, but what it says is engrossing and honest and pertinent — these qualities give the plays of Seamus Byrne a compelling authority.

John O'Donovan is about the closest approach to an Irish Shavian. He was born on January 29, 1921, in Dublin, and he attended the Synge Street Christian Brothers school until he was about seventeen. After a series of clerking jobs, he went to Belfast in 1941 to work in the Auxiliary Fire Service attached to the Royal Victoria Hospital. In the spring of 1945, he returned to Dublin and began submitting articles to papers. He gradually drifted into full-time journalism, working on the *Radio Review*, the *Irish Press*, and for five years on the *Evening Press*, from which he finally resigned to go into free-lancing and radio writing and broadcasting, at which jobs he has labored ever since.

He did a great deal of apprentice playwriting; four early plays were rejected by the Abbey, each with an increasing lack of interest. Finally his play *The Half-Millionaire* was accepted, running for a fortnight in 1954. In 1957, *The Less We Are Together* ran for four months at the Abbey; his next, *The Change of Mind*, ran five weeks, and one of his best plays, *The Shaws of Synge Street*, ran for only a week to small houses. *The Nuclear Station* was a potboiling farce the theatre rejected, and his last play to be staged there, *Copperfaced Jack*, was produced on February 25, 1963.

This production caused O'Donovan some justified anguish. Rehearsals were underway before he learned that the play was even scheduled for production. The theatre made unauthorized changes in the text,[2] rehearsals went badly, and on the Friday before the Monday opening the play had still not been advertised. This was for O'Donovan the last straw; he burst into Ernest Blythe's office and all but assaulted him. After the play had staggered out a week's run, O'Donovan took sick and went into the hospital. He then decided to submit no more plays to the Abbey so long as Blythe remained as managing director. However, the theatre later asked O'Donovan to fashion a Jonathan Swift evening, and the piece has been played in the new Abbey.

O'Donovan's most successful play, *The Less We Are Together*, produced on July 22, 1957, is a satirical farce about partition. "Partition," remarked O'Donovan, "was such a sacred cow in 1956, with De Valera still Taoiseach, that dealing with the subject as I did was equivalent to saying that the Communists weren't wholly demonic when Senator McCarthy was at the height of his power."[3] The play is set in the year 1982 when the R.I.P. (yes, that's what it means) Party has just come into power on the platform of promising to live and work for Ireland rather than "die and moulder in the grave for her." The new Taoiseach or

Prime Minister, Felix Battersby, has promised to end partition within a year. He proposes to end it by bringing Ireland back into the United Kingdom; this prospect horrifies the British and so appalls the Ulstermen that they promptly withdraw from the U.K. themselves.

The situation smacks of Shaw's *The Apple Cart*, but O'Donovan's play is less thickly permeated by ideas, and the ideas are usually put forward as jokes rather than debated thoroughly or seriously. The characters remain only farcical caricatures, some of which, however, are quite droll. These remarks might suggest that I think the play a poor one: on the contrary, it is amusing, often has real point, and almost always has a fine air of high spirits and originality. I can think of no other play resembling it in Irish literature, except for the author's own most recent and as yet untitled play which is discussed below.

The Shaws of Synge Street is a portrait of the family of young Bernard Shaw and of their Dublin circle. As in Johnston's, Carroll's, and Longford's plays about Swift, the author assumes more than can be proved. He has, incidentally, published an interesting book on his subject, as has Johnston on Swift. The play must be judged as a play, however, and not as biography or a necessarily literal truth.

As a play, it is eminently successful. The portrait of Shaw's mother is noteworthy and plausible. O'Donovan draws her as a woman with a frigid reserve and a callous indifference to people's feelings, but this façade hides her passionate attachment to George John Vandeleur Lee, the enigmatic music teacher who so influenced Shaw and whose character O'Donovan also discusses in his book *Shaw and the Charlatan Genius*. Lee appears only in the first two acts, and though I am not sure that O'Donovan makes him psychologically convincing, he certainly gives him enough crotchets and passions to make him a vital stage character. This Lee comes over as an austere, eccentric, and wittily cutting man who cannot control his passion for Shaw's sister Lucy.

The theme running through the many incidents of the complicated plot is apparently the consuming lust that smolders just beneath the crust of Victorian respectability. This theme appears in the fashionable quack of a singing master, Robinson, who gives more lessons in seduction than in singing. It appears in Ann Ellen Shaw, no relation but the wife of George Ferdinand Shaw, a Fellow of Trinity College, in her broad attempts to attract Lee. It appears in the savagery of the husband who beats her. It appears mildly in Edward McNulty's wooing of Lucy Shaw — McNulty, incidentally, was later the author of several successful Abbey comedies, among them *The Lord Mayor*. The whole play is a telling juxtaposition of respectability and reality. In form, it probably is tragicomedy because of its varied and twisting strands of plot and its juxtaposition of the serious and the comic. Probably the best such juxtaposition happens at the end, in the breakup of the family, when George Carr Shaw, G.B.S.'s inept and pitiable father, has a farewell scene with his wife that is totally devoid of overt emotion, even though the audience is aware of his real, acutely felt, hidden sorrow.

O'Donovan's most interesting trick is keeping back G.B.S. himself until the very last moment, after the mother has left for England. Young Shaw enters the room, sees his distraught father, starts to speak, and then departs without having said a word, leaving the elder Shaw in the nearly empty room to sink "weeping, on the wooden crate to find what consolation he can in prayer." George Carr Shaw has no strong scenes until this act, but O'Donovan elicits great pathos from him in it, and gets more than pathos with the wry implied comment of his son's silent exit.

Copperfaced Jack was first produced on February 25, 1963, and later adapted for radio. Several discriminating people who saw the Abbey production have told me they thought the play quite bad. The playscript, however, strongly suggests that the production was at fault. The play, set in 1798, concerns the trial of a patriot named Peter Shanks and his motley handful of rebel followers. O'Donovan's description of Shanks and of Copperfaced Jack is worth noting:

My rebel is, as you've divined, a fictional variation of Emmet, of whom I am not at all an admirer. Adventurers who proclaim a rebellion and sign themselves President of the new republic command neither my respect nor my admiration, especially when they scuttle off up a back street when the going gets hot and then whinge to their serving-maid "It wasn't *my* fault, it wasn't." (Emmet did this.) Jack himself is a notional re-creation of John Scott, first Earl of Clonmell, Lord Chief Justice of the King's Bench, who died of gluttony and drunkenness on the very day that the Rebellion of 1798 (Wolfe Tone's) broke out. On the face of it, his career was that of an unmitigated scoundrel, but I happened to read extracts from his diary and found that he had a clear-sighted view of his own character and behaviour which kept him making attempts to reform himself until almost the day of his death. His great ability (he pulled himself up by his own bootstraps) and his ironic self-portraiture attracted me to him; and although I cannot document every trait I gave him I believe I have re-created him quite faithfully.[4]

He has certainly re-created him richly, for the role is a ripe Falstaffian one which would require almost a Laughton to do it justice. The whole play has a fruity gusto about it that may be suggested by this passage spoken by some prostitutes in Newgate Jail:

VIOLA (*sighing*): Ah Billy-in-the-Bowl, why aren't ye here with us now?

ROSALIND: Was Billy really in a bowl?

BESSIE: He had to be. Both his legs was cut off down to the stumps, so he sat in a little baskety bowl on wheels, and begged from the quality.

VIOLA: He'd just about enough of himself left to sit on.

BESSIE: But he was all there, all the same.

VIOLA: He was, he was indeed, God love him.

BESSIE: And a perfect gentleman.

VIOLA: Even the auld faggots he raped out in Ballybough had to admit that.

BESSIE: They said he took off his hat.

VIOLA: Which is more than a certain viscount I used to know, did.

The theme concerns the kind of act which will secure a man a place in history, and our approval is aroused not for the views of the naively romantic Shanks, but for those of the randy, sadistic, and yet humane Lord Chief Justice. Indeed, Jack is an immense character — this complex, guilt-ridden, autocratic, fallible, wise, and wicked old lecher who grittily, indomitably refuses to die. Despite its Dublin reception, I should say the play comes close to being brilliant.

O'Donovan's latest play is an overlong, untitled, two-act, farcical and fantastic satire opening with this arresting and probably, for Dublin, unstageable exchange:

SPRATT: Morning Mr. Kilgarriff. What's the Prime Minister doing?

KILGARRIFF: Masturbating.

The point of the play is that man is a feckless, bestial, irrational being who will destroy his civilization and who could not be educated to act in any other way. If he had a chance, as he does in this play, to patch up his errors and rebuild his civilization, he would make the same mess of it again.

The satire is better and sharper than that of *The Less We Are Together*; yet it glances rather than cuts deeply. It has none of the weighty thought and brilliant argument of a *Major Barbara*, and it is basically, despite its sobering theme, a lightweight play. I say this to categorize the piece, not to condemn it.

The play's main fault is that it is about a half hour too long. And because most of its incidents are illustrative rather than parts of a causal and developing plot, it has long passages which seem to be going no-where. It might also be argued that the piece is unnecessarily vulgar, but this seems to me a legitimate and Swiftean part of O'Donovan's method, for it well makes his point about man's Yahoo nature. Perhaps the trivial and lighthearted manner of the play is also a comment revealing his opinion of the importance of mankind. At any rate, his method is one of broad caricature, of *reductio ad absurdum* of religion, science, and poli-tics. His method is that of the political cartoonist, not the portrait paint-er. Still, with its devils, angels, prime ministers, and nymphets, the play is a lively and caustic piece of nihilism, a musical comedy without the music but with a stinging point.

John Murphy's *The Country Boy* was accepted almost simultaneously by the Abbey and by the Group Theatre in Belfast, but the Group pro-duced it about a month before the Abbey, in April, 1959. At the Abbey, the play had a first run of seventy nights, and has often been revived, particularly in summer for the tourist trade.

It deals with the old problems of emigration and rural marriage. Ed-die Maher, after fifteen years in the United States, returns home for a va-cation with his American wife Julia to find his younger brother Curly planning to emigrate just as he had, and for the same reason. That reason is largely their father, Tom Maher, a vigorous, old-fashioned, phleg-matic, and immovably opinionated farmer who has no intention of turn-ing control of the farm over to Curly until he is in his grave. The play's strength lies in the full characterization of Eddie, who has felt thwarted by a sense of rootlessness and futility ever since he left home. In trying to convince Curly to stay, Eddie says:

It gets very lonely on the other side of the world, Curly, especially when a lot of the things you long for are behind you. . . . Some guys fit in, Curly. They just become part of the bricks and concrete and the railway lines and the street cars. And they never smell the gasoline fumes or the stink from the chimneys. But the other guys, Curly, are country boys. And if they have a plan to work for it's all right . . . but if they haven't . . . (*pauses*) . . . or if they lose it . . . then they just work because they have to eat . . . or drink. And that's no living for any man . . . unless he's chasing ulcers.

The contrast between the Irish and American ways of life has seldom been seriously discussed in Irish drama, and the attempt at a serious contrast here gives the play much of its interest. Murphy is able to make some telling points in Julia's dialogue. Her finickiness, her restlessness, and her unconscious condescension come across in such remarks as her description of "that ghastly train": "Mary Kate . . . it was a nightmare . . . and the heat . . . the heat. You know . . . I asked the guy who checked our tickets where the air conditioning operated from . . . and he just leaned over me and pushed the window down. Ed, we're going to get a taxi back." Despite his fine ear and his good characterization, Murphy stacks his deck. America comes off as a heartless, chrome-plated, centrally heated jungle in which people lose all of their simple, rural virtues. Ireland, despite Tom Maher, comes off as a little bit of heaven that fell from out the sky one day. This difference was over-stressed in the Abbey production, in which Julia's vulgarity was under-scored. There was probably no malice in the portrayal; it is just that Abbey actresses seem to have gained their conception of the American fe-male and her behavior by watching gun molls in old James Cagney mov-ies.

This Bord Failte propaganda is somewhat balanced by a fine, truthfully written scene between Julia and Eddie in Act III, where we get some deft probing into character: Eddie's steamer trunk has no clothes in it, his expensive movie camera is rented, and he is a drunkard unable to keep a job. There is a hard honesty about this confrontation, although Eddie's quick growth to maturity is truer to the theatre than to life. And certainly the promise that Julia and Eddie will next year again come back to Erin (mavourneen, mavourneen), to the home of simple virtue and true happiness, is a bit much. Still, the character of the anguished drunk-ard brooding over his wasted life is a good one.

Murphy's next play is said to have been poor and was rejected by the theatre. He has since emigrated to Canada.

❦

One of the Abbey's most promising new talents to appear is Tom Coffey, who was born in 1925, in Ennis, County Clare, and educated at St. Flannan's College in Ennis. After graduating, he worked as librarian, clerk, soldier, storekeeper, traveling salesman, private tutor, and office manager. With a scholarship he took a special teacher training course under the Department of Education, and in 1952 qualified as a teacher of English, Gaelic, and mathematics. Since his schooldays he had been active in amateur dramatics, but he took up writing seriously in 1954. In that year he won an Oireachtas [5] literary award for a one-act play in Gaelic, and in 1955 he won a similar award. From 1955 to 1957, he had five short plays in English broadcast by Radio Éireann; in 1958 his first full-length play, *Stranger Beware*, was produced at the Abbey. In 1959 the Abbey produced his most popular play, *Anyone Could Rob a Bank*. His one-act *The Long Sorrow* was produced during the 1960 Theatre Festival. In 1962 *Them* was presented by Orion Productions at the Eblana Theatre and has been nearly as popular as *Anyone Could Rob a Bank*. In 1965, *Gone Tomorrow* won the Irish Life Drama award and was presented at the Gate during the Theatre Festival. In 1965, he wrote his first television play, *A Ship in the Night*, and his latest stage play, *The Call*, was presented at the Abbey in the spring of 1966.

Stranger Beware is a dour and lively melodrama set in the fishing village of Ballycullen on the top of an isolated peninsula in West Kerry. The play is an authentic picture of village life in such out-of-the-way places, but its deeper purpose is to penetrate the personality of these quiet rural people who seem only occupied with gossip, football matches, amiable drinking, and local dramatics. Coffey intends to prove that, as the schoolmaster puts it, "They're like quiet people anywhere in the world. Country people. They keep their feelings hidden — deep down — covered up . . . But if something happens to blow the cover off, they can be . . . dangerous."

The cover is blown off by the murder and robbery of an old man; suspicion falls on a hiker who was staying the night in the old man's house. The rest of the play is simultaneously concerned with the obstructions the villagers put in the way of the police, with their growing hatred of the hiker, and with how the police sergeant and the priest in good detective-story fashion discover the real murderer. When the villagers learn that the murderer was one of themselves, they are as sympathetic to him as they had earlier been savage to the stranger.

The detective-story plot is neatly handled, as is the mounting tension; but the best part of the play is the investigation of the hidden motives of various villagers and the slow emergence of the dead man's character. There is probably not enough emphasis on the theme to make the play more than first-rate entertainment, but it is easily that.

Anyone Could Rob a Bank is a three-act farce — quite good fun, although hardly memorable. The two performances I have seen of the play, at the Abbey and on Telefís Éireann, were played much more broadly than the script suggests. On television, the mother, whom Coffey characterizes as "Dreamy, vague, absentminded," was played by the usually excellent Anna Manahan as a rather middle-brow moron.

The Long Sorrow is a one-act set in a graveyard in Ulster not far from the Border. It tells of a wounded young I.R.A. man who is apprehended by an Ulster policeman. When the policeman is wounded also, both must help each other to escape from freezing in the cold and snow. Their plight has been caused by, as the Ulsterman puts it, "Old men who talk too much. Talking of the good old days and exaggerating like hell. Telling the kids of the heroes they knew, and firing the young imaginations." That speech should be coupled with the I.R.A. boy's reply: "My mother says all Ireland isn't worth one drop of young blood." The play is slight but still a pertinent expression of the new Ireland.

Them, produced in November, 1963, is Coffey's most moving play. The story is about the painful problems that confront the Flaherty family because the youngest son, Johnsie, is an imbecile. The "them" of the title is the world outside the family, which regards Johnsie as a freak and torments him. When he goes to the cinema, people taunt him until he begins to scream. Late in the play, on his twenty-first birthday, some men get him drunk, and he returns home and attacks his brother's sister-in-law.

Each member of the family has had his life complicated by Johnsie. Padraig has begun to drink heavily because he and his wife have had no children. When they succeed in adopting a child, they draw closer together, but his wife fears that Johnsie may imperil the adoption proceedings. Seamus and Maeve in different ways are conditioned by Johnsie to the prospect of marriage: Seamus tries to force his fiancée out of the family conclave, while Maeve is almost pathologically sensitive, and refuses to go out with men. Finally the family votes on whether to send Johnsie to an asylum. When the vote is a tie, the burden of decision rests, as it always has, on the mother Brid. Brid is an interesting role, drawn with terseness and reticence. Nevertheless, it is one of the strongest in the play and demands great presence. Johnsie should be a delight for an actor. There is no false stroke in this depiction of the child mind and no sentimentalizing. Yet the poignancy evoked by the last scene when Johnsie departs is intense. Finally, there is little in the play to interfere with its universality. As Coffey aptly notes, "Almost every small town in the world has one or more Johnsies."

Gone Tomorrow is technically the most interesting play that Coffey has written. Its stage is divided into several fluid acting areas – the garret of a doss house, a bar, a dining room, and a bridge in the town. The action moves easily from one area to another, or happens simultaneously in two areas. Its story of a coming-of-age convincingly depicts, as does Brian Friel's *Philadelphia, Here I Come*, the difficulty one generation has talking with another. Neil Dunne is a likable eighteen-year-old who, in a series of unlucky incidents, becomes less and less understood by his father. What keeps the play from a Henry Aldrich–Corliss Archer triviality is the sensitively drawn portrait of the boy; Coffey really captures something of the agony of maturing youth.

The play lacks the emotional power of *Them*; its early incidents are more illustrative than causally connected, a fact that may make the story seem a little ambling. Still, the relations between children and parents are portrayed with a meaningful accuracy that should transcend any national barriers. The play is also an indication of how even the Abbey playwright, is freeing himself from the strict limitations of conventional realism. The Abbey's playwrights are growing up.

5

Michael Molloy's Dying Ireland

HEN Michael J. Molloy's *The King of Friday's Men* was staged at the Abbey Theatre in October, 1948, many Irish critics hailed him as a second Synge. Their enthusiasm has since cooled, for Molloy is a slow writer, and the memories of journalistic critics are short. Still, the comparison was not inaccurate, for Molloy is the most Syngean of all Irish dramatists — Synge included.

Or, perhaps more accurately, Molloy might be called a more authentic Synge. Synge's strength came from three sources — his use of the character of the Irish countryman, his version of country speech, and his penchant for the grotesque. Molloy knows the countryman more intimately than Synge did, for he is one of them, not a West Briton spending his vacations in Mayo. Molloy's transcription of country speech is more accurate, nearly as rich, and easier to speak. Like Synge, he has a penchant for the grotesque and the violent, to which he adds a quality of brooding melancholy quite his own. Although little known abroad, he is quite close to the stature of Synge, and has given the Irish drama some of its best plays and a galaxy of character parts exceeded in fineness and number only by O'Casey's.

Molloy was born on March 3, 1917, the fifth of eight children. His father managed a shop in Milltown, County Galway; his mother was a national schoolteacher. He went to the national school in Milltown, and then to St. Jarlath's College which he finished at eighteen. He was afterward in a seminary for four years, and was more than halfway to becoming a priest when illness forced him to give it up. He now works a farm of thirty-six acres just outside Milltown — next to the house where he was born and where his brother, a schoolteacher, still lives.

A lot of new houses have been built in Galway in the last few years, but Molloy lives alone in an old stone two-story farmhouse which is scrupulously clean, bare, and a bit spartan. It is his study that gives him away as a writing man, for it has a well-filled cabinet of books and his desk is one that is used. A housekeeper comes in to look after him; a pup named Bob frolics around outside.

He is diffident and stiff at first, with eyes that wander shyly off when he's talking. When that awkwardness wears off, as it soon does, he is a good talker and a good companion. His biggest problem as a writer is that his material is dying out. He gave me the manuscript of a superb play called *The Visiting House*, but visiting houses are things of the past. Now cars allow people to go to the towns easily, cinemas have come to the countryside, and there is no more need for the visiting house. Just down the road from him are the ruins of the visiting house of his play.

When I asked him if people could still be drawn to talk about the legends, memories, and stories he uses in his plays, he said they could, though he also admitted that his Ireland is fast fading away. The new world continues to intrude; emigration continues to carry parts of the old world away. Molloy is ever more thrown back on history for his material, and his plays of today are pervaded by a sadness for a time that is dying.

꿩

Though *The Old Road*, produced at the Abbey on April 26, 1943, is Molloy's first play, it shows his continuing characteristics. The language is richer than that of other realistic playwrights. George Shiels's language, for instance, is basically, save for an occasional locution, General English. Synge's language, especially in its heavy rhythm and the great lengths of its sentences, is more of an artistic translation than a literal transcription. Molloy's language stands midway between Shiels's thinning of the language and Synge's thickening of it. Shiels's dialogue adds little to the literary merit of his plays; Synge's dialogue is one of his chief literary excellences. On the other hand, Synge's dialogue is a problem even for accomplished actors, whereas Shiels's is easy and unobtrusive on the stage. Molloy's dialogue welds the literary richness of Synge to the theatrical fluency of Shiels, and the result is remarkably fine.

Like all of Molloy's plays, the piece is set in the West of Ireland and portrays farmers and laborers. Its theme is almost the basic one of the Irish drama — land and money versus love and life. Or, as Molloy put it, "The OLD ROAD of the title refers both to the old road of emigration and to the still older road of romance." [1] The old people have the desire for land and money and the young people the desire for love and life; the young only win by running away from Ireland.

The theme grows neatly from the characterization and adequately from a rather messy plot. Most of the characters exemplify reactions to the traditional Irish feeling that people should marry for practicality rather than for romance. The most memorable is the crazed old farmer Patrick Walsh, nicknamed the Lord or the Lordeen. Aften a long bachelorhood, he is now roaming the countryside, semi-senile, in a frantic search for a wife. The plight of Brigid and Myles, the impoverished young lovers, suggests how impossible it is to marry for love in the West of Ireland. This plot is well handled until the last act, when there is too much decision and indecision about whether they will emigrate and marry or stay home and be single. At one moment they are going, at another they are not, at another they are, and this back-and-forth is neither strong nor suspenseful. Molloy often takes two years to write a play; this slowness helps to enrich his dialogue, but it also tends to overcomplicate his plots.

Still, in his strong character-drawing, in his rich dialogue, and in his occasional violent theatricality, Molloy is more interesting, even in *The Old Road*, than many of his contemporaries. That theatricality is especially present in this play in the fine fight between Myles and the Lord in Act I. One of Molloy's continuing excellences is this willingness to be violent; after a long succession of low-keyed realistic comedies it is indeed refreshing.

₱

The Visiting House was produced at the Abbey on November 18, 1946. Visiting houses were places to which villagers and farmers came for entertainment, story-telling, singing, and sometimes for dramatized tricks like those portrayed in this play. The deviser of the tricks is the Merryman or Master of the visiting house. The Merryman in this play is Broc Heavy, whom Molloy describes as:

. . . an excellent talker, better than most is he an original phrase-maker, an improviser and master of repartee. An unbroken fifteen-minute solo narrative, whether humourous or serious, comes quite naturally from Broc. The narrative once under way, his gift takes possession of him, and the audience is forgotten; pause, emphasis, repetition, gesture (in the use of his hands he is a master); in fact, every trick of narration is applied with effortless and unconscious skill. As will appear, he is virtually a professional actor, his stage this Visiting House, where he has given nightly performances for many years.

Even more impressive than Broc's skill as an actor is his genius as an author. He is a playwright of real life; the situations he creates among his visitors are the true stuff of drama — funny, full of suspense, intricately plotted, and morally apt.

Some of the habitués of the visiting house are quite as fine. Mickle Conlon, the Man of Learning, is a rare role, a man full of traditional lore and legend; wise, blasted, canny, sad; a kind of folk Lear. Opposed to him is Verb To Be, the Man of Education, who has studied in the primary school, and whose head is full of simple rote learning.

The main plot concerns Broc's daughter Mary who refuses to marry Tim Corry even though he promises to leave for England if she does not. Still, Mary is loath to change her round of dances and exciting nights in the visiting house for marriage and the tending of "screechers." Interwoven with this action are Broc's complicated plots, and threaded through all is a leitmotif of sorrow for the numbered days of the visiting house and, therefore, the numbered days of the old Ireland.

The convolutions of the plot it would be a shame to relate; but this is one play in which Molloy's flair for intricate plotting is both apt and delightful. This is also a rare acting play, one of the most humorous and yet most melancholy of the great Irish comedies. It is Synge with the bitterness left out.

₽

Molloy's best known play is *The King of Friday's Men*, which was first produced at the Abbey on October 18, 1948. Late in February, 1951, it was put on in New York, but, despite Walter Macken's repeating his Abbey role of Bartley Dowd, it was a poor production that lasted only four performances.

The play is set "in the remote and hilly corner where the counties Mayo, Galway, and Roscommon meet"; the year is 1787. Una Brehony, a girl of seventeen, has just become engaged to Owen Fenigan. However, the landlord, Caesar French, has sent out his pressgang to find a new tallywoman, or mistress, for him, and Una is picked. To save herself, she is urged by her uncle to persuade Bartley Dowd, the bullyman from Tyrawley, that she loves him, in order to make him defend her. Bartley is the main character and a unique one in Irish drama. A bullyman was a champion shillelagh fighter, and Bartley has been brought to Kilmacreena to lead the peasants of Caesar French in the annual challenge fight against the peasants of Tulrahan. I believe this is the only attempt the Irish have made to portray these bloody battles on the stage, though a harrowing account of a similar fray is in Carleton's story "The Battle of the Factions." Molloy's bullyman is in his middle thirties, a sober, battered man whose great desire is to wed and live in peace. He knows, however, that he has lost his first youth and whatever looks he had, and he is skeptical when Una approaches him. She convinces him, and, after a magnificent fight scene in which he routs six of Caesar's men, he carries her off.

The second act shows Una coming to love Bartley and being captured by Caesar French's men. In Act III, Caesar, a fine picture of an aging buck, promises not to kill Bartley if Una will convince him that she had never meant to marry him. She succeeds, and as she is leaving she is set upon by Caesar's men; in the melee Bartley kills Caesar and lets Una escape.

The bald bones of the story sound like a wild melodrama out of Boucicault, and indeed if Boucicault had had as much literary talent as he had theatrical genius this is the kind of play he might have written. Several qualities raise this play above melodrama: one is the fine characterization of Bartley, of Caesar, of Una, of her elderly uncle Gaisceen, and of Rory Commons, son of Cormac Commons, the last of the bards. This stress upon character is borne out by a remark of Molloy: "Although I was drawn to *Friday's Men* by its basic story and situation, the theme it finally came to have for me was misfortune and the way people react to it: Bartley, Rory, Maura Pender, etc. The feudal mentality theme which you see as the chief theme is there too, of course." [2]

This feudal mentality is part of the play's vivid flavor of reality. But it is not merely a flavor that gives strength and body to Molloy's evocation of eighteenth-century Ireland; it is also the revelation of certain facets of the Irish character that are startling to modern ears, even though they are still somewhat discernible. I have in mind particularly the peasant morality. Caesar French's peasants pay him an unquestioning loyalty, and not even Gaisceen will fight to save Una:

> GAISCEEN (*Horror-struck, as if he had heard a blasphemy*): Is it raise my hand against the Frenches of Kilmacreena, that all belonging to me are serving since the foundation of the world? I couldn't do it, girl, if he was going to strike me dead itself. My arms'd refuse to rise against him.

Another example of this Irish love of a lord is Boorla, the leader of the pressgang. "For him," writes Molloy, "Caesar French is the Law and the Prophets; for Caesar he is willing to undertake any villainy and undergo any risks. In this he is the typical Irish gentleman's retainer of the period."

One major importance of the play, then, is that it presents a morality in many ways different from ours, and in many ways tragically wrong. Molloy does not quite succeed in raising his play to tragedy, for he seems to get carried away in fashioning a thrilling story. Still, here and there in the play, the ingredients of tragedy exist. His theme, that this slave morality dooms the people caught up in it, is hit too glancingly, but it is hit.

An interesting minor plot parallels Bartley's. Rory Commons, the son of the bard, is an even queerer outcast than Bartley. He is:

> . . . a man of fifty-five to sixty, a wild unearthly looking creature, skeleton thin, haggard, stooped, ragged, with a vast tattered cloak swinging about him. One eye is half closed through some defect or other; his graying hair and beard are long and wild as that of a rambling madman; his movements are spasmodic and unsteady. A man less favoured by nature and fortune one could hardly imagine, yet his whole aspect and behaviour is one of the wildest, most touchy and arrogant pride.

Rory roams the countryside collecting food from the peasants for his father the bard, who as a poet was thought to have a divine gift and was as admired for his art as feared for his curse. Rory has tended his father for years, and Cormac has promised to pass on his gift to Rory. When Cormac dies, Rory finds that he has not the gift, and Bartley says:

> Rory, you have the same mistake made as me. 'Tisn't for good fortune God put our like in the world, but only to do odd jobs for Him. Yourself to give good minding to His composer that was blind, and myself to snatch a girl from the Pressgang, and to keep hunger from my sister-in-law and her orphans. We can no way complain. Himself gave His life for us of a Friday . . .

And the two men go off to hide in the mountains from the law.

The dialogue is fluent if not quite so berry-ripe as Synge would have made it; most of the characters are rounded types; the plot is engrossing, the background true and vivid. But, accomplished as it is, *The King of Friday's Men* cries out to be just a bit better. What happens to Bartley is not shattering enough; indeed, he refuses to be shattered. A hero who bears his fate with Christian resignation is not a tragic hero; tragedy is by its nature unbearable. Molloy did not push his play as far into tragedy as Synge pushed *The Playboy* into comedy, but few other Irish plays might so well serve as a companion piece to *The Playboy* without being made to seem trivial by the comparison.

꙰

Wood of the Whispering was produced by the Abbey in January, 1953, and called by its author a comedy. Despite some Syngean grotes-querie and a happy ending consisting of three marriages, the play is a sad and quiet comedy. Its theme is partly that "ferocious chastity" which O'Casey attacked with gay savagery and partly the ever-present problem of emigration. As Molloy remarked in his Preface:

In 1910 the Great Blasket Island had one hundred and fifty people and a well filled school. Forty years later the population was a handful, there was only one child, so they called their island Tir Na Sean, the Land of the Old. There are countless dying villages and townlands in rural Ireland to which the same title could be applied. The death of a village, like the death of an individual, is usually a painful business, and marked by distressing symptoms. But of this fact our suburban depopulation enthusiasts know nothing.

But country people know all about it, and they know the background of this play, the comedy of the eccentric old bachelors, and the tragedy, too.

All the characters but one are past their first youth, and most are old and cracked. Paddy King is a bachelor almost eighty, a harmless lunatic who fancies himself still a young man and "the irresistible lady-killer of the countryside." His brother Jimmy is a docile, decayed simpleton. Sadie Tubridy is a woman in her late forties who was deserted by Hotha Broderick after he had courted her for twenty years. Now she is a mute recluse living in a deserted gardener's lodge in the woods. The main character, Sanbatch Daly, has allowed his farm to go to ruin and his house to collapse about his head because he has no woman to keep him up to snuff; he lives in the wood in a coffin-like box, with only his dog Leggy for company. The young people include Mark Tristnan, a man of twenty-eight, who "is fearfully thin and pale and hollow-eyed and is highly strung and wild to the verge of madness." What has driven him wild is the lack of a wife and his own poisonous cooking. Sheila Lanigan has returned from England to take care of her dying father. Both she and Con Kinsella, who has also returned from England, hate it, but find they cannot live and marry in Ireland. The whole play is peopled with gentle, sex-haunted characters longing for each other and kept apart by the economy and the traditions of Ireland.

This play might not survive on the commercial stages of England and America, for its first two acts are developed with a caressing leisureliness that would irritate and baffle audiences accustomed to conventional swift plotting. That, unfortunately, is the audience's loss, for the play is superb. Its leisurely pace allows Molloy to develop his collection of grotesques with loving thoroughness and to create many small scenes of lingering charm. Probably the only way to give the flavor of the play is by an extended quotation. Here, then, is a charming scene in which the girl Kitty is teasing those two old numbskulls, Jimmy and Paddy King:

JIMMY (*Fiercely*): Have you the costs for a few pints?
PADDY: No.
JIMMY: You big bloater, you have all our money spent up, buying sweets for every rap in the country.
PADDY (*Fiercely*): Have you any money yourself?
JIMMY: No.
PADDY: You bloody Daniel, we'd be heavy loaded with money if only I could make you work a hard day.
   (*Jimmy settles down to his pipe, Paddy to admiring his moustache in Sanbatch's glass. Kitty tiptoes over to Jimmy, and taps him on the shoulder.*)
JIMMY (*Gloomily*): Hello, there!
KITTY: Jimmy, my aunt was out working in a field, and she left the gate open and caught a cold and is now dying. She's leaving me her publichouse in Curraghmore. 'Twould suit me greatly to have yourself for a husband and master over the apprentices. You wouldn't have a stroke to do only sitting on a barrel behind the counter drinking all you have room for of porter and whiskey and beer and rum and wine. So will you marry me?
JIMMY (*Enraptured by the list of his privileges*): I will . . . But no! 'Tis Paddy's turn to do the talking first.
   (*She runs to Paddy, who has listened to the proposal with indulgent contempt.*)
KITTY: Paddy, d'ye mind if I deprive you of Jimmy, and wed him?

PADDY (*Serenely*): Sure, how could he wed you? He has to stop on my farm and do all work for me.

JIMMY (*Jumping up angrily*): I can wed her if I like. Any more I'll have a house of my own, and I care no more about you than the cat cares about his father.

PADDY (*Jumping up likewise*): You hanging blackguard! How can I wed Sheila if you won't stay and work the farm for us? I don't know how to put wan stone over another to make a wall.

JIMMY: Well, 'tis time you shook hands with work, and 'tis too long I'm digging deep and splitting worms.

PADDY: So you're out to desert me! Well, take notice of this! You belong to the seventies, and you're slaved out and soon you'll be getting the invitation up or down. 'Tis a bit of a wrong age for you to be turning dishonest, but you must do it now. On account of the depopulation no shopkeeper can keep alive unless he waters the drink and sells short weight and robs both rich and poor.

JIMMY (*Overwhelmed*): You have the truth! Girl, I can't wed you! I lived honest all my lifetime, and so long as I burned the candle down to the inch, I'm as well to finish it.

KITTY: Jimmy, we'll have no need for roguery. She's leaving me three thousand paper pounds as well.

JIMMY (*Jumping up in delight*): Three thousand pounds! Then you're a fine plentiful girl and I will marry you.

PADDY: Take notice of this! They're all nice and sweet and wholesome till they get you bound under them, then they aren't happy any day unless they spend a while tongue-lashing and fighting. And you're a man fighting doesn't suit.

JIMMY (*The incorrigible old bachelor in him reasserting itself*): 'Tis the truth, girl! I was evermore a very respectable man that fighting with women wouldn't suit, so I can't wed you.

KITTY: But, sure, if you aren't fighting with me in our house, you'll have to be fighting with his wife in his house.

JIMMY: That's the truth, too! And Stephen's daughter should be wan of the worst divils for fighting in the four red corners of Ireland.

PADDY (*Spitting on his palm like a jobber at fair*): Well, here! No woman'll ever hang up her coat in my house, if you'll come back and do all work for me the same as before.

JIMMY (*Spitting on his palm*): 'Tis a bargain! (*They shake on it.*)

The many scenes like this arouse a curious emotion. There is grotesquerie here and playfulness and absurdity, and over all hangs a muted sadness. Molloy, especially in this play, is a muted Synge, and perhaps because of the difference he is closer to the essence of Ireland.

Act III has much more plot and activity than the earlier acts. There is the wild scene in which Sanbatch pretends madness, the growing delirium of the characters at the prospect of marriage, the poignant wooing of the mute Sadie. It is a play with memorable parts for actors; anyone who has seen the Abbey actor Philip O'Flynn giving Sanbatch's moving curtain speech could hardly forget it. *The Wood of the Whispering* could easily become lost in the more flamboyant experiments of the modern drama, but in its quiet way it is rare and beautiful.

The Paddy Pedlar is a one-act, first presented at the Abbey in September, 1953, and subsequently very popular with amateur groups. It is a historical play, set in the autumn of 1840, during the potato famine. It has the racy authenticity of *The King of Friday's Men* and the benevolent grotesquerie of *The Wood of the Whispering*. When a peasant named Ooshla, a rogue and a thief with pretensions to gentility, decides to rob a wandering pedlar of the contents of his mysterious sack, he discovers that the sack contains the corpse of the pedlar's mother. At first it appears that the pedlar has murdered her, but he is really taking her to be buried with her husband. "If *The Paddy Pedlar* has a theme," Molloy writes, "it is the old Irish proverb and belief that any son who looks after his mother will be lucky, and vice versa." [3]

The play is extremely lively. For instance, when the pedlar, an exhausted rag of a man, is released, he whips out a long knife and:

PEDLAR: Hullabaloo! Hullabaloo! (*Twice he leaps into the air with that hiss of savage joy; drawing back the knife each time as if about to charge at Ooshla. But instead he leaps again, and cries aloud in triumph*) Now, Mamma! Timmy has his knife! Timmy has his knife! Timmy has his knife! No one'll dare harm you no more!

Ultimately Ooshla goes off with the pedlar who promises him to reform him from his roguery:

PEDLAR (*Eagerly*): Maybe I could cure you, sir, the way I cured my father out of hurting mamma, sir?

OOSHLA (*With enthusiasm*): What way did you cure him, Paddy?

PEDLAR (*Taking out knife gravely*): Every time he'd set into lashing her I'd give him a dart of this, sir. I could give you a dart, too, sir, every time you'd commit a roguery.

OOSHLA: Oh, murther! And would it be a deep prod, Paddy?

PEDLAR (*Earnestly*): Sure if it wasn't, sir, 'twould do you no good, sir.

OOSHLA: Oh, murther! Oh, murther! Still you'll cure me. The divil a bit of roguery'll stop long more in me.

The play is a bit long for what it has to say. Its real weakness is that it does not have much to say. Still, the fine one-acts of Lady Gregory were little more than incidents, and this play has a tone lacking in Irish drama since the death of Synge and the early plays of Fitzmaurice.

☙

The Will and the Way was produced at the Abbey on September 5, 1955; it is a comedy with little point except the considerable pleasure to be derived from a stageful of amusing types. In production, the director Ria Mooney added a lot of broadly comic business, and that Abbeyizing runs counter to the tone of the play. When the play is not broadened to farce, quite a bit of legitimate amusement rises naturally from the script. There is not only Molloy's usual rich transcription of country speech, but also an engaging view of the rehearsal and production of a nine-teenth-century Irish melodrama. The play-within-a-play device rarely fails to charm, and this Boucicaultian melodrama has a particular delight because it is so different from contemporary theatre. One would wish that Molloy's trio of elderly playboys — "Fowler" Flynn, "Lanty" Quin-lan, and Jack-the-Cards — had been more than very actable types, but the play remains an amusing work, if not one of Molloy's best.

☙

Daughter from over the Water was rejected by the Abbey and first staged by an amateur group in December, 1962. It was later produced by Siobhan McKenna at the Gaiety Theatre, Dublin, on April 13, 1964. In his Preface, Molloy calls it "a religious problem play," but then goes on to deplore didacticism in the drama: ". . . religious problem plays in general suffer all too often from propagandist distortion for or against religion, and this distortion weakens them as plays and as propaganda. Tragedy or comedy are the dramatist's two safest roads for bypassing the propagandist death-trap." In this play, Molloy has chosen a fine group of comic characters, put them into an absurd situation arising from a crucial religious problem, and avoided a narrow convent-school solu-tion. Tul Higgins is a shiftless farmer who lets his farm go to seed while he composes poems for *Old Moore's Almanac*. He and his wife are en-dangered by several lawsuits for letting their cattle stray into neighbors' fields; in addition, they learn that their daughter in England has lost her faith and is about to marry an atheist. To combat both problems, they pretend that Tul is on his deathbed. There is a great deal of delightful finagling among the neighbors, for the prospect of Tul's death sets off a chain reaction of possible marriages to his wife, his children, and his neighbors. This involved and amusing scheming, most of which takes place before the presumably slumbering Tul, makes up the bulk of the play, and the serious problem of the girl's loss of faith is given much less space and emphasis.

Molloy does not, however, fall into the easy solution of blackly condemning the atheist and reuniting Rita with her Catholic lover. Indeed, the atheist is a nice fellow and Rita is allowed to marry him, even though she does return to her own faith. Still, her change of heart occurs quite quickly and is handled with a thin simplicity that makes this serious part of the play unconvincing. Rita's one brief explanation is really the pat propaganda that Molloy wanted to avoid, rather than a real grappling with the problem. She remarks, "I'm a better-up Catholic now thanks to all Nellie learned in the Legion of Mary in England," but that is not enough. You cannot persuasively discuss a complex and serious theme in stock phrases or by using the traditional comic devices of trickery and overheard conversations, no matter how well you do them. The only way to discuss a complex and serious theme is to take it seriously and to discuss it. That Molloy does not do.

The comic situations, the very actable roles, the moments of strong theatricality, the racy language — all of these are handled, as one would expect, unexceptionably.

<p>

The Bitter Pill is a one-act produced so far only by amateurs. It is a contemporary, realistic play with one fine comic character in its all-woman cast. The script would be improved with about five minutes cut from its ending, but even then it would not quite be topnotch Molloy.

The Wooing of Duvesa was produced by the Abbey during the 1964 Theatre Festival and remains unpublished.[4] Of *Duvesa* Molloy wrote "All Europe in the early eighteenth century was behind either Catholic or Protestant Iron Curtains. *Duvesa* is a study for the Communist one which will engulf us one of these years!"[5]

The play is set in County Galway in the winter of 1715–1716; it tells of the Widow Honora O'Kelly, formerly of Castlekelly, and of her three daughters. Her husband lost the family estate warring against the English, and his family is now poor. They are also proud, and do their work in the potato fields at night so that the peasants will not see them. The peasants think that the farming is done magically by the family saint, St. Grellan.

The complicated plot tells how the youngest daughter is wooed by the old Catholic landowner Sir Walter Burke, by his son Ulick who plans to turn Protestant to save the Burke estate, by Cahal a young wandering harper, and by Donogh O'Higgins a sad wandering middle-aged poet who reminds one of Molloy himself. The plot is complicated and does not really support the theme enunciated at the end of the play by Donogh and Cahal—that Ireland will need much courage to throw off her oppressors. However, I am perhaps reading the play narrowly, for Molloy has also remarked, "I thought the theme would be more the eternal one of the problems of the poet and artist in the world than just the Penal Days theme."

At any rate, the piece is a full re-creation of the times, fuller even than Lady Longford's history plays. Staged well, it should be continuously engrossing. If there were less in it, less of plot and less of theme, it would be stronger. But even that criticism is a compliment. How many other plays and playwrights could be criticized for offering too much richness?

Molloy's latest play *Tess Leitrim, Knight Errant* uses the automobile as its symbol for the changing nature of life in the West. Despite one very funny book-throwing scene, the early draft seems a weary rephrasing of early work. Perhaps Molloy needs a new landscape, for much of what he admired in the old one has changed, changed utterly.

Tomelty, Thompson, and the Theatre in Ulster

BEFORE the twentieth century, Ulster had really no native drama, although a good handful of playwrights, among them Farquhar and Macklin, had come from there. At the beginning of this century, a native drama did take root, but its seeds were sown from Dublin. Inspired by the Irish Literary Theatre, a few enthusiasts in Belfast formed, in 1901, the Ulster Branch of the Irish Literary Theatre. After 1902, the group changed its name to the Ulster Literary Theatre, but it remained influenced by the Abbey group. It produced its own dramatists, although it had little more luck than the Abbey in producing a crop of poetic dramatists. About the only verse plays in the early years were Bulmer Hobson's *Brian of Banba*, Joseph Campbell's *The Little Cowherd of Slainge*, and Richard Rowley's *Apollo in Mourne*. Among the notable realistic plays were *The Enthusiast* of 1905 and *The Pagan* of 1906, both by Lewis Purcell, the pen name of David Parkhill. His plays used homely Ulster speech and sired the kitchen comedy which has been the staple of Northern drama.

There have been six first-rate playwrights to come out of modern Ulster — Rutherford Mayne, St. John Ervine, George Shiels, and, more recently, Joseph Tomelty, Sam Thompson, and Brian Friel. The three early writers are best known for their connection with the Abbey, although Mayne's early plays like *Turn O' the Road* and *The Drone* are identi-

fied with the Northern group. Shiels, the most prolific Northern dramatist, did write three early pieces for the Ulster Theatre — *Away from the
Moss* in 1918, *Felix Reid and Bob* in 1919, and *The Tame Drudge* about
1920. However, after the Abbey's acceptance of *Bedmates* in 1920, he
wrote mainly for the Southern group. Still, *The Passing Day* was first
put on as a radio play in Northern Ireland under the title of *His Last Day
in Business*, and *The Old Broom, Borderwine*, and *Mountain Post* were
written for the Group Theatre, whereas *Moodie in Manitoba* was produced by Ulster amateurs.

The Group Theatre, which produced some of Shiels's work, was the
next notable development in the Ulster theatre after the Ulster Literary
Theatre. The Group was founded in the early 1940's by Gerald Morrow,
Harold Goldblatt, Joseph Tomelty, and others, to stage world, classic,
and Ulster plays. Its most successful Ulster plays were Tomelty's *Right
Again, Barnum* and Shiels's *Borderwine*, both of which ran for fifteen
weeks. The dominant figure in the Group was Harold Goldblatt; toward
the end of 1958, however, he resigned as producer and artistic director,
although he remained on the theatre's board. Other resignations followed, and as the Group was in financial trouble, the company was reduced.

For a brief time in 1957 and 1958, it seemed as if the Group had been
rejuvenated. A new young artistic director, Jim Ellis, was appointed, and
the company became a nonprofit organization with a limited guarantee
against losses by the Council for the Encouragement of Music and the
Arts. A new board was appointed, and younger men came on it. Ulster-
izations of foreign plays like *Sailor Beware* and Priestley's *When We
Are Married* helped to woo back audiences, but there was a need for
good local plays. Tomelty could not be counted on, for he had earlier
left the Group to work in films; then he had had a serious automobile accident which curtailed his writing for several years. However, in 1958
the theatre seemed to have solved the problem: it announced its plans to
produce Brian Friel's *The Francophile*, Jack Loudan's *Trouble in the
Square*, John Murphy's *The Country Boy*, and Sam Thompson's *Over
the Bridge*.

Sam Thompson was born on May 21, 1916, in Ballymacarret, Belfast.
He was the son of a lamplighter in a family of eight of which he was the
next to last child. After he finished school at fourteen, he went to work
in the Belfast shipyards as a ship painter. He was also, like Brendan Behan,
a house painter. In 1947 he was married, and his only son was born in

1953. His experiences as a painter formed the background of his first broadcast work, *Brush in Hand*, in 1956. Its favorable reception led him to write other feature programs for radio. His knowledge of the troubled Belfast shipyards led him to write his first stage play, *Over the Bridge*. The religious lines in Northern Ireland are still drawn hard and fast between Protestant and Catholic, and the efforts of the Catholics to obtain employment in the 1920's and '30's in the shipyards caused great unrest, fighting, and riots. The wounds are still not healed, and Thompson's play took this explosive situation as its subject.

The play was in rehearsal at the Group when pressure was brought to bear to have it withdrawn. Finally Thompson, refusing to make crucial cuts which the theatre demanded, had to withdraw the play. He put up a strong fight for it, however, and the fracas really marked the beginning of the end for the Group Theatre. Ellis and other board members resigned, and there were charges and counter-charges in the press about the immorality of the play. J. Ritchie McKee, the chairman of the board, stated that "This play is full of grossly vicious phrases and situations, which would undoubtedly offend and assault every section of the public — Protestant, Roman Catholic and particularly trade unionists."

Actually, nothing in the play could be considered offensive to any but the most narrow and timid persons. Without being a great play, *Over the Bridge* is an honest realistic study of the effects of religious intolerance. Thompson does not stack his cards in favor of either Protestant or Catholic. He is critical of both sides, and his play is a trenchant demand for reason and tolerance in the conduct of human affairs. It is a good, gripping drama that would not have caused a row in any city but Belfast. As a matter of fact, when it was ultimately produced by Thompson and some friends at the Empire Theatre in Belfast on January 26, 1960, it drew packed houses for six weeks, and then had to be taken off because of a previous booking of the theatre. From Belfast it went to Dublin, where it had a similarly successful season of four weeks; it then went on tour in England and finally wound up at the Princess Theatre in the West End.

Thompson thereafter devoted his full time to writing; his second play, *The Evangelist*, was a study of the Billy Sunday type of preacher. To prepare for it, he haunted revival meetings in Belfast and noted the often hysterical reaction of the congregations. The play, produced in 1963 by Louis Elliman, was very successful in Dublin and Belfast. Curiously enough, Belfast's Catholic, Presbyterian, and Church of Ireland journals all joined together, for once, in praising the play.

In June, 1964, Thompson stood as the Labour candidate for the Northern parliament in a district in which the Unionist candidate had been for years returned in great strength. He lost, but made a good showing. Nevertheless, Mrs. Thompson thinks that the campaign took a lot out of him. He had already had a heart attack in 1961, and on February 1, 1965, he had a fatal attack in the Labour office in Belfast.

His most recent television play, *Cemented With Love* of 1965, met with some opposition, for it was about past election practices in Northern Ireland. In his last years, he turned to acting. He had, for instance, played in the Ulster production of *The Quare Fellow*, in *Over the Bridge*, in Friel's *The Blind Mice*, and had begun to do television work in England. His work generated a great deal of healthy excitement, but I do not think that he was basically a stormy petrel or an *enfant terrible*, but a thoughtful, honest man, courageous enough to take as his subjects some central issues of his time and country. None of his work has been so far published, and I have only been able to run down an imperfect copy of *Over the Bridge*; it strikes me as an accomplished realistic play written with restrained power and containing great promise.

The timidity about *Over the Bridge* was symptomatic of the weakness of the Group Theatre. McKee, the chairman of the board, had said that the theatre was "determined to avoid the staging of any play likely to offend the religious or political sensibilities of the man on the street whatever his denomination or class. Above all they were determined that nothing they would do would give rise to sectarian or political controversy in any extreme extent." Such a policy is antithetical to the vitality of an art theatre. However, after the Thompson debacle, the Group managed to stagger on for a few more productions; then it fell hopelessly into debt and finally threw in the towel. The Arts Council took over the theatre temporarily, later giving it over to James Young, a Belfast comedian who stages long-running lowbrow comedies.

※

The Belfast Arts Theatre was formed in 1947 by Hubert Wilmot; in its early years it produced an impressive list of plays, ranging from *Huis Clos* to *Sweeney Todd, the Demon Barber of Fleet Street*. The theatre played Ibsen, Chekhov, Wilde, Pirandello, Evreinov, Čapek, Claudel,

Cocteau, Auden and Isherwood, Fry, Eliot, O'Neill, Rice, Anderson, Miller, Williams, and Joyce. It did European premieres of Wilder, Saroyan, Kingsley, and J. J. Bernard, and world premieres of Wolfgang Borchard's *The Man Outside* and Donagh MacDonagh's *God's Gentry*. It did such fine period pieces as *The Drunkard, Maria Marten,* and *The Colleen Bawn.* For a few years, a Belfastman might have got a tolerable education in the modern drama by attending productions at the Arts Theatre. In more recent years, the quality of the plays has begun to tail off. The theatre would still produce an occasional fine play like *Epitaph for George Dillon, Roots, The Long and the Short and the Tall,* or *The Big Knife,* but more often commercially successful plays by Coward, Rattigan, Van Druten, Maugham, and N. Richard Nash crowded better work off the stage. Most recently, the theatre has turned almost exclusively to light commercial fare, such as *Salad Days* or Agatha Christie mysteries, Belfast farces by Sam Cree, or British farces of the kind made popular by Brian Rix's London company.

The theatre is now on a firm financial basis. It is a modified repertory company, with a staff of ten Equity actors, a resident producer, stage director, and designer, a stage manager with a couple of assistants, and a permanent front-of-the-house staff of eight people. The group moved into a new theatre in 1961 — a handsome, modern, beautifully appointed theatre seating about five hundred people. It is an unsubsidized theatre, formed as a nonprofit distributing company with Wilmot as president. The only play I have seen there is the Aldwych farce *One for the Pot.* Without approaching the Rix standard, it was done with some *élan.* Certainly, the theatre will be on the Belfast scene for some years to come.

The theatre has reached a comfortable middle age. It depends upon its box-office receipts for its existence, and has understandably become oriented to the box office. It is, in other words, an arts theatre nowadays in name only. When I suggested to Hubert Wilmot several serious unproduced plays by established professional writers, plays which had not been able to get a commercial hearing, he patiently explained that such plays would only succeed in giving a depressing evening to the tired businessman and the weary housewife upon whom the theatre depended. He had in mind a new Sam Cree farce for his next production.

🎭

Since the disintegration of the Group and the commercialization of the Arts, one vital theatre has emerged in Belfast — the Lyric Players

Theatre, which was founded in 1951 and whose moving spirit is Mrs. Mary O'Malley. It was founded mainly as "a medium for poetic drama," and it is the only theatre, not excluding the Abbey, to have worked its way through all of Yeats's plays. It has also produced poetic plays by Robert Farren, Austin Clarke, Valentine Iremonger, and Donagh MacDonagh among the Irish writers, and it has done an impressive number of poetic dramas from the range of world literature. Among these are Aristophanes's *The Frogs*, Euripides's *Hippolytus*, Shakespeare's *Hamlet*, *Lear*, *Othello*, *Julius Caesar*, and *Macbeth*, Jonson's *Volpone*, Milton's *Comus*, Ibsen's *Peer Gynt*, and plays by Lorca, Eliot, Fry, and Dylan Thomas. It has tried such demanding pieces as O'Casey's *The Silver Tassie*, Mary Manning's *The Voices of Shem*, Robinson Jeffers's version of *Medea*; it has performed Chekhov and O'Neill and several prose plays by modern Irish writers, among them Keane's *Many Young Men of Twenty*, James Plunkett's *The Risen People*, G. P. Gallivan's *The Stepping Stone*, and Eugene McCabe's *King of the Castle*. For its lovingly done Yeats productions, it has had special music composed and paid great attention to costume and set design. Without being myself convinced that many of Yeats's plays are theatrical, I must admit that the Lyric Players Theatre does them well.

In its fifteen years, the theatre has spread its wings impressively. From a beginning in a private drawing room, it moved on in 1951 to its own studio theatre. In 1956, it enlarged the theatre and opened a drama school. In 1957, it began to publish the literary magazine *Threshold*. In 1959, a children's theatre grew out of its drama school, and the theatre paid its first visit to the Dublin Theatre Festival. In 1960, the group was established as a non-profit-making association; its first trustees and honorary directors included such people as Padraic Colum, Denis Johnston, Rutherford Mayne, and Thomas Kinsella. In 1962, the group opened a shop in the center of the city for selling Irish handicrafts and for use as the theatre's booking office. In 1963, a gallery was opened above the shop to display exhibitions of paintings. Also in that year, the group founded the Belfast Academy of Music. In 1964, a site for a new theatre was purchased, and on June 12, 1965, the foundation stone was laid. It sounds as if Mrs. O'Malley is attempting a total renaissance of the arts for Belfast.

The theatre has not drawn a group of playwrights to it yet, but it has been most determinedly an art theatre. It has presented a large body of worthy plays and masterpieces that Belfast would otherwise not have seen. So long as Mrs. O'Malley's energies do not flag, the theatre would seem to have a secure, honorable future.

❦

The writings of Joseph Tomelty are little known outside of Ireland, but he is the most interesting Ulster playwright to emerge between Rutherford Mayne and Sam Thompson. In some ways, his career resembles that of Walter Macken, for he has been an actor and a novelist as well as a playwright. He was born on March 12, 1911, at Portaferry near Belfast, and he went to school there until he was twelve. In his early twenties, he became involved in amateur dramatics in Belfast. His first play, produced by amateurs, was a one-act called *The Beauty Competition*, which he later expanded into the three-act called *Barnum Was Right* and which was then published under the title of *Mugs and Money*. *The Beauty Competition* was accepted by B.B.C. radio, as were several other short plays. Tomelty also wrote a radio serial, but none of this work has been published.

The three-act version of *The Beauty Competition* was played at the Empire Theatre, Belfast, and was so successful that it was one of the impulses behind the founding of the Group Theatre. In 1951, Tomelty left the Group, which was then flourishing, and with Tyrone Guthrie and Alan McClelland formed a company to perform George Shiels's *The Passing Day* at the Ambassador Theatre during the Festival of Britain. Incidentally, the play which succeeded *The Passing Day* — put on as a stopgap measure — was Agatha Christie's *The Mousetrap*, which at this writing is in its fifteenth year.

During the Shiels run, the film director David Lean dropped into the theatre, was struck by Tomelty's playing, and hired him for the film *The Sound Barrier*. Since then Tomelty has appeared in about thirty films and many television shows. He has continued to write prolifically, fiction as well as plays and television scripts.

He lives in a sprawling, comfortable old house with a large garden on the outskirts of Belfast. He is married, has two daughters, and is now in his middle fifties, a heavyish man with a superb actor's face, a mane of thick white hair, a good brow, and craggy, shaggy black eyebrows. He looks as if he might have stepped out of Dickens or perhaps out of *Juno*, in which he actually did play Captain Boyle. He is an actor in his conversation — volatile, alive, full of anecdote, and always about to jump up and act out a scene or illustrate a point. He sums up his own work by saying that his comedies are local and have no universal content, and that his serious plays are not quite good enough. I would agree that he has written no masterpiece, but he has written a good deal of sound work over the years.

Mugs and Money or *Barnum Was Right* is a comedy of Belfast family life. Rabby Marley, like Captain Boyle, is a heavy drinker, an out-of-work loafer, and also an ex-soldier. His wife Martha, like Juno, holds the family together, though she is as Protestant as her husband is Catholic. The daughter Mugs is entered in a beauty contest which turns out to be a fraud, and her dreams of a film career under the name of Dolores Del Monte are shattered. The son Willie John, who aspires to be a live-wire journalist, always has his efforts short-circuited. Rabby has a couple of Joxerish cronies — one Scotty Sturgeon who is ever breaking into song, and the other Barney Brudge whose "split personality" makes him go into momentary comas when he begins to preach against drink, of which he is normally abnormally fond. The comedy is local stuff, but the dialogue has much ripe, colloquial banter to it.

Right Again, Barnum was first produced by the Group Theatre on December 7, 1943, and is a sequel to *Mugs and Money*. Like most sequels, it is not as good, but its dialogue has lost none of the racy flair of the earlier play.

The End House was produced by the Group and, on August 28, 1944, by the Abbey. It is a domestic tragicomedy set in Belfast a year and a half before the Second World War. The MacAstockers are an impoverished Catholic family: the father is out of work, the mother loses her insurance money, the son is an Irish Nationalist just released from jail, and the daughter is an independent new woman. Intentionally or not, the play seems a Belfast *Juno and the Paycock*. It shows, like *Juno*, the disintegration of a family — the father falls from a ladder, the son is shot by policemen, and the daughter is seduced and deserted. Tomelty's son and daughter are better characterized than Johnny and Mary Boyle, but the father and mother are much thinner than Boyle and Juno. The language, as one would expect, is more than adequate but less inventive than O'Casey's. The comic scenes are milder than those in *Juno*; the ending is unrelievedly tragic, lacking O'Casey's extra dimension of mingled emotions. Still, the play is fairly stated and a moving portrait of the plight of Catholics in predominantly Presbyterian Belfast.

All Souls' Night is Tomelty's best tragedy. It was first performed by the Group in September, 1948, with the author playing John Quinn, the father, and later produced by the Abbey on April 16, 1949. A tragedy of North of Ireland fisherfolk, it is also a reminiscent play, but suggests Synge rather than O'Casey — particularly the Synge of *Riders to the Sea*. Tomelty, however, uses the folk legend that on All Souls' night the dead can return, and two dead sons of the family do return. The second son, Michael, has just been killed because his greedy mother will not allow him any of the money that she has saved and he, eager to buy a larger boat, is driven out to sea on a stormy night to plunder a wrecked ship. The progress of Tomelty's tragedy is more predictable than inevitable, and drawn out rather than suspenseful. Unless excellently done, its final impression might well be gloomy rather than tragic, sluggish rather than powerful. Its diction is straightforward rather than evocative, and its characterization is adequate but never memorable. Having made so many strictures, I should also say that I have not seen the play and have a nagging suspicion it might be more powerful than I have allowed.

Tomelty's best-known play is *Is the Priest At Home?*, which was produced by the Group Theatre in May, 1954, and performed a hundred and twelve times at the Abbey before and after Christmas, 1954. It starts with a bald, unpromising statement of its theme in a scene between a priest and another overdrawn stage-American. Once past that initial scene and into the central reminiscence in the priest's mind, the play settles down to being one of the most reasonable and effective statements about the life of an Irish priest that I know of. The thesis is that the priest is powerless outside of purely spiritual matters and that he is not very effective even there against the peculiar nature of his countrymen. As the priest's wise old handyman tells him, "Forget the Church Universal and remember you are in the Church Hibernicus." Doubtless this view is not the whole story, any more than that opposite view of tyrannical clerics that we get in Carroll's *Things That Are Caesar's*, is the whole story. Yet Tomelty makes his case with great persuasiveness.

The discussion scenes hold the attention as closely as the best of D'Alton, and the illustrative actions are justly chosen and authentically evocative. Even better, he does not make the mistake of winding up his individual stories patly or artificially. Indeed, he usually does not wind them up at all. Such a device, though true to life, is often false to art; but Tomelty has so stressed his theme that the audience is caught up in it and satisfied to accept the stories as illustrations rather than the end in themselves. Really, Tomelty's play proves that realism is not outworn; all it requires for continued vitality is an author who can bring to it a significant and complex statement rather than a stage platitude.

Among Tomelty's recent unpublished plays is *To Have a Little House*, an effective realistic melodrama with a compelling main character in John Brush, an illiterate handyman. A realistic but somewhat experimental play is *The Sensitive Man*, a piece which suggests the direction Tomelty's recent writing is taking. At the end of the play, a character remarks to a wandering actor-playwright, "You must make it a tragedy about life. . . . Our lives . . . Life differs from the play, only in this. . . . It has no plot. All is vague, desultory, unconnected . . . with the mystery unsolved." The description applies as well to *The Sensitive Man*, and that fact makes the play both weak and interesting.

In his recent work, Tomelty is trying to make the dramatic form jibe more with the sprawling reality of life. To him, form on the stage demands compression, simplicity, and structure — all qualities opposed to the confusions of reality. His latest play, on which he was working when I spoke with him, is a three-character one which tries to convey a sense of the life beyond the stage by having offstage characters who try to come on and who are always barred. Much of *The Sensitive Man* is taken up with sketching what happens to these people who never appear, and who bear only more or less directly on the story, which gives the play, in spots, a weakly discursive effect. Much of it has a repetitive anecdotalness which one finds in life, but which seems a bit leisurely for the drama. Although Tomelty, like Keane and Molloy and Sam Thompson, is an avid listener to stories and scraps of dialogue, his main action has little impelling forward movement, little developing story. The problem of whether Rosena Rapple will win her fight with the landlord and be allowed to continue strewing fish innards on the seawall for the birds — this problem is smothered in conversation and static situations. There is much in this portrait of a small town in the North that is broodingly lovely and almost lyrical, but there is little that is dramatic. Still, the play is an intriguing experiment in a field which Tomelty is yet exploring, and experiment has so far been notably lacking in the drama of Ulster.

II REACTIONS FROM REALISM

6

At the Gate Theatre

ALTHOUGH the modern Irish drama originated partly in a nationalist impulse, there were other allied impulses even from the beginning. Yeats, of course, was the champion of a poetic drama which in a few early plays was allied with nationalism, but which grew ever farther away from such a public statement until in the later Noh plays it seemed to have retreated almost into an art-for-art's sake privacy. There was also a third impulse behind the early blossoming of dramatic activity, an impulse centering on that interesting and curious man Edward Martyn.

Of the founders of the Irish Literary Theatre, the one most aware of the modern drama outside of Ireland was Martyn. Some of his early plays were influenced by Ibsen, although it was an Ibsenism diluted by his own vague and personal brand of Catholic-Celtic mysticism. Martyn, however, was the least forceful figure in the early dramatic hierarchy, and his own efforts were inevitably submerged. Yet he had a tenacity of his own, and after his split with Yeats he went his own way and founded his own theatre, which was known from time to time as the Irish Theatre, the Theatre of Ireland, or the Hardwicke Street Theatre.

He gathered around him an able group that sometimes included Thomas MacDonagh, John MacDonagh, Joseph Plunkett, Padraic Colum, Maire Nic Shiubhlaigh, James Stephens, Rutherford Mayne, and, for a short while, the young Micheál Mac Liammóir. But Martyn's theatre produced plays infrequently, and, according to that indefatigable first-nighter Joseph Holloway, the productions rarely came within hailing distance of Abbey standards. Yet from 1906 to 1916, Martyn produced several good Irish plays that were not done by the Abbey — among them works by Colum, Stephens, Seamus O'Kelly, Padráic Ó Conaire, and himself. But more germane to our present argument is that Martyn also produced some notable foreign plays — pieces by Ibsen, Chekhov, Ostrovsky, Strindberg, and Villiers de l'Isle Adam.

This international impulse was kept alive when, in 1918, Yeats, Lennox Robinson, and others, feeling a certain parochialism in the almost solely Irish repertoire of the Abbey, formed the Dublin Drama League. It used the Abbey stage and many of the Abbey players to present a wide variety of foreign works ranging from the Greeks to Pirandello, O'Neill, Lenormand, Sierra, Toller, Andreyev, and Cocteau. "The League," Lennox Robinson remarked, "ceased to exist in 1928, exactly ten years after its birth, and Hilton Edwards and Micheál Mac Liammóir arrived with their plays and their ideas." When Edwards and Mac Liammóir founded the Dublin Gate Theatre in 1928 they kept alive this international impulse within the Irish theatre. They produced the most exciting of classic and contemporary dramas, no matter what the style of the play, and during the 1930's and the 1940's the most vital theatre in Ireland was the Gate.

꽃

Hilton Edwards is an Englishman who toured with Charles Doran's Shakespearean company and played with the Old Vic before being hired in 1927 for a tour with Anew McMaster's company in Ireland. There he met McMaster's brother-in-law Mac Liammóir, who was playing with the company, and in 1928 they began their long partnership by producing Mac Liammóir's Irish version of *Diarmuid and Grainne* in Galway. In October of that year, they opened the Dublin Gate Theatre Studio at the Abbey's little Peacock Theatre with an impressive production of *Peer Gynt*. Since then, Edwards has directed more than three hundred plays for the Gate and acted in many of them. He is a superb character actor and probably the most experienced director in the country. His influence on the Irish theatre is well summed up by Mac Liammóir, who wrote:

It was his arrival on the Irish scene that was the first signal for the searchlights of interest and understanding to be turned, not away from the author, who at the Abbey had been pre-eminent from the beginning even over the actor, but equally upon the director and his art. It was he who introduced to Dublin methods of production, decor, and lighting, handling of mass effects, experiments in choral speaking, in scenic continuity, in symphonic arrangements of incidental music, of mime and gesture, hitherto barely understood. It is impossible to see the work of any of the younger directors without tracing a great portion of its inspiration to him. Production, as it is understood in Dublin today in what I must call the resident companies would undoubtedly exist in one form or another, but it would not be as it is.[1]

Mac Liammóir himself is a fascinating figure who began his career as a child actor in *Peter Pan* and with Beerbohm Tree in *Oliver Twist* and other plays. Really he seems a man born out of his time: he should have been about fifteen years older in the Yellow Nineties and hobnobbed with Wilde and Beerbohm, for in manner and appearance he is the last of the dandies. His prose suggests the ornate elegance of Pater, his drawing the feline elegance of Beardsley. Certainly he would be one of the few actors still able to pull off the grand romantic manner. His contributions to the Gate over the years have been as significant and various as those of his partner. The effect of a typical Gate production — if one could call any production from such a disparate repertoire typical — derived not only from Edwards's perceptive direction, but also from a sense of taste and style inherent in Mac Liammóir's designs for sets and costumes. As an actor, Mac Liammóir must rank with Cyril Cusack and Siobhan McKenna as the best known outside of Ireland and as among the best within it. His most popular recent vehicle is his delightful one-man show based on the writings of Oscar Wilde and called *The Importance of Being Oscar*. As a writer, he has given the theatre both original scripts and adaptations. The originals include his *Diarmuid and Grainne*, his *Easter, 1916*, his *Ford of the Hurdles*, *Where Stars Walk*, *Dancing Shadows*, *Ill Met by Moonlight*, *Portrait of Miriam*, *The Mountains Look Different*, *Home for Christmas*, and *A Slipper for the Moon*. His adaptations include *Jane Eyre*, *The Picture of Dorian Gray*, *A Tale of Two Cities*, *Trilby*, *Juliet in the Rain* from Lenormand, and *An Apple a Day* from Jules Romains's *Dr. Knock*, as well as his most recent adaptation, *The Informer*, from O'Flaherty's novel. His other writings include an invaluable and witty volume of reminiscences, *All for Hecuba*, and a memoir of the filming of Orson Welles's *Othello*, *Put Money in Thy Purse*.

For its first two seasons, the Gate's plays were done in the Abbey's small experimental Peacock Theatre. For the third season, the Gate moved into the Rotunda, where the architect Michael Scott had converted a second-story ballroom into a moderate-sized theatre. The stage was small, there was little room for the storage of sets, and no fly space. Despite these handicaps, the theatre's productions were the most visually exciting to be seen in Dublin.

A pictorial record of the theatre's first seven seasons is preserved in *The Gate Book* whose many photographs attest to the taste and ability of Mac Liammóir as a designer. The photographs make it apparent that the theatre was attempting to develop no one style, but rather to find the appropriate style for each of the widely varied shows that were produced. There are realistic interiors for plays that demand them — a simple cottage for Mary Manning's *The Happy Family*, a parlor of a Big House for Lady Longford's *Mr. Jiggins of Jigginstown*, a spacious drawing room for *Lady Windermere's Fan*. There are stylized interiors — a whimsical overdecoration for *The Importance of Being Earnest*, an almost Dali-esque amusement park scene for *Liliom*, a child-like agleyness for *Ten Nights in a Bar Room*. Some plays or scenes in plays were merely done in front of painted backcloths — the minute cartoon of the Coliseum for Lady Longford's *Queens and Emperors*, the formal decoration for *A Bride for the Unicorn*, and the suggested interiors for *The Old Lady Says "No!"*, both by Denis Johnston; each aptly interprets the style and spirit of the play.

For many years, Edwards and Mac Liammóir were able to hold a company together — despite secessions of some good actors, among them the young Orson Welles, Geraldine Fitzgerald, the young Cyril Cusack, James Mason, and Peggy Cummins. Of course the most telling secession was not by an actor, but by Lord Longford, who was the chairman of the theatre's board and who for several years had footed many of its bills. In 1936, when Edwards, Mac Liammóir, and part of the Gate Company were touring in Egypt, they learned to their surprise and dismay that Longford had formed a company which was appearing in England billed as the Gate Theatre. A compromise was eventually worked out whereby the Edwards–Mac Liammóir group kept the name of the Gate, and each company played in the theatre for six months and toured for six.

During the war, tours outside of Ireland were impossible, and Edwards and Mac Liammóir played several seasons at the Gaiety Theatre in Dublin, which had a seating capacity three or four times as large as the Gate, at which, of course, they also played. In recent years, despite

Mac Liammóir's success in *The Importance of Being Oscar* and his travels over the world in it, and despite a stint that Edwards put in at Telefís Éireann, the Gate still produces a show or two a year. The tragedy is that the theatre had to be a commercial one, and no commercial management in modern times has been able to keep its head above water. A few years ago the Arts Council recognized the contribution of Edwards and Mac Liammóir by paying off the theatre's debts. But that was no real answer, for Edwards and Mac Liammóir have not maintained a permanent company for several years, and any new Gate productions are cast from the reservoir of available Irish actors. Practically speaking, this means that the tradition of the Gate will die with its two major figures who, though vital and productive, are no longer young. The loss of their knowledge seems an enormous waste; the Irish government should at some time have subsidized the Gate and put it on a permanent basis, so that what Edwards and Mac Liammóir have learned could be transmitted. Mac Liammóir himself once suggested "a division of the Abbey's year into, let us say, eight months for its present programme, artists, and direction, and four for Hilton and me and our manner of looking at things." Even at this eleventh hour it is not quite too late for some sort of subsidy which would allow the discoveries of Edwards and Mac Liammóir to become a permanent part of Irish theatrical tradition.

In his interesting book *The Mantle of Harlequin*, Edwards wrote:

When the Dublin Gate Theatre was started by my partner, Micheál Mac Liammóir, and myself in the late twenties theatrical revolution was in the air. Just as the Abbey had been swept along on the tide of naturalism, not in itself a native product of the soil, so the Gate bore a more obvious evidence of foreign influences. The Gate, although it has presented many plays by Irish authors and on Irish themes, is not a national theatre. It is simply a theatre. Its policy is the exploitation of all forms of theatrical expression regardless of nationality. It embraces upon occasion, the naturalistic play, but its concern has always been with the whole gamut of the stage.[2]

All forms of theatrical expression and the whole gamut of the stage really are represented in the Gate's long and distinguished list of productions. Indeed, this list might serve as a model for what a vital repertory theatre should do. The Gate presented examples of about everything from Aeschylus to Brecht — including fourteen of Shakespeare's plays, eleven of Shaw's including the complete *Back to Methuselah*, three of Ibsen, two of Chekhov, two of Strindberg, and six of Wilde including Mac Liammóir's adaptation of *Dorian Gray*, as well as traditional English classics by Congreve, Vanbrugh, Farquhar, and Sheridan. Despite this well-rounded selection, the larger part of the Gate's plays were drawn from what was the most theatrically exciting in the contemporary world drama. By "theatrically exciting," I mean that the Gate's bent was toward the drama as theatre rather than as literature. They would produce Noel Coward, Guy Bolton, and Kaufman and Hart nearly as often as they would produce Pirandello, Kaiser, and Cocteau. Americans are well represented on the Gate's list, with seven plays by O'Neill, three by Rice, and others by Maxwell Anderson, Wilder, Behrman, Hellman, and Miller.

The Gate did not depend mainly, as did the Abbey, on its own writers, but it produced a respectable number of new plays by Irishmen. Its most notable discovery was Denis Johnston, whose work is discussed in another chapter; it also produced Frank Carney's *The Doctor's Boy*, Austin Clarke's *The Hunger Demon*, two plays by Dr. Robert Collis, Padraic Colum's *Mogu of the Desert*, St. John Ervine's Shakespearean sequel *The Lady of Belmont*, M. J. Farrell's *Guardian Angel*, Brian Friel's *Philadelphia, Here I Come*, Conor Farrington's *The Last P.M.*, Andrew Ganly's *Murder Like Charity*, three plays by Maura Laverty, nine plays by the Longfords, two by Donagh Mac Donagh, three by Mary Manning, T. C. Murray's rejected Abbey play *A Flutter of Wings*, Padraic Pearse's *The Singer*, Lennox Robinson's adaptation of "Boule de Suif" and also his *When Lovely Woman*, Richard Rowley's *Apollo in Mourne*, Elsie Schauffler's *Parnell*, four plays by David Sears, and two plays and a translation by Yeats. Not all of these plays are published, but some I discuss in this chapter and some others elsewhere in this book. My most notable omission is probably the work of Maura Laverty, which was well received, but which is unpublished and which I unfortunately have not read.

Probably the best Gate writer to start with is Mac Liammóir, for he has been a prolific and successful writer for the theatre. Only two of his scripts — *Where Stars Walk* and *Ill Met By Moonlight* — have been published, and they are both adroit, accomplished, and rather similar. *Where Stars Walk* was first produced at the Gaiety Theatre, Dublin, on February 19, 1940. In general, it resembles the later and better *Ill Met By Moonlight*, inasmuch as Mac Liammóir combines a brittle modern comedy with a seriously treated fantasy. In the later play, the fantasy is melodramatic, but here it is romantic and treats the Irish legend of Etain and

Midhir. The play takes as its premise Etain's return to earth as a country girl who does not remember her divine past. Then Midhir, her lover, appears as a boy from the country who awakens her consciousness, and they both finally go off together.

Etain and Midhir, using the names Eileen and Martin, are servants in the house of a retired middle-aged actress who is acting in a friend's play about the legend of these same two lovers. The scenes with Sophia Sheridan and her friends take up most of the space and are in the vein of neo-high comedy, in the manner of Noel Coward and Ivor Novello. Much of this dialogue is purely theatrical stuff, light fluff, bright banter with a soupçon of satire, insult rather than pure Congrevian wit. Still, it is much better than the usual specimen of this style, and with actors able to manage an airy, Luntian delivery it should convey much charm. I have a personal distaste for the Noel Cowardice that Mac Liammóir practices here, and that doubtless prevents me from waxing as enthusiastic as the play's merits would allow. Its emotions, however, are more theatrical than real; its manner is copied more from theatrical artifice than from life; and its theme is charming in a way that makes it seem inconsequential make-believe. However, the play has worked on the stage precisely in the way that Mac Liammóir wanted it to, and that is a considerable accomplishment.

Those same qualities are even more evident in *Ill Met By Moonlight*. But that play is a curious one, not only for its subject matter, but also for its attack and for its being not quite of a piece. It is set in the home of Professor Sebastien Prosper in Connemara. Prosper, folklorist, lives, with his young daughter Susan and his Irish servant Lee, in a house supposed to be built within a fairy ring; the action of the play illustrates a folk tale told to Prosper in the play's first scene:

The newly married bride in this story walks out in the moonlight on Midsummer Eve, meets the fairies, and is stolen by them under the withered rowan tree at the corner of the house . . . The changeling who is left in her place returns, a woman bewitched, who cuts up hell with the family, kills her old father-in-law, and on the same day seduces her husband's friend, who was probably best man at her wedding . . . Enfin, she was banished by a wreath of flowers . . . sprinkled with salt and goat's blood . . . thrown over her neck by her old nurse and by her husband giving her . . . a good puck in the gob . . .

Told baldly, Mac Liammóir's illustration of this story seems a half-whimsical melodrama. The excellence of the play lies, however, in its

treatment: Mac Liammóir brings to the story such a theatrical characterization and such a civilized dialogue that the play seems fuller and more
meaningful than the ordinary thriller. Partly, his J. B. Priestleyan treatment of the kink-in-time theme gives a more substantial base to his fable;
but mainly the effective evocation of malignancy in the changeling suggests a frightening relevance to human psychology.

The play has faults. For instance, its first half contains the delight, and
its second half the terror. Given Mac Liammóir's plot, there is possibly
no way out of this problem; much laughter in the second half would dis-
sipate the intensity, just as much foreboding in the first would reduce
the air of reality. And in places Mac Liammóir reaches back into the
nineteenth-century melodrama for his effects, as in the changeling's
fiendish laughter that concludes Act II.

Much of the charm comes from Prosper and Susan. Prosper is only a
stage type, a humor, a curmudgeon with a heart of gold, but he is a
splendid one. What could be more featly Jonsonian than the scene in
which Prosper goes swimming while insulting his unwanted guests, his
nephew Robert and Robert's new wife Catherine?

Put up with you? But, of course! I adore matrimony. Yes, do stay. Plas-
tically, at any rate, you have many points. Your head's superb. I hope,
Madame, that you are not one of those pampered, feather-brained young
things (*He unties his tie*) who, like my nephew, here, seems to think
nothing of upsetting the orderly ways of a household (*His shirt begins
to come off*) where there is serious work to be done, who have no reverence for the most ordinary observances of family life (*He wrenches himself free of his sleeveless singlet*) and who seem to imagine there is a virtue in kicking over the traces of convention to an extent that is beyond
the limits of common decency. (*His trousers are half off: He notices
Catherine's amusement*). What are you laughing at?

However, Mac Liammóir's real triumph is Susan. Half woman and half
gamin, her freshness springs partly from her youth, partly from her casual upbringing, and partly from her attempts to appear older. She mixes,
for example, a cocktail for Catherine with considerable aplomb, but she
puts into it brandy, gin, Cointreau, and vodka. Her moments of affec-
tation, however, are balanced by moments of naturalness. Even when
lecturing Prosper on his language, she drops back into her basic naturalness: "it's all right *en famille*, it's like fishermen in a pub dropping into
Irish after hours; but in front of nice refined people it sounds lousy, honest to God it does." Indeed, the best test of Susan's excellence is the critic's temptation to quote and quote from her. Suffice it to say that she is

nearly as fine as the Brigid of *Shadow and Substance* and the Blanaid of *The Moon in the Yellow River*.

꿥

David Sears was an influential Irish drama critic who had several plays produced at the Gate — *Juggernaut* in the second season, *The Dead Ride Fast* in the 1931–1932 season, *Grania of the Ships* in the 1933–1934 season, and *The Forced Marriage*. Only *Juggernaut* has been published. Although it won the drama prize at the Tailteann Games of 1928, it was rejected by the Abbey; but was popular enough at the Gate to be revived. The play is a realistic portrayal of the divided loyalties of a middle-class Irish family during the Troubles. Their difficulty is tautly dramatized when a wounded gunman bursts into their home demanding shelter. Their first impulse as law-abiding citizens is to give him up. Then, slowly, although they still disagree with his methods, they grudgingly admit his claim on their loyalties and help him escape. The theme is restated in more personal terms by the case of the daughter who is the last to give in. She loves a British officer who will be marked for assassination if the gunman escapes. Yet finally the girl also agrees to the escape, and here the play becomes psychologically unconvincing. The Juggernaut of the title is the symbol for patriotism; Sear's attitude toward patriotism is emphasized by the overtheatrical curtain line of the daughter:

> MARGERY (*Raising herself in the chair and looking, in the strange light, like one demented*): . . . Juggernaut! Inexorable Juggernaut. I am crushed beneath your insensate wheels and you roll on. (*She collapses . . .*)

Most of the dialogue is much less hokey, but despite the adequacy of the characterization and the excitement of the situation, the play seems dated. Now, more than a generation removed from the emotionally charged atmosphere of its time, the play seems only a patriotic paean, too bald to be convincing.

꿥

Mary Manning was born in Dublin of an Anglo-Irish family from Kerry. She was educated at Morehampton House School and Alexandra College in Dublin, and later studied art in London and Boston. She studied acting at the Abbey school and played with the Irish Players in England and with the Abbey in Dublin before joining the Gate. There she was publicity manager for the theatre and editor of *Motley*, a magazine it published. In *All for Hecuba*, Mac Liammóir wrote how her "brain, nimble and observant as it was, could not yet keep pace with a tongue so caustic that even her native city . . . was a little in awe of her." This gift for wit and satire was evident in *Youth's the Season — ?*, which was produced at the Gate on December 8, 1931, in the one-act *Storm over Wicklow* produced in 1933, and in *Happy Family* produced in 1934. Shortly after, she left Dublin for America and married Mark De Wolfe Howe, Jr., of Boston, a lawyer and authority on Justice Holmes. For some years, her husband and three daughters absorbed all her time, and she did no writing for the theatre. She did, however, publish two novels — *Mount Venus* in 1938 and *Lovely People* in 1953. In 1955, she returned to dramatic writing with an adaptation of *Finnegans Wake* called *The Voices of Shem*. Recently she has dramatized O'Connor's novel *The Saint and Mary Kate*.

Dublin had never seen a play quite like *Youth's the Season — ?*, and perhaps it has not seen one since. Such a strong and smoothly written play would have been remarkable no matter who had written it, but it was even more remarkable for a girl barely out of her teens. In comparison with the sense of style in this play, Shelagh Delaney's *A Taste of Honey* really seems like notes for a rough draft. Miss Manning creates a fuller world inhabited by cleverer young people who have a sense of intellectual malaise and spiritual fecklessness that almost reaches the intensity of tragedy. Her group of young, Anglo-Irish, middle-class Dubliners is at that crucial moment just before their lives are set in permanent patterns — before they decide finally what to do or whom to marry. Her point is that youth is really not the season of thoughtless joy, but of exacerbating indecision and lacerating self-scrutiny.

In the brilliantly funny party of Act II, for example, the main characters suffer agonies during their dancing, joking, love-making, and drinking. Desmond, who has given himself this party on his twenty-first birthday, keeps groaning, "This is a terrible party." His sister Deirdre is eaten up with jealousy at her fiancé's apparent interest in another girl, an interest brought about by Deirdre's own pose of stuffy intellectuality. His sister Connie, having just been turned down by Terence Killigrew, announces in a flourish of masochism her engagement to a budding Colonel Blimp. Killigrew, the twenty-seven-year-old poet manqué and drinker rampant, flays himself satirically for taking refuge from the world in his own selfishness. Even a minor character like the inordinately conventional Philip Pryce is eaten up with an absurdly unrequited and gnawing-ly painful love for the American girl, Priscilla Converse. And at the end of the evening, after all of the insults and quarrels and brawls and after Priscilla has fallen down the stairs, Desmond says to his friend Willie:

> DESMOND (*staring hopelessly in front of him*): My future — I must think of my future! (*He drinks the remains of a glass, and starts singing* — "*Youth's the season made for Joy, Love is then a Duty*" —.) Come here, Willie. (*Willie trots over to him obediently, carrying a load of bottles.*) Listen, Willie. (*He sings the first two lines again.*) Listen, Willie, if you hear anyone singing that song, strike him across the face.
>
> WILLIE (*stupidly*): . . . strike him across the face.
>
> DESMOND: Yes, because it's a bloody lie. Do you hear, a bloody lie.
>
> WILLIE (*Repeating it mechanically*) . . . a bloody lie.

In form, the play is probably a tragicomedy because it has various strands of plot, ranging from the farcical to the tragic, and each strand shows how a character reacts to the coming of responsible adulthood. Deirdre, for instance, sheds her pretensions and gets her man; Terence sheds himself of his ego, and, seeing how mediocre he is, shoots himself; in horror, Desmond gives up his hopes of being a designer and sheds his artiness for a bowler hat, a rolled umbrella, and his father's office.

What makes the play so funny, moving, and convincing is a pervasive sense of style. And the style is all the more convincing for being not an artificial collection of Wildean epigrams, but the fluent, brittle, and imitative cleverness that is about as close to real wit as conversation usually comes. For example:

> DESMOND: Now let's gossip. Let's be vilely libellous. Let's be salacious and treacherous. Let's stab our best friends in the back. Let's betray our relations; let's wash our dirty linen in the drawing-room. In other words — let's be Dublin.

It would be difficult to find a more accomplished first play.

Miss Manning's other early work can be disposed of fairly quickly. About *Storm over Wicklow*, she remarked, "I was only 22 when it was produced at the Gate, and it seems very immature now. I think its success was due to the fact that people in Dublin were fed up with the going native British and Americans — so anything that satirized them was all right." [3] "Immature" is probably the wrong word for this amusing little comedy of a group of people gathered together in a summer hotel. After all, the piece was only meant as a light comedy. Although the characters are types, much of the dialogue is deft and much of the satire still pointed. *Happy Family* has not been published, and I have not read it. Of it, Miss Manning wrote, "I'm ashamed of it. It was really a bad play except for the maid's part. So don't even think about it." [4]

The Voices of Shem, her adaptation of *Finnegans Wake*, was first produced by the Poets' Theatre in Cambridge, Massachusetts, on April 25, 1955. Later, when it appeared at one of the Dublin Theatre Festivals, it was received with a general approval mingled with reservations about its intelligibility. Those reservations seem to me just, although the piece does provide a fascinating evening in the theatre. Despite its high spirits, its fun, its songs, the wit and the theatricality of its chorus, there is still the barrier of a language much too thickly intellectual to work as stage dialogue. It is nevertheless hard to think how the spirit of this long, complex book could have been transposed to the stage in any more lively or fairer fashion.

₱

Dr. Robert Collis is a Dublin pediatrician born in 1900; he has written — in addition to several medical works — an autobiography, a travel memoir, and two plays for the Gate. Only the first play, *Marrowbone Lane*, has been published. It is a simply told story of a young girl from Mayo, just married and brought to live in a Dublin tenement. More than fifty people are crammed into the house which is full of the stench and grime of years, and so rickety that it is dangerous to live in. The story tells of the girl's frantic effort to escape, of a fall on a dilapidated stairs which lames her and makes her unable to have more children, and of how in one semi-expressionistic scene she carries her one sick child from hospital to hospital, of how it dies, and of how she and her husband are then at last allotted a new house.

The play is made all the more harrowing by its simplicity. Collis propounds no thesis and no solution, but merely draws an accurate picture of an intolerable situation, of overcrowding, squalor, dirt, and disease so overpowering that government bureaus and hospitals and public health nurses are unable to cope with them. The characterization is adequate but the emphasis is mainly on situation and story, which come across with great force. Collis's Mary is no Juno Boyle, but he has made the situation which entraps her so stark that Mary sometimes gets almost the same effect as Juno. Here, for instance, is her last speech, after her baby has died and she has learned of the new house:

My God! – "All right – all right!" That's what you've always said, Jim Kane, ever since you brought me to this place. "It's all right." It was "all right" when they told us we couldn't have a home unless we had eight children or were dyin' of consumption, and now they're after murderin' the only baby we can ever have, it's all right. (*More hysterically.*) I'm glad he's dead. (*Takes a step towards the others.*) I'm glad I can't have any more children to be born in this city to die in sickness and pain. (*She crosses the room, looking wild, almost mad; the others back away from her. As she reaches the cot she stops, pauses for a moment, cries out, and sinks on her knees beside it in uncontrollable tears.*) Oh, Mother of God! Brendan, my baby!

This is certainly one case in which a theme was so searingly stated that it transformed a straightforward play into art.

¶

At a financial crisis early in the career of the Gate, the Earl of Longford averted the premature demise of the theatre by buying up its remaining unsold shares. In the next few years, time and again his money kept the theatre afloat, and eventually he became chairman of its board. It was natural that an intelligent and sensitive man such as he should become interested in the artistic side of the theatre, and, as he learned more about the practical stage, it was inevitable that he should raise his voice about the selection of plays or the hiring of actors. In *All for Hecuba*, Mac Liammóir complains that Longford imperfectly understood the economics of the theatre and caused many difficulties by, for example, insisting on hiring unnecessary and untalented actors. It is impossible at this date for an outsider to determine the justice of the charge, but it was understandable that such a closely knit team as Edwards and Mac Liammóir might have difficulty in aligning their notions of theatre with those of a man who could only seem to them, at the time, a talented amateur.

Earlier I mentioned that Mac Liammóir and Edwards, while on tour with part of the Gate company in Egypt, were surprised to learn that Longford had formed his own Gate Theatre Company. In a souvenir program which Longford Productions issued in 1939 appeared the Longford side of the story:

. . . the Company presented plays till early in 1936, in spite of increasing financial and other difficulties. Eventually it gave up all active work in theatrical production, and ceased to maintain a Company of actors.

Early in 1936 Messrs. Edwards and Mac Liammóir departed on a tour of their own to Egypt with many of the old Company, and Lord Longford founded a new Company, at first with the intention of occupying the theatre temporarily, till the initial success of the undertaking encouraged him to put it on a permanent basis. The Company was under the management of Harry Fine and was composed of the rest of the old Company, together with other actors well-known at the Gate and Abbey Theatres. It was known as Longford Productions.

The new company's first seasons were distinguished ones for in addition to productions of *Everyman, Tartuffe,* Marlowe's *Dr. Faustus, King Lear, Twelfth Night, As You Like It, The Merchant of Venice, Henry IV, The Duchess of Malfi, Ghosts, A Month in the Country, The Cherry Orchard, Lady Windermere's Fan, A Woman of No Importance, Saint Joan,* and such moderns as J. B. Priestley and Emlyn Williams, the theatre produced such Irish plays as Longford's adaptation of Le Fanu's *Carmilla,* his *Yahoo* and *Armlet of Jade,* Lady Longford's adaptations of *Pride and Prejudice* and *The Absentee,* her original play *Anything But the Truth, The Uncrowned King* by V. A. Pearn and Brinsley Mac-Namara, Austin Clarke's *Sister Eucharia,* and revivals of Mary Manning's *Youth's the Season — ?* and Johnston's *A Bride for the Unicorn* and *A Moon in the Yellow River.*

After this auspicious beginning, the theatre became rather less adventurous. Its new Irish plays were usually written by either Lord or Lady Longford, and the rest of its repertoire was mainly drawn from the English and Continental classics. On the other hand, the Longfords' own plays were often quite good, and Dublin might well never have seen much of Shakespeare, Sheridan, Shaw, Wilde, Chekhov, and Ibsen had not the Longford Company presented them. In staging, the company hardly rivaled the Gate, but some photographs of Longford productions look quite intriguing, and many people have spoken to me enthusiastically of particular shows. The company never gathered together as distinguished a group of actors as did the Gate, and probably was not always an excitingly first-rate group. But although it did not measure up to the Abbey or the Gate, its contribution to the Irish theatre should not be underestimated. Consistently the Longfords presented the great plays of the Western world, in days when the Abbey, for instance, was doing chiefly kitchen comedies. The difficulties of maintaining a company and managing a theatre are immense, and the theatre ate deeply into Lord Longford's purse. In 1956, when the Dublin Corporation demanded certain physical changes in the building, a costly remodeling was necessary, and Lord Longford's portly and dignified figure, carrying a small box for contributions, became a familiar sight on the streets of Dublin. He did not create a great theatre, but it was a respectable one that filled a real need, and he maintained it for a quarter of a century. That is yeoman service for the art of the theatre.

中

Edward Arthur Henry Pakenham, the sixth Earl of Longford, was born on December 29, 1902, a descendant of a family that had come to Ireland in 1641 with an English occupation force. His father died at Gallipoli in 1915 when Longford was thirteen years old and a schoolboy at Eton. He went up to Christ Church, Oxford, and received an M.A. in 1925. He then returned to Ireland where his family had extensive estates in County Westmeath. In 1931 he became chairman of the Gate Theatre board, and in the same year the Gate produced his first play, *The Melians*. This play was followed by *Yahoo* in 1933, *Ascendancy* in 1935, *The Armlet of Jade* in 1936, *Carmilla* in 1937, and *The Vineyard* in 1943. With his wife he translated the *Oresteia*, and alone he did translations of Sophocles, Euripides, Calderon, Molière, and Beaumarchais. He also made many translations of Irish poetry, including a version of Merriman's *The Midnight Court*. On the nomination of De Valera, he served for two years in the Irish Senate. He died on February 4, 1961, in Dublin.

Probably Longford's only play of lasting interest is *Yahoo*, first produced on September 19, 1933. The play suffers somewhat by comparison with Denis Johnston's later version of the Swift story, *The Dreaming Dust*. Lord Longford's play has a secret, unconsummated marriage between Swift and Stella, which Swift engineers when Vanessa becomes too urgently demanding. The weakness of *Yahoo* appears later, however, when Stella, near death, pleads with Swift to recognize the marriage and he violently refuses. The violence of Swift's refusal and the reason for it are unexplained, and there is consequently an inexplicable hiatus in Swift's character. Johnston's explanation of Swift's strange relations with Stella may not be the true one either, but it does give the character a dramatic plausibility. Lord Longford's Swift remains something of an enigma. Lord Longford's Swift is thus a kind of early-day angry old man. Like John Osborne's Jimmy Porter, Longford's Swift is full of spleen and Weltschmerz with which we can never fully identify because we can never fully understand them.

Johnston's version seems the better acting play. It allows for eight meaty roles for actors, whereas Longford's has strong parts only for Swift, Stella, and Vanessa. Curtis Canfield suggests that Longford's Berkeley is a comic character and cites three absurdities; to me these three seem to exhaust the comic possibilities of the role. Johnston's version should also act better because his dialogue is easier to speak. *Yahoo* is written in a rather stiff imitation of eighteenth-century speech. Professor Canfield admires this dialogue, asserting that its flavor of formality keeps the play from being taken as realistic, and prepares the audience for the expressionistic conclusion. My own feeling is that the dialogue of *Yahoo* is less a structural aid than a hindrance to the actors who must wrestle with it.

Yahoo also diverges from *The Dreaming Dust* by spending more time on "The Drapier's Letters" and by having as its eminently theatrical conclusion an expressionistic journey through time that tots up Swift's subsequent reputation ironically and attempts to make a statement about his real value. This fine scene is the best part of the play, although a few earlier scenes have some dramatic power. However, Longford is always in danger of dissipating that power. For instance, in the confrontation with Vanessa, Johnston builds his play to the point where Swift throws down the letter, turns, and leaves without a word, and he achieves great tension and strength. Longford has Swift throw down the letter, turn away, and then turn back for a long dialogue with Vanessa. The dialogue is not bad, but it lacks the intensity of Johnston's pantomime.

In sum, *Yahoo* is an interesting play with excellent touches, but finally the portrait of Swift is one of exacerbated irascibility with no real psychological reason given for it. An actor playing Lord Longford's Swift would have to bring much to the role to make it understandable.

❧

Lady Longford's original work falls into two categories — plays of contemporary Irish life and plays from Irish history. Both types are notable for their ease of dialogue and deftness of construction, but the contemporary plays genially reflect the foibles of Irish life with an accuracy hardly matched since the comedies of Lennox Robinson.

Christine, Countess Longford was born Christine Patti Trew in 1900 in Cheddar, Somerset. She attended Somerville College, Oxford, and received an M.A. In 1925, she married the Earl of Longford and has since lived in Ireland. Her books include *Vespasian and Some of His Contemporaries*, *Making Conversation*, *Country Places*, *Mr. Jiggins of Jigginstown*, *Printed Cotton*, and *A Biography of Dublin*. Her translations for the stage include *The Eumenides* of Aeschylus and the *Antigone* of Sophocles. She has made stage adaptations of novels by Jane Austen and Maria Edgeworth. Her original plays include *Queens and Emperors* of 1932, *Mr. Jiggins of Jigginstown* of 1933, *The New Girl* of 1934, *Anything But the Truth*, *Lord Edward*, *The United Brothers*, *Patrick Sarsfield*, *The Earl of Straw*, *Tankardstown*, *Mr. Supple*, *The Hill of Quirke*, and *Stop the Clock*.

Lady Longford's first original play, *Queens and Emperors*, has not been published; however, her second, *Mr. Jiggins of Jigginstown*, has. First produced by the Gate on March 28, 1933, the play is set in a big house in the Irish midlands owned by Horatio Jiggins. Mr. Jiggins is an elderly sage whose clarity and benevolence appear eccentric to the relatives and the Church of Ireland vicar who hope to profit from his will. The clash of selflessness and selfishness is nicely dramatized in the well-drawn characters, and Lady Longford is able to make many telling criticisms of morals and manners. Here, for instance, is a speech from Georgina, Horatio's cousin, which suggests both the quality of the dialogue and the nature of the criticism:

What I should like would be to settle down in this part of the country for a few months every year, in a nice place with good stabling and fifteen or sixteen hunters, hunt three days a week and come back to a good dinner and a bottle of port in the evening. But I can't afford it. I can't afford anything but my little maisonette in Kensington. I couldn't send Hugo to his father's school, though I sent him to quite a good school. And he can't go into his father's regiment so he has to go to Cambridge next year instead, and after that I hope we shall be able to wangle a job for him in the Colonial Service, if there are any colonies left. One never knows in these days. What I say is, the Sweepstake money ought not to be given to the lower classes, who don't know what to do with it. It ought to be divided up among the poor gentry like ourselves.

The comedy is thoroughly professional — not in a slick sense, but in the sense of highly competent craftsmanship. Its serious criticism is embodied in an adequate story peopled by more than adequate theatrical types and conveyed by deftly ironic dialogue.

Lord Edward was the first of several historical plays which Lady Longford wrote in the 1940's. It was first produced on June 10, 1941; its hero is, of course, Lord Edward Fitzgerald, the Ascendancy patriot. Al-

though the simplest and thinnest of her historical plays, it is a clearly organized recital of the sprawling events of Lord Edward's career. Similarly, the dialogue is a model of ease and clarity. What clarity of dialogue
and tightness of plot can accomplish, Lady Longford has done. Memorable drama needs a bit more, but still *Lord Edward* may stand as pain-
less educational theatre.

The United Brothers, first performed on April 4, 1942, is set in the
same period as *Lord Edward* and is another example of the treachery
from within that wrecked the carefully laid plans for a Rising. This
play's John Sheares is a fuller character than Lord Edward, partly because of the love-story subplot which Lady Longford has attached. Also, most of the play occurs in drawing rooms, and the women with their
gossip and banter play a larger, more engaging role than the women in
the earlier play. The whole play grows excellently in intensity, from
badinage to tragedy. It has the clarity of *Lord Edward*, plus a greater
urbanity of dialogue and a greater development of character.

Better yet is *Patrick Sarsfield*, which was first produced on May 18,
1943.[5] The events of the play stretch from April in 1690 to August in
1691, and depict the resistance of James II's forces, under Sarsfield,
against the forces of King William. Technically, this is the most difficult
of the first three histories, for the events are more sprawling and complicated and also less conventionally dramatic. Both *Lord Edward* and *The
United Brothers* ended in the failure of an endeavor, but the deaths of
the protagonists could give to the plays a sort of tragic finale. At the end
of *Patrick Sarsfield*, when the hero has capitulated and is preparing to
leave with his army for France, there is no dramatic finale, but only depression and failure. Still, this historical play is a finer achievement than
the earlier two. Sarsfield is not exactly vivid, but there is more to him
than there was to either Lord Edward or John Sheares. Some of the
minor characters — particularly James II and the Duke and Duchess of
Tyrconnel — are quite full. The collapse of the Duke in the penultimate
scene is particularly well done; his character has a great deal of racy gusto. Even though the cast list is not a long one, there is enough fullness to
the characters to suggest a fullness of events.

Lady Longford's finest history play, *The Earl of Straw*, was first produced on October 10, 1944. The play is set in 1600 and 1601, during the
rebellion of Tyrone against Queen Elizabeth. Its plot is loosely progressive rather than tightly knit, showing the various attempts to capture the
Earl of Desmond, James FitzThomas. Although its cast is not large, the

play, like *Patrick Sarsfield*, gives the feeling of large groups of people. It is also a straightforward but vivid glimpse into the rebellion and the reasons for its failure. Not merely lack of money, men, and weapons defeats the Earl, but also greed for money and outright informing among the Irish nobility. Curiously, although the audience's sympathies are all with the dashing Desmond and although the plot details the progressive dissolution of the rebellion, the most triumphant moments come at the end when one would have expected the gloomiest. After his capture, in a fine Shavian scene Desmond demonstrates to his captor, Sir George Carew, Lord President of Munster, that he, Desmond, really is the master of the situation, and that the English are in an untenable position. They will lose the war if not the battle.

The play must have, on stage, something of the excitement of a swashbuckling movie. The characterization is not scanted, however. The pragmatic and urbane Carew, Dermot O'Connor the Irish general who plays a greedy but cautious game of selling out to the highest bidder, Lady Margaret his wife who is really a spy and Carew's mistress, Myler Magrath the Queen's Archbishop of Cashel, and his cousin Darby Mac Craghe the Pope's Archbishop of Cork — all of them are engrossing and plausible characters. Mainly, though, the play is Desmond's. He has a swinging dash that brings the play excitingly alive. In sum, this is as vivid and accomplished a historical play as any dramatist has written in modern Ireland.

Tankardstown; or, A Lot To Be Thankful For was first performed on July 13, 1948. It is a mildly wry, mildly ironic play of contemporary life — contemporary meaning shortly after the Second World War. The situation and the frequent references to shortages date the play a bit, but most of the characters are still significant Irish types. The character of the businessman, Michael Manifold, is particularly well observed and unfortunately still quite apt. He is a director of Tankardstown House, a Georgian mansion recently converted into a "luxury hotel." He has his finger in many other pies, and has made a pile of money out of the war. But he has not been much concerned about the niceties of the law, and at the end of the play it is convenient for him to move for awhile to England. However, Lady Longford makes it clear that this is a temporary setback: Manifold and his kind will be a feature of Irish life for a long time to come.

A peculiar point about the satire is its mildness. With many small, deft touches, Lady Longford creates a play full of plausible and worthless people, but she finally avoids condemning them. Actually, the play ends with a warm tolerance for Manifold and the others, and Lady Longford seems here a more sophisticated John McCann — the only difference being that he writes approvingly about the lower middle class and she about the upper. The other main weakness of the play is its slimness of plot. Probably one's major enjoyment comes from the absolute rightness of her dialogue.

Mr. Supple; or, Time Will Tell, which was first performed on October 4, 1949, also tilts at the faults of the upper-middle-class businessman and his family. It is better than *Tankardstown*, for its plot is stronger. Patrick Supple is an auctioneer, house agent, and alderman in the town of Kilgobbin. He and his industrialist friend Joe Fortune are trying to involve Major Bellairs, a stage Englishman and a new settler in town, in one of their money-making schemes, not realizing that Bellairs and his wife are really inveigling a great deal of money out of them. When Tom and Angela, Supple's son and Fortune's daughter, unmask the scheming English, the play ends, presumably, happily. The legitimate criticism the audience should have for Supple and Fortune is camouflaged, however, by the supposedly greater criticism they should have for the Bellairs. And at the end, Tom and Angela seem well on their way to becoming even more schemingly canny than their fathers.

The dialogue so deftly exposes the faults and foibles of these well-chosen Irish types that one cannot suspect Lady Longford of being blind to their faults. One wonders, particularly in this play, if her refusal to criticize is a two-edged weapon. On the one hand, the play may succeed in flattering a middle-class audience; on the other, it may still succeed in making its points to the perceptive.

The Hill of Quirke, produced at the Gate in October, 1953, is Lady Longford's best contemporary play. Set in the small town of Ballyquirke, the play tells of the plans for a civic festival. Largely, the festival seems to have been dreamed up by Sean Merriman the hotel owner and publican and by Paddy Fox the owner of the dance hall and cinema, in order to promote business. They succeed in involving most of the village in the project, especially the reluctant parish priest Father Crowe, the Church of Ireland minister Mr. Argue, the Anglo-Irish landowner Captain Blood, and the enthusiastic young technical instructor Frank Furey. The finest parts of the play are the committee meetings these men attend in preparation for the festival. The circular discussions, the beside-the-point arguments, the paying off of old scores, the violent passions about nothing important – all these are common to committees everywhere, but Lady Longford has transcribed them with uncommon skill. Probably the best way to recommend this droll play is to extract a typical exchange from one of the committee meetings:

CROWE: Have you got an agenda?

FRANK (*Hands paper*): I made a few notes. The name's not fixed yet.

PADDY: We could call it a Carnival.

CROWE: No, no, Paddy. I won't have the word Carnival. A Carnival means amusements and nothing else.

ARGUE: I agree with you, father. Most emphatically. I'm against the word Carnival.

CROWE: We want no amusements in connection with the Festival.

ARGUE: Hear, hear.

CROWE: And I'm running a Carnival myself in October, in the aid of the new schools.

FRANK: Agreed to drop the word Carnival. I thought of a Civic Week.

SEAN: Now a Civic Week's nice, very nice. It sounds well.

ARGUE: I'm in favour of Civic Week. Very strongly. It's a more modest conception than a Festival, if I may say so, and we must remember our resources are limited. Ballyquirke is not a large town, as towns go. And when one thinks of the Edinburgh Festival, or the Festival of Britain, or even of Wexford, I think we should hesitate –

BLOOD: I'm not keen on Civic Week. Sounds a bit new-fangled to me.

PADDY: Now there's one thing we have to consider, and that's the publicity. What's it like on a poster? (*Scribbles*) Ballyquirke Civic Week. Come to Civic Week in Ballyquirke. Come to glorious – no, glamorous – no. There's no glamour in Civic Week. Something lacking.

SEAN: And here's another thing. It could last more than a week. Why tie ourselves down to a week in these early stages? It's early yet.

ARGUE: It's a small town, Mr. Merriman.

SEAN: There's a good surrounding district.

BLOOD: By God, you're right, Merriman. Some of the best country in Ireland. Where would the town be without the country?

SEAN: Hear, hear.

FRANK: As an alternative, we could call it a Rural Week.

BLOOD: That's better. Rural Week's better.

PADDY: There's no glamour in Rural Week.

BLOOD: I'm a countryman myself and no townsman, and I say we should call it a Rural Week. The Ballyquirke and District Rural Week. How's that for you?

PADDY: It's too long.

SEAN: And it could be a fortnight.

BLOOD: All the better if it's a fortnight. The more the merrier. The Ballyquirke and District Rural Week or Fortnight . . .

Lady Longford's last play is the unpublished comedy, *Stop the Clock*. Despite a sadly funny picture of the genteel poverty endured by a Church of Ireland minister, the play is not up to her usual standards. Yet, like all of her contemporary plays, it has a basic competence and is a wittily pertinent commentary on the new Ireland. In these plays, Lady Longford's range is restricted, but she always hits her target.

꿯

The Gate Theatre and Longford Productions have made notable contributions to the Irish stage. They have lessened the parochialism of the audience by producing both classics and interesting new plays from the world repertoire. The Gate, particularly, created by its eclectic staging a milieu for experiment. And although neither group specialized in new Irish plays, they did provide a platform for the dramatist whose manner was too experimental or whose matter was too unconventional for the Abbey. And, most important, they provided a theatre for the early masterpieces of Denis Johnston.

The Adult Theatre of Denis Johnston

I T IS necessary to correct a widespread impression, put about by unscrupulous enemies, that I died of some unspecified disease in the summer of 1933, and have never written anything since." So writes, with engaging wryness, Denis Johnston in a preface to *The Old Lady Says "No!" and Other Plays*, a collection of most of his dramatic work. Johnston's joke about his reputation is unhappily accurate. *The Moon in the Yellow River* "is still performed not only on the stage and on TV, but also in Danish, German, French, Spanish and Polish." [1] But his other plays are seldom performed by the commercial theatre and little known by the general public of playgoers. When he is known, it is as the author of *The Moon* or of *The Old Lady*, and these plays are usually dismissed as interesting but obscure.

Really, though, Johnston's plays should be both an audience's and a critic's delight. They are alternately strong and funny; their characterization is fuller than that of most plays; their themes are far from conventional theatrical platitudes; and their manners are widely varied. The six plays in Johnston's collection range from an Expressionist tragicomedy to a Shavian anti-war tract to a philosophical courtroom melodrama, a historical tragi-fantasy, and two others as difficult to pigeonhole as they are absorbing to read. After a theatrical diet of strident absurdity, foppish ambiguity, pedestrian "reality," puerile soul-searching, and the glamorizing of masochism, homosexuality, cannibalism, and just plain boorishness, Johnston's thoughtful matter and varied manner should seem an oasis of intelligence in a desert of triviality.

Intelligence, of course, may be Johnston's biggest hazard, for the drama is still a public and, therefore, a preeminently naive art. Audiences tend to be nonplused by any theme much subtler than "Honesty is the best policy" or "Cattle rustlers should be shot," and drama critics tend to be baffled by the rare dramatist who insists on making intelligent observations and who refuses to work till the end of his days in one dramatic manner.

Johnston's virtuosity is apparent in his life as well as in his plays. Born in 1901, the son of a lawyer and Irish Supreme Court judge, Johnston has had a restless, active, distinguished life. He was educated at Cambridge and Harvard, and practiced law in Ireland and Britain. While still in his twenties, he wrote the brilliant *The Old Lady Says "No!"* and directed *King Lear* for the Abbey. In 1931 he became a director of the Gate. The Gate produced some of his plays, as did Longford Productions, and for both groups he did some producing and acting. In the late thirties he was a writer and director for the B.B.C., first in radio and then in the pre-war days of television. He is one of the very first writers to do original scripts for television, and he has since written many scripts for both television and radio. During the war, he was a correspondent in the Middle East, Africa, Italy, and Germany, and later he wrote *Nine Rivers to Jordan*, a disconcerting, not entirely realistic book about his experiences. After the war, he was for two years or so a program director for B.B.C. television. In his early fifties, he began teaching in American colleges, first at Amherst, then at Mount Holyoke, and then at Smith. In 1955, on a Guggenheim Fellowship, he wrote a book called *In Search of Swift* which has proved more disconcerting to scholars than his plays have to drama critics.

Johnston's plays have not had the popular impact of O'Casey's or Carroll's or Behan's, for none of them has a simple theatrical theme as even the best plays of O'Casey do. His plays are not obscure in the way that Beckett's are, for Johnston is not, I think, an ambiguous writer. He does use the drama as an intelligent rather than as a simple-minded art. To that extent, he is at war with his form; this conflict makes him both interesting and somewhat unproduced.

Perhaps the best way to make sense out of his diversity of styles is to note how in succeeding plays he seems to be searching for a compromise between significant statement and theatrical necessity. His first play,

The Old Lady, is his most unbendingly intellectual. It is perhaps a young man's play, because of its brilliance, its brittle ironies, its dazzling reliance upon allusions, and its uncompromising demand for an amount of information no audience has ever collectively had. As Johnston became more a man of the theatre — came to know more about audiences, acting, directing, set design, theatre construction, the college and the commercial theatre — he became less willing to settle for excellence *in vacuo*. A play in the theatre must touch its audience constantly, and his later plays attempt to do just that. However, they attempt to touch the audience not merely emotionally, as O'Casey and Behan do, but more fully — both emotionally and intellectually. This poses a knotty problem and is probably the reason Johnston once remarked, "The variety of style that the plays disclose is simply a reflection of my search for an adequate means of communication." [2] He has certainly not reached the end of his search; but in an ideal theatre in an ideal civilization, with an audience composed of Shavian He-Ancients, Johnston might appear a better playwright than either O'Casey or Behan who, despite their excellences, used the stage as a primitive and naive art.

Johnston's first play, *The Old Lady Says "No!"*, is one of the few plays to use allusion as thickly as does modern poetry. Its strong theatrical merits can hardly be fully appreciated unless one has studied the playscript closely, chased down many unfamiliar allusions, and understood their historical context. That seems an unusual demand for a play to make, but modern poets like Eliot and Pound have made even more burdensome demands. One may laboriously disentangle the wealth of allusions in *The Wasteland* or *The Pisan Cantos* without being able to bring either work into intellectual focus. Not so of *The Old Lady*. When one has the information, the play has the clarity that the theatre demands.

I have no space to write a gloss of the play,[3] but I can appropriately theorize about Johnston's technique and intention. His intention is to criticize Ireland by creating provocative ironic contrasts between ideals and practice. Mainly, he contrasts a romantic patriotism of the past with a modern sentimentalizing of that ideal and with an even more modern emptiness of spirit. The effect is sardonic negation: the ideal has been punctured, the sentimental has been made to appear spurious, and the tawdry emptiness has triumphed.

The play proper is a disjunctive dream sequence taking place in the mind of an actor who had been playing the role of Robert Emmet in an old-fashioned romantic drama. Hit on the head during performance, he falls unconscious and imagines himself wandering about a modern stylized Dublin in the guise of Emmet. He stands for the romantic ideal, and Johnston makes his satiric points by the incongruous juxtaposition of Emmet's ideals and the satirically viewed practices of modern Dubliners. The plot does not consist of logically connected incidents, but rather of a series of meaningful ironies which, like themes in a symphony, recur, meld, and reappear with ever more pertinent intensity. So many satiric points are made that it is impossible to discuss each, but there are two notable scenes that might stand for the rest.

Early in his dream, the Speaker finds himself in College Green beneath Grattan's statue, but the statue has the face of Major Sirr, who arrested Emmet. Lest the irony be missed, Johnston underlines it by the ensuing incidents and dialogue. None of the passersby recognizes Emmet, and one even breaks away from him, explaining that he is late for his Irish class. That lip service to patriotic ideals is contrasted with the real preoccupations of modern Dubliners when a passing flapper remarks, "Brown Thomas for panty-bras and Elizabeth Arden to rebuild drooping tissues. Max Factor, Chanel Number Five and Mum's the Word. Has your car got a strap round the bonnet?" One girl mistakes Emmet for a masher, and the point is doubly stressed when a man, insisting that Emmet be heard, introduces him as one who "will need no introduction from me to a Dublin audience. . . . His fair fame . . . his zeal in the cause of the Gael . . . his unbounded enthusiasm for the old cause . . . have made his name a household word wherever th' old flag flies. . . . Mr. Robert Ellis."

Later a scene in the drawing room of the Minister for Arts and Crafts attacks the cultural pretensions which overlie a really imperturbable lack of taste.[4] Its tone might be suggested by this brief exchange:

CHORUS: The State supports the Artist.
GRATTAN: And the Artist supports the State.
CHORUS: Very satisfactory for everybody and no favouritism at all.
MINISTER (*confidentially*): And of course, then you see, it helps us to keep an eye on the sort of stuff that's turned out, you understand.
CHORUS: Clean and pure Art for clean and pure people.
LADY TRIMMER: What we need most is a small Salon.
GENERAL: That's right. A small Art Saloon.

The most intricate example of ironic juxtaposition occurs in this second part when three speeches go on simultaneously. The passage is too long to quote, but each speech suggests a different attitude. The idealistic Speaker quotes from the opening playlet such lines as "If there was a flame in every Irish heart to put an end to slavery and shame!" The General sings Moore's sentimental ballad, "She is Far from the Land." The artists — O'Rooney, O'Mooney, and O'Cooney — chime in with Joycean and O'Caseyan parodies as well as such modern debasements as "My good woman, I said, I'll tell you what's wrong with you. Virginity, my good woman, that's all. And believe me, it's nothing to be proud of." If it is possible to drag coherence and not a mere babble of sound from this scene, it should be savagely effective.

A third telling device is the use of a woman to symbolize Ireland. Ireland has been traditionally pictured as a Dark Rosaleen or a Kathleen ni Houlihan, and she appears here as Emmet's romantic ideal, Sarah Curran. The actress who plays Sarah, however, must also play a foul-mouthed old harpy who would be quite at ease in a Brendan Behan brothel; each character is an aspect of the same conception.

There is, finally, too much in the play for any swift summary to do it justice. It has a wealth of satiric incident, a mordant and frequent use of popular song, and a multitude of witty ironies. It may be too densely textured for our present theatre, but it is impossible to call this brilliant mélange untheatrical.

※

The Moon in the Yellow River is a straightforward realistic play, but its Broadway production by the Theatre Guild emphasizes my point that Johnston's plays are almost too intelligent for the theatre. In his introduction to the play, Johnston reprints a dialogue between him and the Guild's governing board which reads as if it were lifted from a play satirizing theatrical imperceptivity. The play is not obscure if considered by the standards which would be applied to a reasonably thoughtful novel; it is obscure only when compared with the blatant obviousness of the commercial drama. Its characters are more fully drawn than those in most realistic plays; its problem has more meaning than whodunit or whether boy gets girl.

The theme is partly stated in Dobelle's speech:

It is right that men should murder each other for the safety of progress. I admit it. That is why I am against right and believe in wrong. When I look back over my life, it's as plain as a pikestaff to me. It is always evil that seems to have made life worthwhile and always righteousness that has blasted it. And now I solemnly say that I believe in wrong. I believe in evil and in pain and in decay and, above all, in the misery that makes man so much greater than the angels.

This theme is developed mainly by the story of the power house built by the Free State government. Heading the operation is Tausch, a German who believes that material progress will elevate the soul of man. He is opposed by Darrell Blake, an I.R.A. captain who plans to blow up the power house. Blake, a man of considerable human value, is cold-blood-edly shot by his friend Commandant Lannigan who understands that this death is necessary if the power house is to be preserved. Tausch is appalled by the murder and refuses to learn the lesson it teaches — that the right causes pain and evil.

The theme is repeated in a minor plot: Dobelle's wife was allowed to die in childbirth in order to save her child, an incident that pushed Do-belle toward his view of good and evil and so soured him that he ignores his daughter Blanaid, a girl of thirteen. But the murder and the events culminating in the destruction of the power house shock him into love and sympathy for her. This ending is no sentimental negation of his basic opinion, though he has now learned to feel deeply as well as to see clear-ly.

This is a witty and beautifully characterized play. Dobelle's daughter is a charming, whimsical, eminently natural picture of a young girl. And even a merely theatrical portrait like Blanaid's Aunt Columba should seem on the stage persuasively human as well as theatrically eccentric — a trick that often eluded Shiels and even O'Casey. The play's theme affirms the need for human sympathy even in a coldly malevolent world. This view is realistic, but affirmative; few other dramatists of Johnston's generation could have embodied it so consummately.

🙰

Johnston's next play, *A Bride for the Unicorn*, was first staged by the Gate on May 9, 1933. Its stage directions call for a revolving stage with which the Gate was not equipped, and the play was done there on a sta-tionary platform and a ramp before a front curtain. Photographs suggest that the production did not do justice to the play; I doubt whether it has ever been properly staged. It offers, however, a challenge to a director with imagination, money, and a really well-equipped theatre. A Joan Littlewood might make a fine show of it, and it is one of those plays that our theatre has never thoroughly grappled with.

Part of the fault is Johnston's; the play may be too symbolic for strong emotional pertinence. Broadly, it seems to be a parable about the life of man, told in a striking blend of styles — from Greek choruses to Elizabethan lyrics to snatches of "For He's a Jolly Good Fellow." It is pervaded by a welter of references eclectically chosen from the history and literature of Western man. There seems no thoroughgoing allegory, though the hero and his seven companions are early compared with Jason and the Argonauts. This quest motif, however, seems not to be pursued throughout: at other points the hero and his companions are compared with Charlemagne and his Paladins and to the sun and the seven planets.

The tone is belligerently modern and clever, allowing for a wide variety of effects, from straight emotionalism to high poetry, from low buffoonery to caustic satire. Many specific moments should be most effective. For instance, The Ultimate Observer in his role of a Drunken Bust whose oracular remarks only emerge when he is tight is quite droll. Despite such moments, the play does not, to me, jell into the blatant coherence that the drama still demands. I may, however, be being unfairly stupid here; so here is Johnston on his intentions:

They were to write a play on the theme that the fear of Death is an illusion. That a Death at the proper time is our subconscious objective, whether we imagine we are scared of it or not; that what we think is chasing us is in fact the thing that we are chasing; and that when we find out what it actually is, we should feel greatly relieved. . . . It is supposed to be a statement that the business of life is itself, and that its crown is its ending, and that consciously or subconsciously we are aware of this, and that most of our activities show our awareness.[5]

🙞

Storm Song was first performed at the Gate on January 30, 1934. Describing it as more a burp than a song, Johnston has explained that it was a conscious attempt to win a popular audience. The play is the only one of Johnston's not occasionally revived, but it has certainly the ingredients of a commercial success: a love interest, strong curtains, melodramatic highlights, theatrically effective characters, clever dialogue, and a glamorous subject. Also, despite its slickly contrived surface, it has a thoughtful point. It is really only at the end, when boy does not get girl, that entertainment-hunters might be disappointed.

The play is set on an island off the west coast and tells of the making of a documentary film like Robert Flaherty's *Man of Aran*. The main strands of plot are the struggle to complete the film and the love story of Gordon King and Jal Joyce. Both plots are connected by the theme, which explores the character of the artist; most of the characters portray different attitudes about that point. Szilard, the great director, is fanatically devoted to his work, and nothing — neither women nor success nor critical adulation — can deflect him. Johnston has written this full role with much canniness, not romanticizing the character and not making him an intellectual.

Some other characters play a part in the creation of the work of art, but are not themselves artists. Bob Bristow, who develops the films, is "an efficient chemist" and "a thorough-going lowbrow." Alf Quilt, the film company's Cockney accountant, represents the amiable, tolerant public. The movie magnate Solberg, who appears only at the final curtain, is a Sam Goldwyn figure willing to tolerate art if it will make money. Some characters make pretensions to artistry: chief among these are the satiric parts of Raymond Chenevix, an imitative dabbler, and Deirdre Dobbs, an enthusiastic amateur.

The main character is Gordon King, the film cutter, and the only person besides Szilard to whom art is a passion. In King, Johnston emphasizes the nature of the true artist, posing for him the dilemma of love or art. Perhaps Johnston does not quite face up to the dilemma; he lets King be tricked into choosing art. But the point is made that an ascetically selfless devotion is required from the artist.

The scenes in which Johnston explores the attitudes toward art are done with a light, satiric touch. Without philosophizing, he makes his points by means of character, and there is much dialogue in that Katherine Mansfieldian vein which both he and Mary Manning can command. The play is not thematically so complex and its characters are not so deeply etched as those of *The Moon in the Yellow River*, but it is one of the most euphonious burps I have heard.

#

With *Blind Man's Buff*, first presented at the Abbey on December 26, 1936, Johnston won his popular audience. The play is an adaptation of

Ernst Toller's *The Blind Goddess*, but a comparison of *Blind Man's Buff* with Edward Crankshaw's literal translation of Toller shows that Johnston took little more than a bare and considerably modified outline. Besides shortening Toller's plot and adding several developments of his own, Johnston set his version in Dublin and permeated it with local color. Although the plot concerns a murder trial, the play is more than a thriller; it has more point than the honesty-is-the-best-policy one that usually arises from this genre. Johnston really has the excitement of the thriller's plot and the significance of the serious play; that combination is rare in a theatre largely given over to what Arthur Miller calls effects. Indeed, the play is typical of Johnston's mature compromise with the theatre.

The story tells of the trial of Dr. Frank Chavasse for his wife's murder, how he is wrongly convicted, and how he is subsequently released. The main character is not, as in Toller's play, the doctor, but his former mistress, Dr. Anice Hollingshead. They have separated, but Chavasse's wife has continued to make his life a hell, and she finally commits suicide. Anice is unfortunately the examining physician. Chavasse is indicted for murder because of the allegations of Mary Quirke, a querulous former maid in his home. The crucial point in the trial scene, which is entirely Johnston's work, is that Chavasse can be acquitted if he does not impugn Quirke's character. He cannot resist striking at her, and it is then possible to admit evidence about his own character. This evidence — his intimacy with Anice — supplies a motive and convicts him.

The point at issue is the tortuous backwardness of the law. Justice will be done only if the central issue is not broached; when that issue comes to light, Chavasse is wrongly condemned. Anice, however, persuades an official to reconsider the case, and new evidence fortuitously turns up to clear Chavasse. The theme, then, is that the law, despite its convolutions, does reach justice. This point Chavasse is too small to see, and the play ends with Anice leaving him.

The characters are well drawn — particularly Dominick Mapother, a modern stage Irishman of the Joxer Daly or Rabit Hamil variety. Even some minor characters, such as Thin and Poer, are neither thin nor poor. The theme, the absorbing plot, the strong characterization, and the vivid evocation of Dublin all combine to make *Blind Man's Buff* thoughtful and satisfying theatre.

Here it seems necessary to skip forward a few years to *Strange Occurrence on Ireland's Eye*, which was first presented at the Abbey on August 20, 1956. In his preface, Johnston explains that he wrote in 1936 an unperformed radio play about the nineteenth-century trial of William Burke Kirwan. Later, Toller persuaded him to adapt *Die Blinde Göttin*, and *Blind Man's Buff* is really a combination of Johnston's radio play and Toller. Years later, sensing that the combination was "inept," Johnston took his own work out of *Buff* and refashioned it into *Ireland's Eye*. The central acts of *Ireland's Eye* are close paraphrases of Johnston's own material in *Buff*, and this revision was made "with the purpose of avoiding the suggestion that I was plagiarising myself." [6] Both versions are good. *Buff* might have a bit more humor, but probably there is a greater coherence in *Ireland's Eye*.

The Dreaming Dust was first presented at the Gate on March 25, 1940, and has since undergone many revisions. The play grew out of Johnston's irritation at the reception of a paper he had read in Dublin in which he suggested a novel theory about Swift's parentage and his relation to Stella. His view that Swift was the illegitimate brother of Sir William Temple and that Stella was Temple's illegitimate daughter irks scholars but has some suggestive evidence to support it. One product of Johnston's interest was his book *In Search of Swift*, which also irks scholars but is a salutary reminder that they are sometimes slovenly in their researches.

The play does not stand or fall on Johnston's theory. As he remarks in his preface, the established views of Swift would lead us to regard the Dean and his friends as "a Bedlam of eccentrics, from which nothing in the nature of an intelligible play could possibly emerge." Johnston's theory makes the characters in the play psychologically plausible, and that, after all, is no more than what Shakespeare did to Richard III or Shaw to Saint Joan.

The play is about more than Swift. It is concerned more "with the seven deadly sins, their relative deadliness, and the curious phenomenon that it is usually our own particular sin that we find really unbearable in other people." This theme is cleverly introduced. A troupe of actors has been performing a Masque of the Seven Deadly Sins in St. Patrick's Cathedral in Dublin. In the course of repairs to the church, the tomb of Swift and Stella has been opened, and the actors pause there to speculate on the relation of the Dean to Stella. The matter becomes so absorbing that each propounds his own theory, and each discovers in Swift that sin which he himself had just portrayed.

The play may be performed by eight actors if each takes two or three different parts. "It is," remarked Johnston, "an exercise for actors and actresses with a flair for character, who seldom get enough opportunity to display their versatility in the course of one play." Swift is a particularly demanding role which requires an actor to portray the man at different ages and in moods ranging from gaiety to anger to anguish to lunacy. The play has some big acting scenes, especially the confrontation between Swift and Vanessa in which not a word is said. Also, the final baiting of the imbecilic Swift by the mob, in which he rises to an instant of raging coherence and hurls the Bible at them crying "Yahoos, Yahoos!" is magnificent.

Without accomplished acting, the skeleton of the seven illustrative scenes becomes a bit too obtrusive: they seem almost the seven deadly scenes. Yet this is hardly Johnston's fault; the play remains highly original and fluent.

<p>

The title of *The Golden Cuckoo*, Johnston's next play, must refer to the main character Mr. Dotheright (pronounced Duthery), an eccentric old obituist (that is, a free-lance writer of obituary notices). Mr. Dotheright rebels against society by breaking a post office window and proclaiming "a sovereign, independent Republic, conceived in Peace, and dedicated to the triple slogan 'One Truth, One Law, One Justice' — a Commonwealth where men shall be given to dignity, and not Dignities to men, and where Liberty and Equity are as free as the winds of Heaven."

In this play, Johnston poses the problem of "the tyranny of Democracy." When we have "a society that is subverting the Common Law for the convenience of the Policeman, and that maintains itself by a mass of regulations that have no basis in social morality at all," then "the problem of the individual against the State . . . is rather more acute than ever." In today's circumstances, Mr. Dotheright's thesis "of the moral duty of the put-upon to break the law from time to time — assumes a significance which grows with the tendency of the State to become, itself, the biggest lawbreaker within sight."

By genre, if such a consideration be not hopelessly inadequate here, the play is a comedy with strong elements of rowdy farce. The characters are stereotypes, but original ones of considerable charm. Mrs. Vanderbilt, the charwoman with a tendency to kleptomania; Mr. Penniwise, poet manqué and lawyer; Mr. Hooley, the cabman who finally admits that he was not out in 1916: none of these is a major character, but each is far from a familiar theatrical silhouette. It is curious how developed a role Mr. Dotheright is, considering in what a minor key Johnston presents him, how long he is offstage, and how often he is dwarfed by the showiness of the others. What puts him at the center of attention is his unshakable fidelity to his highly original views. He is remarkable in the way that Shaw's Saint Joan is remarkable. Joan may stay offstage through an entire scene; she may have less to say in the crucial trial scene than the other characters; her death may occur offstage. But her forceful ideas keep her at the center.

There are in fact reminiscences of Shaw's Joan in the play, especially in the last act when Dotheright's friends deny his cause in the way that Joan's friends do in Shaw's Epilogue. Like Joan, Dotheright admits hearing voices and protests against an entrenched society. Johnston's ending is more caustic than Shaw's weary but not quite hopeless one, however. Mr. Dotheright had been consigned to an asylum from which he had been rescued by his friends, but he insists on returning because "As a Saint, I am a failure. But as a Madman — ah, there at least, I am in the forefront of the field."

Perhaps the play does not quite conclude wryly, for Dotheright by returning to the asylum retains his integrity, and integrity is so rare that a joyous comic miracle is passed. Dotheright's cock, bought on the assumption that it was a hen, lays an egg which falls down from the loft and breaks on someone's head. That touch, incidentally, suggests the conclusion of the first scene of *Saint Joan*.

Of all of Johnston's plays, this is the warmest and liveliest. The original characters, the mad-tea-party situations, and the dialogue which runs a gamut from quip to rant should all make the piece a delight on the stage. Here, Johnston finds his finest compromise between the naïveté of the theatre and the originality of the perceptive mind.

꽃

The Scythe and the Sunset, Johnston's play about the Easter Rising, was produced on May 19, 1958, at the Abbey after a first presentation at

the Poets Theatre in Cambridge, Massachusetts, in March. By its title
and subject, it demands comparison with O'Casey's *The Plough and the
Stars*. O'Casey's great tragicomedy, despite its subtle ironies, is a play
that exists mainly as an emotional experience. Its intellectual content is
simply that war is senseless; the senselessness is brought home with great
emotional force in agonizing scenes of human suffering and waste. In individual characterization, in human comedy and tragedy, *The Plough*
has it all over *The Scythe*. But when we contrast rather than compare
the plays, Johnston's real excellences emerge. His play exists on a different intellectual level. I do not mean that it is aridly devoid of emotion
any more than O'Casey's is a brainless evocation of tears and laughter.
The culmination of O'Casey's play, however, is his most pitiable evocation of suffering, whereas the culmination of Johnston's is a debate about
motives. *The Scythe* is a companion to and not a rival of *The Plough*.

Johnston's play is set in an upstairs cafe across from the general post
office in O'Connell Street, and the cafe is used as a Red Cross station by
the rebels. Johnston uses four kinds of illustrative character: his rebel
leaders, of whom Tetley is the most conscious of issues; his Anglo-Irish
officer in the English army, Palliser, who has been wounded and captured; his common people, in the persons of Maginnis an ordinary soldier and Roisin the waitress; and his *raisonneur*, Dr. Myles MacCarthy;
and perhaps also his chorus, the real-life character of a well-known Dublin looney, Endymion.

At first the rebels are inept amateurs who cannot work a captured
machine gun and who leave the telephone unguarded so that Palliser may
ring up Dublin Castle. The crucial point in Act II shows the rebellion in
danger of collapsing; truce feelers have been sent out, and Palliser has
succeeded in postponing the bombardment of the city. Angered at the
disdain of the amateur soldiers for him and his class, he shows a rabid
woman patriot how to fire the machine gun at the British envoy in the
street, and thereby ensures that the Rising will be fought out to its tragic
ending rather than ignominiously curtailed.

In Act III, the rebels have weathered fire and become more than play
soldiers. Even the sardonically critical attitude of that voice of the public Roisin has changed to admiration. Tetley can now surrender knowing
that the executions of the rebel leaders will solidify the opinion of the
country behind them and mean that they have ultimately won. Palliser
refuses to be taken from the now burning building because he, and what
he stands for, must show as much Face as Tetley — must be able to take

it as much as Tetley. Palliser's death in the collapsing building suggests the passing of the old order, but the play does not end in a patriotic paean to the new as, say, G. P. Gallivan's *Decision at Easter* or David Sears's *Juggernaut* do. Johnston has Palliser remark to Tetley about the future of Ireland that "You don't give a damn about liberty. All you care about is a cause. And causes always let you down."

Obviously, it takes more space to discuss even cursorily Johnston's theme than it does O'Casey's. O'Casey's play makes its points by means of some of the deftest comic characterization in the modern drama. His points are implied by the revelation of human folly and courage, they emerge in human terms, and they are rarely stated overtly. Johnston's play is full of explicit remarks, and his overt argument is rather more engrossing than the human relations between his characters. The love story of Emer and Tetley or that of Roisin and Maginnis hardly exists on the same plane of emotional reality as does O'Casey's love story of Jack and Nora Clitheroe.

The fine part of Dr. MacCarthy is a case in point. He is a sardonic on-looker who runs an insane asylum and has no illusions and few ideals, despite a considerable residue of sympathy. He is not, however, the same kind of character as Fluther or Bessie Burgess. O'Casey's characters are really humanizations of Jonsonian humours. They have a memorable existence like Falstaff or Micawber. MacCarthy is not in that way memorable. He is an intelligence more than an individual. Although he gets the most laughs, we laugh at the wit of what he says rather than the absurdity of what he is. This pervasive intelligence is the big difference between Johnston's play and O'Casey's. Their intentions and manners are quite different, and one cannot condemn Johnston for losing a game he was not playing.

Johnston's play is more narrowly Irish, whereas O'Casey's is more universal; in its own way, however, Johnston's play is nearly as fine as *The Plough and the Stars*. It would be ideal to have a dramatist who combined the best qualities of both writers. At any rate, *The Scythe* does reinforce my main point about Johnston's writing: his work increasingly acknowledges the limitations of the theatre and strives at the same time to lessen those limitations. His experiments are not frivolous. Unlike the writers of the absurd, he knows how far it is possible to strain against theatrical necessity. It is only absurd to label him, as did one critic, as a writer who never fulfilled his promise. He has more than done so. The promise that has not been fulfilled is that of the theatre itself.[7]

8

The Experimental Theatre of the Poets

THERE is a vast mass of criticism that analyzes and appreciates the plays of W. B. Yeats, and I do not propose to add appreciably to it. It would seem an impertinent casualness to sum up in a few pages the dozen plays which Yeats wrote in our period, when so many astute critics have subjected them to minute and searching analysis in so many lengthy articles and books. The bulk of that comment, however, is so uniformly eulogistic that I can perhaps perform a service by playing the devil's advocate.

Much of the critical discussion about the Yeats plays has concerned their themes and their poetic craft, but some of the more lively academic commentators have also defended the plays for their dramatic worth. Vivian Mercier and John T. Unterecker, for instance, have enthusiastically claimed that Yeats is not merely a real dramatist, but a great one. In one persuasive article, Mercier calls *Purgatory* "one of the most shattering experiences that the modern theatre has to offer," and remarks that the Greek's scream in *The Resurrection* is "one of the great *coups de theatre* of the twentieth century." [1] Unterecker sums up this position by remarking that "Yeats was one of the most conscious craftsmen the theatre has ever known, and . . . he may well, in the long run, be one of its most successful artists." [2] Obviously, Yeats's plays do not lack champions. But as Yeats's view of the theatre seems to me an unhealthy one, I propose to put in general terms the case against Yeats as a playwright.

1. It is now about seventy years since Yeats seriously began writing

plays, but his work has never been really successful in the theatre. Most of his plays are rarely performed, none is frequently performed, and even an enthusiast like Professor Mercier will admit that without superb performances the plays are painfully dull.

2. Yeats's later plays, which are currently more admired than his earlier ones, are private statements. As he remarked in his last play, "I wanted an audience of fifty or a hundred." The theatre, however, has traditionally been one of the most public arts. The Greeks watched plays in great public amphitheatres; in the Middle Ages plays were performed in public squares; most of the great modern theatres play in buildings, often expensive and beautiful ones, that are in one way or another publicly supported. Yeats wanted his last plays performed before a small group of kindred spirits in a drawing room; he wanted to dispense with both the public and the physical theatre. Of course, no aesthetic policeman forbids an author to create a work of art under such conditions. But when an author does dispense with two chief necessities of theatre, he can hardly object when it is pointed out that he has created something other than theatre.

3. Most of Yeats's plays are undramatic. Aristotle thought that the chief elements in a play were plot, characterization, theme, language, song, and spectacle; and the first of these he thought by far the most important. In most Yeats plays, the important element is language, although in the Plays for Dancers song and spectacle are also stressed. I heartily favor poetry, music, dance, and imaginative costumes and sets as antidotes to a barren realism, but I think that these elements must emphasize the plot rather than minimize it.

In such writers as Yeats, Hofmannsthal, and Maeterlinck, language tends to be used as exposition, lyricism, or speculation. In exposition, the plot is explained rather than dramatized; in lyricism, the plot is halted; in speculation, the plot is obscured. The language of truly dramatic poets — a Sophocles, Shakespeare, or Racine — almost at every moment clearly embodies a clash of forces. To take but two undramatic examples from Yeats, note the high proportion of exposition in *Purgatory* and *At the Hawk's Well*.

The spectacle in a Yeats play usually minimizes whatever elements of drama reside in the plot. The reason is largely that Yeats so formalizes the spectacle that he makes it unspectacular. His use of the Gordon Craig screens had the effect of reducing what the audience had to look at. Indeed, the screens had the same effect as his later drawing-room plays of abolishing the set. The folding and unfolding of the cloth in the later plays is spectacle so formalized that it is undramatic. When dance is used, it is often intended to supply the action that the poet has not himself created. The crucial dramatic action of *At the Hawk's Well* must be conveyed by the dance of the Guardian of the Well. The dance can be effective if staged by a choreographer who is himself an artist, but if the dance is not done well the play is ruined. Yeats has not done his job as a dramatist here; rather he has left the crucial clash of the play to his choreographer. In Act III of O'Casey's *Red Roses for Me*, song and dance and poetry are also the chief means of furthering the action, but O'Casey has specifically spelled out in his stage directions what he wants. He does not allow the effect of the play to escape from his own hands. In *At the Hawk's Well*, Yeats has little control over the play. It is as if Shakespeare had written *Julius Caesar* as he did until he came to Antony's funeral oration, and had then inserted a stage direction which read "Here I want Antony to sway the crowd to his view; so the actor should ad lib in order to gain the greatest dramatic spontaneity."

Yeats's treatment of the major elements in a play — plot and characterization — tends also to be undramatic. Static exposition makes up an inordinate part of his plays, and the actual development of the plot is often so truncated that dramatic tension is nonexistent. The characterization is usually so formal that it does not exist in the usual sense. There are no great roles in Yeats; indeed, there are almost no roles at all. An actor playing Forgael or Cuchulain has nothing to characterize. He does not have to be an actor at all — only an elocutionist.

4. Yeats was never interested in theatre and knew little about it. I am not saying that he took no interest in his own lyrical dialogues, but that he took no interest in what have ordinarily been called plays. Granted, he could hardly have been connected with a theatre for forty years without learning something, and he did learn something in spite of himself. Some of his advice to playwrights was sound and penetrating. But generally he learned only what he wanted to learn; he was less interested in learning the necessities of the drama than in staying true to his own brand of experiment.

This point seems borne out by testimony from people who worked with him at the Abbey. Much of this testimony seems impelled by the jealousy of the moderately talented for the genius, but there would have been less catty criticism had Yeats in the theatre not wrapped around him the cloak of his poetic pose. A haughty aloofness is hardly the healthiest attitude for a cooperative venture, and the players resented it. At hardly any time did everyone in the Abbey pull together; often many were disaffected and irritated at being treated as second-class citizens of the theatre. When Yeats did try to take a practical hand in the staging of a play, the players were usually baffled, amused, or covertly contemptuous. The results themselves were frequently droll and have occasioned a host of stories. There is, for instance, the story of Yeats working and working with the limelight man to get the proper lighting effect on the stage. After many experiments, he called up to the balcony, "That's it! That's just what I want!" And the limelight man replied, "But Mr. Yeats, the limelight box is on fire."

A less apocryphal story is related by Joseph Holloway after attending a rehearsal of *On Baile's Strand* conducted by Yeats:

. . . I say without fear of contradiction that a more irritating play producer never directed a rehearsal. He's ever flitting about and interrupting the players in the middle of their speeches, showing them by illustration how he wishes it done, droningly reading the passage and that in monotonous preachy sing-song, or climbing up a ladder onto the stage and pacing the boards as he would have the players do. . . . Anon he would rush on and erase or add a line or two to the text, but ever and always he was on the fidgets. . . . Frank Fay I thought would explode with suppressed rage at his frequent interruptions during the final speeches he had to utter.[3]

Holloway also watched the rehearsal of a production of *Deirdre* featuring Mrs. Patrick Campbell; he remarked, "Yeats kept busily walking up and down in front of the stage, and his gesticulation occasionally sent Mrs. Campbell off in a laugh until she finally had to tell him to sit down."[4] On May 27, 1915, Holloway had a conversation with A. Patrick Wilson, who had just resigned as the theatre's manager and producer:

Wilson spoke of Yeats in rehearsal speaking to one of the supers in *The Green Helmet* and telling him he did not come on right — he should walk on as if he were taking part in some great ritual, as if inspired by some great religious emotion, etc. The super couldn't understand the poet, and no wonder. So Yeats turned to Wilson with, "Let you explain." Wilson merely said, "Walk on and pause a moment; then proceed as if you were attending your grandfather's funeral." The super understood, and Yeats had got the effect he in vain had sought to explain.

Again in *Shanwalla*, Yeats started speaking to Hutchinson thus: "Victor Hugo in one of his books writes of Napoleon I going into Russia in an ecstasy of hope and returning utterly crushed and defeated. I want you to look like Napoleon did then, as you say these words." Hutchinson looked at Yeats, tried to do something, but didn't please the mighty man of words, and he appealed to Wilson to explain. Wilson said to Hutchinson, "Arise suddenly as if to go, and then sit down again and look at the footlights till the end of the scene." He did so, and Yeats's Napoleonic look was realised.

Again Yeats addressed Miss Drago, who is a great actress, but not burdened with intelligence to an excessive degree, and started by saying, "Balzac in one of his books says so and so, and so and so, and so on! Now I want you to realise that on the stage just here!" She kept saying, "Yes, sir! Yes, sir!" — not understanding one word he was saying. . . .[5]

There is a degree of malice in Wilson's account, but Yeats's pose did foster malice among workers at the Abbey. Although many of them were fine artists in their own right, Yeats seemed to regard them as employees rather than as colleagues. He was never a leader like Molière or Stanislavsky, and although great credit must be given him for holding the theatre together, he was also its greatest disruptive influence.

⚜

After years of relative obscurity, Austin Clarke is at last being recognized as a major Irish writer. He is primarily a poet, but like Yeats he worked in other forms and is, in the best sense of the term, a man of letters. He was born in Dublin in 1896 and, like Joyce, attended Belvedere College. Later he went to University College, Dublin, where Douglas Hyde was one of his teachers. In 1917 he was appointed lecturer in English there, succeeding Thomas MacDonagh, but in 1921 his appointment was not renewed when it was discovered that he had been married in a registry office. He then went to England and spent several years as a book reviewer and editor. His first volume of poetry, *The Vengeance of Fionn*, was excellently received, but his subsequent work was in a lyrical, Celtic twilight vein at a time when the major movement in poetry was most influenced by Eliot and Pound. In the 1930's he returned to Ireland and began broadcasting for Radio Éireann. In 1940, with Robert Farren, the poet and playwright and subsequently Abbey Theatre director, he formed the Dublin Verse-Speaking Society which produced verse plays for radio. From this group he formed the Lyric Theatre Company, which once or twice a year rented the Abbey for a week of plays. The work of the group deserves to be studied, for it kept alive the tradition of verse drama in those post-Yeatsian days when the Abbey was almost wholly given over to prose realism. In addition to Clarke's own work, the company resurrected some Fitzmaurice and did pieces by Bottomly, Binyon, T. Sturge Moore, and MacLeish as well as first productions of Yeats's *The Herne's Egg* and *The Death of Cuchulain* and of Donagh MacDonagh's *Happy as Larry*.

I should like to suggest that the interested reader supplement my discussion of Clarke's plays with a couple of more appreciative essays listed in the bibliography. Many of Clarke's plays still seem to me, after much brooding about them, dull and untheatrical; however, I have seen none staged and do not wholly trust my judgment. Several of his most admired religious plays — such as *The Flame, Sister Eucharia,* and *The Moment Next to Nothing* — seem to me only tedious, repetitive, and eminently undramatic. A case in point is his first play, *The Son of Learning,* or, as it was earlier called, *The Hunger Demon.* It is based on a medieval Irish tale, *The Vision of Mac Conglinne,* which is about a hunger demon that enters the body of a king and makes him fantastically ravenous before it is finally expelled by the wandering scholar Mac Conglinne. Clarke explains that the keynote of the play is exuberance and that it "is meant to be acted in high spirits." I should think it would need to be, for the first act is mainly exposition which would seem strenuously to resist the liveliest efforts of most producers and actors. There are moments of theatre in Act III, when the scholar exorcises the demon, but the play's general dullness is pervasive — a point even more noticeable when the play is compared with Padraic Fallon's brilliant radio version of the same legend.

Black Fast, first presented by the Abbey in January, 1942, was also intended to be broad and is described as a poetic farce. The description, I think, stretches the usual meaning of the term farce. Set in the seventh century, the play dramatizes the controversy over the exact date of Easter by making it a domestic argument between Conal More of Ulster and his wife Blanaid Fairnape. The argument centers on whether they should be observing fast or feast days; it is droller in its conception than its execution.

More amusing is *The Kiss,* a short one-act performed first at the Peacock by the Dublin Verse-Speaking Society in May, 1942. An Irish adaptation of a piece by Theodore de Banville, its couplets are neatly adroit and it is quite charming.

As the Crow Flies is a short radio play in six scenes, first broadcast over Radio Éireann on February 6, 1942, by the Dublin Verse-Speaking Society. Suggested by a Middle Irish tale in Hyde's *Saints and Sinners*, it is an extremely effective playlet which might work well on the stage, although it would certainly have to be done in a stylized and imaginative manner. Some scenes take place in a boat on the Shannon and some in a high cave where the priest and two monks have taken refuge from the storm. The other scenes — between the Eagle of Knock, the Crow of Achill, the Stag of Leiterlone, the Blackbird of Derrycairn, and the Salmon of Assaroe — would be even more difficult, but they could be done. This folk parable, which gives us a frightening glance into man's prehistory, seems to me Clarke's best work up to this time.

The Plot is Ready was first done at the Peacock by the Dublin Verse-Speaking Society in October, 1943. The action takes place in November of the year 534 when Muriadach Mac Erca, the high king of Ireland, is dying. Great pressure is brought upon him to repent of his sins, particularly his having taken a mistress and put his wife away; but he dies unrepentant and his mistress is swept up in a blaze of light to join his spirit and those of the fallen angels. Clarke pays a good deal of attention in the script to the staging of the play, but it is still not very dramatic. The mistress's love is conveyed in a long soliloquy, the king's conscience-stricken dream is not particularly imaginative or differentiated from the real scenes, and his death, which happens offstage, is described by exposition.

The Viscount of Blarney is based on a folk tale and was first performed by the Lyric Theatre Company at the Abbey in December, 1944. Its heroine is a charmingly drawn young girl, and the play recounts her adventures with a Pooka, Jack O'Lantern, and the devil costumed as an eighteenth-century gallant. Its visual effects are theatrical, its language the raciest and most colloquial to be found in any of Clarke's plays.

The Second Kiss is a light one-act comedy, first performed by the Lyric Theatre Company in June, 1946, at the Abbey. Its language is more dramatically feasible than is usual for Clarke: playful, supple, spontaneous, even mildly witty.

One of Clarke's most theatrical plays, *The Plot Succeeds*, was first put on at the Abbey by the Lyric Theatre Company in February, 1950. Based on the legend of Mannanaun Mac Lir, the sea god who was able to transform himself and others into various shapes, it tells how Mongan, the king of Ulster, after losing his wife in a chess game with the king of Leinster, takes on the form of various other characters in order to get his wife back. The device causes plenty of farcical mistaken identities, and should be good fun for the audience as well as for actors who must play both their own roles and the disguised Mongan. Clarke calls the play a poetic pantomime, and, although it is more theatrical than much of his work, it is pretty far from *A Comedy of Errors.*

One untheatrical element is the rhyme scheme, which was partly suggested by Gaelic prosody. One of the rhyming words in each couplet is dissyllabic and only the first syllable is rhymed. The pattern is carried out with skill, but when the verse is spoken it conveys little sense of rhyme at all. For instance:

> Then let us swear the summer is too rash
> For us and trinkets fashioned on the ash-tree
> May dangle in shame since matter is unsteady.
> Forget that thistles grow so light of head —
> Their seed is carried down, that every fly
> Is furious and all we give the lie to
> Crackles and bursts the pod. Keep house like women
> Who fear a bite or sting may pink their limbs.
> Hide, fancy, lest the honeysuckle catch you:
> This world's extravagance must meet its match!

To me, this invisible technique suggests that, despite his occasional successes as a dramatic poet, Clarke has always been more interested in the poetry than in the drama.

⚜

Donagh MacDonagh, the son of the executed patriot Thomas Mac-Donagh, was born on November 22, 1912. Like Clarke, he was educated first at Belvedere College and then at University College. He has a B.A. and an M.A., and he became a Barrister at Law in 1935 and a Justice of the District Court in 1945. He is a member of the Irish Academy of Letters; his poems were collected in the volume *The Hungry Grass.* Two of his plays, *Happy as Larry* and *Step-in-the-Hollow,* have been published in Penguins, and the first has been twice produced in New York. His other plays include *God's Gentry,* an Irish adaptation of Anouilh's *Romeo et Jeannette* called *Fading Mansion,* and *Lady Spider.* With A. J. Potter, he has written a ballet called *Careless Love* and an opera called *Patrick.*

Happy as Larry is one of the better-known verse plays of recent years, and MacDonagh has described it like this:

The story goes back to 1941, when poetic drama was a dirty word. I thought that it might be possible, by using the technique of the Marx Brothers and the circus, to lure the unsuspecting public into the theatre and then land dollops of verse in their laps. At this stage Liam Redmond drew my attention . . . to a story in Goldsmith's *Citizen of the World* . . . it is the basic plot of a hundred stories, including *The Widow of Ephesus* and *A Phoenix Too Frequent*. I decided to write the thing in the Dublin *patois*, a very suitable vehicle for wit and satire. I can't remember why I planned to have a chorus, except that it seemed to be a standard device in verse plays. After a time it began to be a bore, so I brought it right into the play which was a good thing.[6]

To this statement should be added E. Martin Browne's remark that "The style and rhythms of *Larry* are derived from the popular ballads of which the author is a collector, and which are sung in the pub or in the street."

The play is one of the more successful modern attempts to weld together poetry and drama. Its language is clear enough for the theatre and not burdened with an abundance of conceits, images, and metaphors which obstruct the forward impulse of a sentence. Also, in attaining this constant clarity, MacDonagh does not sacrifice, as T. S. Eliot often does, the effects of verse. He constantly varies the form of his lines, their length, meter, and rhyme scheme, but he never changes the pattern so thoroughly that it becomes vague. Much of his clarity is determined by the ballad form. The short line lengths demand a simplicity of diction, and the simple ballad meters are already so implanted in people's minds that when MacDonagh uses them the memory is jogged into an instant recognition.

Despite these theatrical qualities, the verse does not seem successful throughout. MacDonagh often intends wit and satire, and so his verse requires a tightness of form which it does not always have. Much of the play is probably of necessity doggerel, but the doggerel is often either too irregular and rough or too flat and uninspired. Either, for instance:

> Why break your heart with all this hurrying?
> Is there another waiting with a ring?

Or:

> Fair enough; if you won't talk
> I'd better continue with my walk.

MacDonagh also allows himself a similar slackness with his rhyme. Sometimes in the same passage he will use exact rhyme in an exact pattern and then suddenly shift into irregularity for no apparent reason other than inability to hold to his form. In the same passage, he will rhyme exactly, then give an off-rhyme or an assonance, and then drop rhyming entirely.

Having been so nigglingly critical, I should point out that the play has many successful passages. Perhaps one quotation may suggest their general quality:

> We are the first explorers, the pioneers that came
> Out of the virgin country. Our flag's a question mark,
> Quandary is our name; our sun and moon are dark,
> Our faces featureless, our country unnamed.
> All that you're doing now is done this fifty years,
> The murderer and victim picked clean in the same earth,
> The laughter and the tears, the misery and mirth
> Are nothing but a story to titillate our ears.
> Every action is predestined, you do what you must
> Like God, we stand in loneliness anatomizing dust.

A better play is *God's Gentry*. It was first staged by the Belfast Arts Theatre in August, 1951, and then shortly after was produced at the Gate in Dublin for a long run. It is a ballad opera about tinkers, and its fanciful story is set in County Mayo. It tells how a band of "laughing, cheering, dancing, drinking" tinkers robs the shop of John Melody, "a cantankerous gombeenman," and how a young tinker runs off with Melody's daughter. When the tinkers are caught, they resurrect the old god Balor of the Evil Eye and invoke his protection. He then turns the world topsy-turvy so that the tinkers have all the money, all the porter, and all the poteen they want. They live like lords for a year, and at the end of the year the former gentry are leading the free and easy tinker life and even stealing from the tinkers. Fortunately, when Balor's power gives out, all is restored to its normal order.

It is impossible to convey in words the theatrical potential of this script — the staged effect of its dancing, singing, spectacle, and high spirits. The verse, both in the recitative and the songs, is tight, fluent, and funny, easy for the actor to speak and the audience to understand. All in all, it seems a much more colorful and theatrical show than *Happy as Larry*.

Lady Spider is a dramatization of the Deirdre story which had been previously dramatized by AE, Yeats, and Synge. MacDonagh's poetry is less beautiful than that of his predecessors, but probably more feasible for the stage. In form, it is generally free verse with varying line lengths and an occasional use of rhyme at dignified or formal moments. Dignity, however, is a quality more evident in the versions of AE and Yeats; simplicity and conversational ease are the hallmarks of MacDonagh's version. His rhythm is quite loose, and his language at times indistinguishable from good prose. Its poetic quality resides in the frequent images and metaphors occurring mainly in the longer speeches. These embellishments appear more frequently and are more fanciful than what we would expect in prose; yet they are not obscure and not so profuse as to clog the forward impetus of the action. Generally, the language has more of the urgency and abruptness of dramatic dialogue than almost anything in *Happy as Larry* or *God's Gentry*.

Another notable quality, lacking in many verse dramas, is the realistic psychology given to the characters. In AE and Yeats, if not quite in Synge, the characters have about as much individual humanity as figures on a medieval tapestry. Many poetic dramas are unbelievable not because of the poetry but because of an artificial, lifeless, coldly formal characterization. Here, however, Naoise is far from the stock lyric lover. He is no Yeatsian Forgael, but a virile, vigorous, ambitious Hotspur who has no intention of marrying Deirdre at all, who when married is casually unfaithful, and who is not nearly so perceptive as either Deirdre or his older brother Arden. If some dignity and grandeur are lost by this realistic dramatization, the well-built plot and the intriguing characterization serve to make it the most effective version for the modern stage.

Step-in-the-Hollow was first presented by the Gate at the Gaiety Theatre, Dublin, on March 11, 1957. The main character, Justice Redmond O'Hanlon, is a lusty old lecher who has been caught in the bedroom of a none-too-bright girl named Teazie O'Sullivan and who only barely (no pun) manages to escape. His various derelictions of duty are about to be brought home to him when a government inspector arrives to investigate his court. Teazie's mother insists on bringing her daughter's case to court, and the justice is unable to avoid hearing it. The court scene is complicated in its twists of plot; indeed the whole plot is a quite adequate series of intrigues and mistaken identities. It bustles along, it is fast-paced, it is lively.

The play might have been funnier, however, had it been written in fluent prose. MacDonagh uses, with some success, contemporary diction, clichés, and slang. He does not handle language with a debilitating poetic reverence, and he is a lot closer to W. S. Gilbert than to Stephen Phillips. Nevertheless, despite some ease and even raciness, the dialogue is often not quite right. For instance:

> JULIA: Control meself. That's all I've heard all day,
> But I'm here now and I'm going to have my say,
> And if anyone tries to stop me I'll raise such a stink

That it isn't only Jembo who'll be out of a job as quick as a
wink.

This is not a bad passage, but it takes longer to convey its message than
would good prose, and it really has none of the compensating virtues of
good poetry. The real virtue of the play is not that it is in poetry, but
that it is not in other respects a bad job.

⊕

At least a mention must be made of Conor Farrington, a young actor-
playwright born on June 17, 1928, in Dublin. After graduating from
Trinity College, he worked for a year in a bookstore and then joined an
English touring company, playing for a year and a half in such diverse
places as Malta and India. The experience taught him much about the
practical stage and allowed him to play about forty Shakespearean roles
in addition to parts in other staples of the company such as *Charley's
Aunt.*

By Christmas of 1954, Farrington was back in Dublin. He auditioned
for the repertory company of Radio Éireann and has worked with this
group ever since, save for a year he spent on a scholarship at the Yale
Drama School — an experience he describes as "interesting in a perverse
sort of way." His first staged play was *Glenmore*, which was put on in
the Dagg Hall at the Academy of Music in 1955. His *Conquest of Mexico* was written with Mac Liammóir in mind, but remains unperformed.
His *The Last P.M. or Stella and the Big Bang* was performed at the 1964
Theatre Festival by the Gate. It was also written for Mac Liammóir who
enthusiastically called it "the best Irish play in forty years." Farrington
more justly considers it a "damn good play of the kind I don't write
well."

The production of this satiric prose play convinced Farrington that
the proper medium of the actor is verse.[7] He believes, correctly I think,
that much realistic dialogue is mere "one-dimensional banality," and that
only by verse can the drama reach again the emotional peaks that we
now experience in opera, but rarely in the drama. The verse he favors is
not the elusive, faintly stressed kind of Eliot's late plays, but a verse
whose rhythm is strong enough to arouse emotion. He has enough acting
experience to realize that the stage line must be not only evocative, but
also immediately apparent. For most poets, these qualities are contradictory. At any rate, Farrington thinks that he has really only now found

his forte, and that most of his work up to this point has been faulty and uncertain. That would certainly seem true of *Glenmore* and *The Conquest of Mexico* whose mouthfilling rhetoric seems an almost insuperable hurdle to both actors and audience.

The Last P.M., however, is a moderately successful attempt at a crisp and witty satire on a modern theme. The real problem of the play is that its individual lines lack wit. The story is a fable of power politics, a satiric condemnation of man as destructive and nihilistic; the main character is Stella, a girl from outer space who spends most of her time trying to fulfill our moral dictums by being unhappy, by suffering, and by hoping to set off a nuclear explosion. Indeed, that is how the play ends. The fable has some trenchant things to say, and although the speeches keep listing toward a lengthy lyricism, they do not quite overpower the story.

Much of what Farrington has to say about contemporary dramatic dialogue strikes me as eminently sound and healthy; his conclusions about lyrical dialogue are persuasive; his plans for a series of poetic historical plays are interesting. Still, he has a heavy load of theory to carry, and so far his plays have sunk beneath the burden.

⍟

Finally a word must be said for at least the two — and I use the word deliberately — greatest plays of Padraic Fallon. Neither *Diarmuid and Grainne* nor *The Vision of Mac Conglinne* could be staged, and, in fact, neither was meant to be. Both are plays for radio, originally produced by Micheál Ó h Aodha for Radio Éireann. The quality of imagination in both is so superb that I approach them with considerably greater feelings of inadequacy than usual. There is just too much in these sprawling, funny, beautiful plays for a page or two of summary to do justice to.

Unlike most modern versions of myth and legend, they preserve the wonder and magic at the same time that they infuse the story with meaning. Most modernizations fall into one of two categories: they either become dramatic by reducing the legendary characters to realistic human stature, as in the Synge and MacDonagh versions of the Deirdre story, or they preserve something of the heroic stature but become formalized, lifeless, and undramatic, as in some of Yeats's plays. On the one hand, we have the way of Mark Twain and T. H. White; on the other, the way of Tennyson and Charles Williams. Perhaps halfway between we get such rare works as those of Tolkien the novelist or of Fallon.

159

Fallon's rhetorical method is an improbable but fluent wedding of formality and simplicity. To take one typical passage:

NARRATOR: I bring you to Allen in the dawn, the great earth worked palace of Finn, Finn the leader of the Fianna, the soldiery of Ireland who are independent of High King, Kings, or sub-Kings. Only the black bird is awake over the vague blur of the country. In the big hall the serfs are drugged in the ashes alongside Finn's mighty hunting dogs. Only the black bird and the thrush and now the lark are awake. And Finn, yes Finn himself. The great man strides softly through the sleepers. He climbs the earthworks. He leaps floating like a bird, to the ground forty feet below. He walks to a stone bound well and drinks. He squats on his heels like a great bird and stares wide lidded into the half dark that is Ireland. He is an eagle, he is darkness, he is an aging soldier of fortune, his hair is spindrift for whiteness, he is a winter-morning.

And suddenly the white day is on the land; and as though at the summons of a great gong the cashel of Allen is awake. Cows low, bulls bellow, pigs squeal, and the cocks, the cocks make every breath a trumpet, blue smoke rising from the cooking pits, and floating down from the great earth wall come two long striding men with hunting dogs. One is Ossian the son of Finn, the other doesn't matter —

VOICE: Do I not matter? My name is Diorruing, the son of Dobar O Baoisene.

NARRATOR: Hush, nonentity. . . .

Much of the formality comes from heavy parallel structure, but what keeps the formality from stiffness is that the single units of parallelism are simple and usually quite short. Also, the diction is both precise and, in every sense of the word, easy. The majority of words in the above passage are of one or two syllables; the few longer words are mostly common ones like "suddenly" and "independent." The quality of the description also wars against any static formality. This is no purple passage that exists for itself; it describes — and rather beautifully — but it also moves right along rather than palely loitering. Finally, there is some fluent variation in the length of sentences and clauses. Though it may sound paradoxical, this is a controlled style which is at the same time very free.

The style flows often and easily into verse with no disconcerting shifting of gears; the reason is probably that the main characteristics of the prose are also those of the verse. The verse uses rhyme and off-rhyme quite satisfyingly, though. For instance, here is Grainne choosing between Diarmuid and a personified force of nature called the Green Planet:

I stand between two
One burns low and one is a tall green candle
My right hand does not know.
This new feeling my left hand fondles.
The low-wicket boy on my right,
I leave in his flower pot. I choose the wicket
Eye, I pick the thick bright thighs
Of the man from the North whose fist is on my neck.
He is salt and savour. He rolls from the Sea;
My sailor man. Our days will be short and full;
He will beat me but he will know me.
And I will shine from his window sill.

The rhetorical method of the play seems to parallel the entire dramatic method, for the play weaves back and forth between scenes of stylized reality and scenes of fantastic myth-making like this:

The hurt and furious Diarmuid runs madly over the snow fields of the North. He throws great bergs around. He thaws icecaps, under him the mighty glacier runs into calm blue water. And the blood streams warm from the wound in his thigh. About him is the cry of birds and great migrations. Light wakens the white bear and he lumbers from his lair with red eyes. And trailing all this tumult walks the weeping Grainne. She has no difficulty with the path for her lord has thawed the way. She walks in great hues of flowers and blossoms. Sometimes she spreads out into mighty meadows and the reindeer seek her and the furred Eskimo, sometimes flowerhead, the sweeter for being just a pinpoint of colour in a waste of snow. And always, though she hurries, hurries, she is just behind him, till at last she comes upon him with his anger, an anger that never sets, so that there is no night in that part of the earth.

It is difficult to suggest the quality of such creatively legendary scenes as the battle with the Green Planet or the great concluding battle with the boar of Ben Bulben or the curious and fascinating scenes in the sacred wood of Dubhros with the giant of the Quickentree. Really Fallon is doing much more with the legend than anyone else who has ever handled it. It is as if, by making Diarmuid and Grainne larger than nature — magical — by even making them blend into the elements of nature, he intends a parable illustrating fully and finally certain aspects of man's nature. Into his mixture he has poured a strange blend, perhaps consisting of bits of Jung and Freud and anthropology as well as legend. Micheál Ó h Aodha described the play well when he remarked, "it is not set in pre-Christian Ireland nor in an Irish Other-world of pagan belief, but in a mythopoeic universe where Orpheus, Jung, Hercules, Sir James Frazer, Adonis, Robert Graves, Demeter, Freud, and Dionysus can wander at will." [8]

Ó h Aodha has made also a good summation of Fallon's later play, *The Vision of Mac Conglinne*:

It is a blend of myth and the comic spirit, of wild fancy and Rabelaisian humour. It has the satirical quality of a "Land of Cockaigne" and, on another plane, a symbolic meaning, cloaked under mountains of food, which derives from the hidden harmonies of the seasons. Austin Clarke in his *Son of Learning* was content to take the story much as he found it and to embroider it with assonantal patterns. Fallon aims much higher — at cosmic significance.[9]

"Cosmic" may be the wrong word, although the characters, as in the previous play, take on such a legendary size, and the actions are of such a free-wheeling, expansively imaginative nature, that one fumbles among such huge adjectives as "immense, titanic, gargantuan" to describe it. I think, however, that basically the play is a paradoxical paean to and a mournful analysis of the lamentable effects of woman on man. The action seems to show that woman fills man with a sense of glory, romance, security, passion, and is also the source of man's greatest agony and humiliation. The woman in the play is Ligach, a combination of witch, wife, mistress, mother, white goddess, and black goddess. For half the year she is the delight and torment of Fergal, King of Ailech, in the north, and for half the year the joy and agony of Cahal, King of Cashel, in the south. The play tells of her return to Cahal, who is quite at peace without her. Her meaning for man is portrayed by symbolic actions which also work as parts of a superbly imaginative story. For instance, Mac Conglinne, the poet whom she makes use of, is beaten, tortured, insulted, humiliated, and tormented by serving her; finally, in his exorcism of Cahal, he is reduced to a gutted old age. The chief symbolic action is the hunger demon which possesses at various times Mac Conglinne, the Abbot, and Cahal; the greatest comedy is derived from the grotesque, exaggerated descriptions of the torment of hunger. For instance, the Storyteller opens Part Two with this description:

I open this scene with a madness of feasting. Cahal is delighted with his appetite at first. He displays it to ten chieftains on his way home to Cashel. They are not as pleased as he is, for he eats them out of house and home. He eats them to the scullery, he eats them to the piggery, he lays bare the fowl run and then climbs to the pigeon-cote. He walks into the stubble-field and gnaws the sheaf in the pointed stock. He is forever nibbling. He picks the leaves from the trees as his chariot passes beneath them, he catches at the tops of the grasses. His face is green with grass-juice, greasy from fat bacon, gray with dust, and he is anything but royal as the gates of his city open to him and he climbs up the great rock of Cashel.

The temptation is almost irresistible to quote at length — especially from the superb scene, overflowing with puns, in which Mac Conglinne is whipped. Indeed, one can open the script at practically any place and find speeches of sheer delight. I have just tried the experiment and have hit upon this minor speech in which a sergeant is reading out a corporal: "You son of a stunned pimp, you brothel of a boy, you stuffed and stifled grandson of a Munster woolmerchant, how did you get your stripes? Have you been to school to any master except the paymaster?" The wit and humor in the play are as fantastic as anything in *Diarmuid and Grainne*, although the earlier play is, by the necessity of its story, the more moving; it has also the more beautiful lyrics. However, this comic play is so much more inventive in incident, stirring in language, and meaningful in theme, that one is finally convinced: despite all of the contrary evidence of sapless poetic drama, from Tennyson to MacLeish, poetry really can bring fullness and glory to the modern drama.

The Genius of George Fitzmaurice

W HEN George Fitzmaurice died in 1963, he was given only a couple of short paragraphs in the *Irish Times*, which remembered him mainly as the author of *The Country Dressmaker* and a few one-acts performed early in the century by the Abbey Theatre. Despite this scant notice, a few perceptive poets, such as Padraic Colum and Seamus O'Sullivan and Austin Clarke, had always regarded Fitzmaurice as a master dramatist. That regard was based upon the volume *Five Plays* which appeared in 1913 and upon the handful of plays which O'Sullivan brought out over the years in the *Dublin Magazine*. These magazine publications and about a half a dozen amateur productions were the only attention that Fitzmaurice's work received in the last forty years of his life. He was ignored as few writers of the first rank have ever been, but he was a rare and original genius.

❦

Fitzmaurice was born on January 28, 1877, in Bedford House near Listowel,[1] that amazing little town in County Kerry which later gave to Irish literature Maurice Walsh, Bryan MacMahon, and John B. Keane. The Fitzmaurices were an old family going back at least to the fourteenth century in Ireland, and the playwright was born only a few miles from Fitzmaurice Castle. His father was a Church of Ireland minister who married a Catholic girl, Winifred O'Connor, in 1861, when he was thirty-nine and she about nineteen. A mixed marriage was unusual then, but twelve children came from the marriage. George was the tenth child and the third son; when he died he was the last direct surviving member of the family, for none of his seven sisters and four brothers had married.

After his schooling, Fitzmaurice worked briefly in a bank in Cork, but, disliking the job and in poor health, he quit to take a temporary clerkship, on November 9, 1901, with the Congested Districts Board in Dublin. His starting salary was 25 shillings a week — not a princely wage, but comparing quite favorably with that of an ordinary laborer.

Apparently he had a bit of spare money, for from his early days in Dublin he was an ardent devotee of the music halls, and there is some indication that he was equally interested in the legitimate stage. Most certainly these were fertile writing years for Fitzmaurice. *The Country Dressmaker*, his only popular success, was produced at the Abbey on October 3, 1907. On March 10, 1908, the Abbey did his one-act *The Pie-Dish*, and on April 24, 1913, his one-act *The Magic Glasses*. Also in 1913, his *Five Plays* was published, containing the plays just mentioned and also *The Moonlighter* and *The Dandy Dolls*. It was a collection of masterpieces.

At the same time, his job was suffering. It is impossible now to know whether he was genuinely ill or merely bored and malingering, but in 1908 he lost 102 days from sickness, and in January, 1909, he took a formal sick leave. He lost his job in April when he did not return from leave. At the end of December in 1913, he was reinstated, but soon after joined the British army and served in France as a private. After the war, he returned to Dublin to work with the Land Commission, and in 1919 he wrote *'Twixt the Giltinans and the Carmodys*. This was his last play staged by the Abbey; it was produced on March 8, 1923, about a month before the first production of O'Casey.

He continued to miss work. In 1920, he was absent 190 days, and in 1921 he was absent 79. Probably because he had missed so much work he was not promoted until 1925. In 1932, he transferred to the Department of Agriculture, having complained that he could no longer handle the large record books in the Land Commission. In 1935, at the late age of fifty-eight, he at last reached his maximum salary.

He was continuing to write, but exactly what and when is a matter of conjecture. After his last Abbey production of 1923, he went for more than two decades without a single production. He was, save for the occasional appearance of a play in the *Dublin Magazine*, forgotten. In the last two decades of his life, however, he got a few semi-professional and amateur performances. Austin Clarke's Lyric Theatre produced *The Dandy Dolls* and *The Magic Glasses* in 1945. The Earlsfort Players produced *The Moonlighter* and *The Magic Glasses* in 1948; *The Magic Glasses* was also performed in 1949 by the Green Circle Theatre Club. In 1952, *One Evening Gleam* was done by the Studio Theatre Club, and St. Mary's School put on *There Are Tragedies and Tragedies*.

His scant success may have heightened a tendency to shyness and general oddness that seemed to run in his family. He was, for instance, over-scrupulously tidy; he had a strong fear of crowds; he avoided riding in a bus or car. He had very few friends and practically no close ones. Even writer acquaintances, like O'Sullivan and Clarke, would sometimes have difficulty finding him; he would just seem to drop out of sight for long periods. His scant success may also be reflected in a theme that runs through many of his later plays — stoic acceptance of less than the ideal and putting up with second best.

There are indications that, toward the last, he had some low moments about his plays. For instance, Lord Longford once wrote him for permission to stage *The Enchanted Land* at the Gate. Fitzmaurice drafted a reply on a torn-off inside cover of the *Dublin Magazine* allowing the performance, but the reply was found among his papers at his death, still unsent. Also in his papers was found this laconic and therefore all the more poignant note: "Author is prepared to sell outright all rights in 14 plays dealing intimately with life in the Irish countryside. Most have already been either produced or published. Suitable to which to build musical, television, etc. Pass to any-one interested." He died May 12, 1963, in his room at 3 Harcourt Street, an old man who had nourished his talent for fifty years with almost no encouragement. There are few sadder stories of neglect in Irish letters.

※

The Country Dressmaker was Fitzmaurice's first produced play, though probably not the first he wrote. Holloway records that he had had a play rejected by the Abbey before the acceptance of the *Dressmaker*. At any rate, Yeats was enthusiastic about the *Dressmaker* and thought it inflammatory enough to cause a repetition of the rows that had greeted *The Playboy* earlier in the year.

It is a story of matchmaking in Kerry, and of how two factions scheme to win Pats Connor, a returned American. When the scheming gives way in Act III to an outright fight, it would seem that this portrait of Irish country people is scarcely more flattering than was Synge's. Yet the play was unpredictably successful and remains the fifth most revived in the Abbey repertoire. The crafty matchmaker from the mountains, Luke Quilter, is a delightful part on both the stage and the page, while the scheming farmer Michael Clohesy is larger than but very true to life. In Clohesy, Fitzmaurice drew a character that hit people with a shock of recognition at its accuracy and yet had some of the complexity of life rather than the mere simplicity of the stage. The central character of Julia Shea, the dressmaker who has been faithful to Pats for ten years, is an adequate part that screams to be made a bit fuller. Julia is like Lydia Languish: she has idealized love out of all resemblance to actuality by reading romantic novelettes. She refuses Edmund Normyle because of her love for Pats; then she refuses Pats when she learns that he has not always been romantically faithful, but was once married in the States; finally she is persuaded to accept him and with him, reality, saying sadly, "I'm willing to make the best of it." Her remark might stand as the major theme of most of Fitzmaurice's plays — and perhaps of his life.

The play has minor flaws, though they would probably hurt it little on the stage. The subplot of the Clohesys trying to win Pats away is more interesting than the main plot, and Julia is not good enough to hold the center of the stage against either the exuberant Clohesys or the inimitable Quilter. There are also a couple of characters who have practically nothing to do, but it is a ripely funny play, with fine characters, racy speech, and a complex but never absurd plot. It is not quite up to the standard of *The Playboy*, but easily on a par with the best realistic comedies of Lennox Robinson and George Shiels.

Fitzmaurice's next long play was *The Moonlighter*, which he worked on in 1909 after he returned to Kerry. It was optioned by the Abbey, but never produced there. Indeed, it remained unproduced for thirty-eight years. It is a four-act play about the Land Struggles. Peter Guerin, an old Fenian farmer, has sent his other sons to America because they took part in nationalist activities; his youngest son Eugene is now a hot-headed rebel who joins the Moonlighters. The first three acts build to a pitch of excitement, with the Moonlighters going off to raid the Big House and Eugene being left behind. Angered and abashed, he seeks to prove himself by seizing up a gun and dashing out to kill his uncle, Big William Cantillon, a grabber. Act IV is somewhat disconcerting: twelve months have passed, Big William has been killed, Eugene has disappeared, the Moonlighters have been betrayed in their raid, and Eugene's friend Tom Driscoll has been accused of Big William's murder. On the eve of Eugene's return, his rusty gun is found unfired; when he appears he is subdued and wants only to live quietly. When the soldiers come for Driscoll, however, the old Fenian sympathies break out in Eugene's father, he rushes out to aid Driscoll, and both are shot.

There is a poignantly tragic last scene, with one of the women crying:

Ah, what signifies it now what any one did or didn't, since he is dead? But it is for him and the like of him that the flowers smile, and always smiled, in the green soil of Ireland. But he is dead. . . . Tom to be dead! Oh, Tom! Oh, love of my heart, is it dead you are! Is it dead! (*Throws herself on corpse.*)

Fitzmaurice does not quite allow a stock patriotic reaction here, for the figure of Eugene is standing by, a silent, stubborn negation of patriotism. Fitzmaurice was writing more than a patriotic play; he was also writing a comment on human psychology. He was remarking that men in middle life often turn from the ideal to the practical. To an Abbey still half enveloped in the Celtic twilight, such a view would have been heresy.

Fitzmaurice's early one-acts seem to be about the position of the artist — or at least the extraordinary man — in society. *The Pie-Dish*, produced on March 10, 1908, tells of old Leum Donoghue, who has been fashioning an ornamental pie dish for twenty years and who now, almost on his deathbed, is about to complete it. His relatives have little sympathy with his whim, but the old man frenziedly fights off death, first calling on God and then on the Devil to give him more time. As soon as he calls on the Devil, he falls down dead, and his pie dish breaks. Old Leum is probably not onstage long enough to arouse the pity of tragedy sufficiently, though he does elicit the fear and the shock of it. *The Pie-Dish* is a very short, very remarkable play.

The Magic Glasses, done at the Abbey on April 24, 1913, is a fantasy. Jaymoney Shanahan has a set of magic glasses through which he can see amazing and beautiful sights. He spends his time in the loft of his father's house peering into his glasses, and his parents call on Mr. Quille, a sort of local medicine man, to cure him. At first Quille seems to succeed, but Jaymoney cannot finally resist the lure of the glasses and returns to the loft, which instantly collapses with him. He is found in the rubble, his throat cut by the glasses.

Holloway, the great diarist whose reaction was usually that of the typical man in the audience, thought the play "the silliest production ever attempted on the Abbey stage." What would have won the day for the play would have been a genial, happy ending like that of T. C. Murray's *A Pipe in the Fields*, but Fitzmaurice ends his fantasy with a disquieting sting. As *The Moonlighter* was patriotism laced with a sobering dash of practicality, so this play is fantasy with a hard cold dash of seriousness.

The best of the short plays is *The Dandy Dolls*, which is quite fit to rank with *Riders to the Sea, The Gaol Gate, Nannie's Night Out,* and *The Words upon the Window Pane* as the best one-acts of the Irish drama. It is the most fantastic of the early plays and the most evocatively written, I think, of any of his work. The play is set in a Kerry farmhouse where Roger Carmody makes Dandy Dolls in those moments when he can suppress his passion for chicken-stealing. Whenever Roger finishes a doll, the Hag of Barna's son swoops down from the Barna Hills, rips up the doll, and pulls out its "squeaky-squeak." Despite help from one of the Grey Men of Doon, who are dollmakers to the King and Queen of Spain, and despite help from Father James, who baptizes the new doll, the Hag and her son both swoop down from the Barna Hills, engage in a terrific fight with everyone, destroy the doll, and carry poor Roger off:

Riding on two Spanish asses they were, holding him between them by a whisker each, and his whiskers were the length of six feet you'd think, and his eyes were the sizes of turnips bulging outside his head. Galloping like the wind they were, through the passes of the Barna mountains, sweeping him along with them, for ever and ever, to their woeful den in the heart of the Barna Hills.

It may have been the "blasphemous" baptizing of the doll and the randy folk-like character of Father James that deterred the Abbey from accepting this play, but its characterization, its dramatic force, its grotesque folk humor, its fantastic imagination, and its brilliant language make it a masterpiece fit to rank with the best of Synge and the later O'Casey.

One might suggest a reading of the play on these lines. The artist sublimates, but only partially and ineffectually, his passions in his art. His art, however, rises from these passions and is inevitably destroyed, and no power, not even God's, is capable of saving the artist or his work.

Some of Fitzmaurice's best work was discovered after his death among his papers, unpublished and unproduced. Among these scripts was *The Toothache*, a wild one-act farce which was apparently very old and which may be the rejected first play that he submitted to the Abbey. It tells how a credulous young man came down to the village to get his tooth pulled by the blacksmith. The blacksmith's cronies persuade him to spend more money on drink than he would originally have spent having the tooth pulled at home. The piece is slight, but combines blackness with farce in a quite original way. Certainly the scene in which Mulcair, with the pincers in Patsey's mouth, whirls the poor fellow furiously around the room to extract the last tooth, would be a show-stopper.

The Simple Hanrahans is a grotesque three-act comedy. A family of farmers named Munnix hope to trick the presumably simple Hanrahans into a marriage of Pete Munnix with Lena Hanrahan. But it soon appears that the Hanrahans have really diddled the Munnixes — and, indeed, with other trades and bargains, everyone else in the neighborhood. On his wedding night, Pete Munnix discovers that Lena has a wooden leg, false teeth, and a wig. There is nothing to be done, however, and after recovering from his initial shock Pete falls back in love with Lena and everyone else must also be content. Again, we have Fitzmaurice's constant idea that reality never comes up to the expectation, and that the wise man must be content with reality, poor substitute though it is for the ideal.

The action is fairly slim and static, and much of the play's humor depends upon the dialogue. The most-used device is a long series of semi-Malapropisms upon polysyllabic words. The play is discursive and conversational rather than conventionally progressive, though in this day of Beckett, Ionesco, and Pinter its illogical grotesqueries could easily be appreciated for their sheer delight.

There were three versions of *The Ointment Blue; or, The Ring of the Barna Men* among Fitzmaurice's papers. It must therefore have been an early work which he tinkered with considerably in later years. It is a three-act comedy set presumably in 1850, though actually in some never-never Ireland as colorfully fantastic as that of *Cock-a-Doodle Dandy*. It is possibly Fitzmaurice's greatest play, a brilliant masterpiece shot through with wit, superb comic characterization, exciting dramatic action, and dialogue as playful as that of Synge, O'Casey, or Joyce.

It is the story of the champion fighter of Carraweira, Dermot Rua Mullarkey, and of a tournament that the King and Queen of Ireland hold to determine who shall marry their elder daughter. Dermot's previous prowess came from a little box of ointment given him by an old Hag. His ointment has now run out, and the attempts of his uncles, Teig of the Trees and Donacha, are not able to prevent the Hag from giving the ointment to Cormac O'Rourke. At the tournament there is a splendid onstage fight that eliminates all the heroes save Dermot and Cormac. Finally, although Cormac defeats Dermot, Dermot does win the second daughter and a legacy from her rich uncle in Texas.

Relating the bare plot of a fantasy is like making a précis of a fairy tale; it takes away the charm and leaves the skeletal absurdity. A fantasy depends upon the originality of its characterization, whimsy of its plot, and charm of its dialogue. All of these qualities *The Ointment Blue* has abundantly. It is the sunniest Fitzmaurice play and should be sheer magic upon the stage.

The Waves of the Sea is a somber, more realistic fantasy. It tells how the Red Danaghers trick Rich, one of the White Danaghers, out of an inheritance and then exile him to an island in the Bay of Doon under the care of the frightening Donal Bluebeard. Thirty years later the Red Danaghers are all prosperous but unhappy. One is a compulsive eater, another cannot eat at all, one is stricken by religious remorse, and another is a hypochondriac. Then, on the island, Rich by chance throws his magic ring into the sea, and the sea covers the land and sails the island into the mainland. Rich escapes, but ignores the servant girl who has waited for him and goes out on a spree under the impression that he is rich rather than impoverished. The Danaghers go forlornly off to salvage what they can, and the poor servant girl ruefully surveys herself in the mirror, contemplating the waste of time and the injustice of fate. That wry point seems the theme of the play: nothing is black and white and there is no just distribution of rewards and punishments. No one wins as much as he wants, and no one's loss is tragic. This unconventional theme and story offer an adult reading of reality rare in the theatre, and offer it in the surprising embodiment of a folk or fairy tale.

From 1924 to 1957 eight Fitzmaurice plays appeared in the *Dublin Magazine.* The first was *The Linnaun Shee,* a one-act comedy published in October, 1924, and produced by Austin Clarke's Lyric Theatre Company at the Abbey on May 5, 1949. Fitzmaurice told Clarke that the play was a satire on Yeats and his cult of the fairies. The play seems more a comment than a satire, and the comment was hardly noticeable in the 1940's when the Celtic twilight had receded so far into the past. At any rate, Jamesie Kennelly is a middle-aged farmer who has determined to leave his wife and follow his first love, the Linnaun Shee. When the Shee appears, she is not the beautiful girl of Jamesie's dreams, but a hideous hag. Entranced, however, he follows her, but she deserts him for a younger man. He returns home, a haggard but now practical and business-like farmer. The play is not one of Fitzmaurice's best, though the conversation of Jamesie's wife and her two gossipy cronies is a sharply observed bit of satiric realism.

The Green Stone is a one-act published in the issue for January–March, 1926, and as yet unproduced. It is another semi-realistic fantasy and, despite a stereotyped stage American, one of his more amusing. Mortimer Collopy has been given a green stone which allows him to see the future. His relatives find him and his stone a nuisance, and in a series of amusing scenes try to hide the stone. But when the American arrives to buy it, the relatives themselves cannot find it; they sell the American a false stone. Then the mermaid who originally gave Mortimer the stone returns, and Mortimer smashes the stone on the hearth. After the great explosion the smoke clears and all the relatives are clasping pots or shoes full of gold. Whenever they loosen their grip, however, some of the gold flies away. They give Mortimer five shillings to enjoy himself with, and he goes airily off as they sit grimly clasping their disappearing money. Fitzmaurice is trenchantly contrasting the values of the outsider against those of the society in this satiric and yet curiously amiable little play.

'Twixt the Giltinans and the Carmodys was published in the issue for January–March, 1943, but had been produced twenty years earlier, by the Abbey on March 8, 1923. It is a mordant parable about idealism and practicality. To get a legacy, Billeen Twomy must marry, but he is unable to decide between Bridie Giltinan and Madge Carmody. After much crafty plotting to snare him, both families turn on him in another of Fitzmaurice's glorious stage fights. At the last minute Billeen, now rejected by both girls, marries Old Jane, a dour, elderly servant who discovers to her chagrin that he really has little money. At the end, the two decide to make the best of it; they come together, "showing signs of antagonism rather than affection. They embrace grimly and determinedly, and a loud kiss is heard." Fitzmaurice has given us another wryly unromantic view, embodying it in such a gay farce that our laughter is probably as delighted as it is rueful.

There Are Tragedies and Tragedies is a one-act published in the issue for July–September, 1948, and first produced at St. Mary's College, Rathmines, Dublin, on January 4, 1953. It is another wry comment embodied in an absurd situation. Humphrey Doolin and his wife have lost their money in a bank failure. Yet Humphrey is more concerned with buying a public house than with his loss, and his wife Kytie is absorbed in her aching corns. When the news comes that their money is safe, they are no more enthusiastic than they were sad when they thought it lost. They are still wrapped up in their petty problems rather than in their immense ones. Fitzmaurice's earlier heroes aspired greatly and lost; his later people sometimes win, but they have learned to aspire only after limited goals.

One Evening Gleam is a one-act published in the issue for January–March, 1949, and first produced by Liam Miller at the Studio Theatre Club, Dublin, on September 15, 1952. It is a remarkable short tragedy about a blind man lying asleep in a tenement room and about his mother and two neighbor women who chat through most of the play. Then the man wakes, regains his sight for an instant, and immediately dies. The mother stays alone by the body, sobbing. The talk is first-rate and full of reminiscences of the Dublin music halls in the early years of the century. The theme seems to be that people are immensely gregarious no matter how they may dislike each other, but opposed to the gregariousness is the solitary grief of the mother at the end. One woman leaves reluctantly, thinking that she should really bring in the neighbors for a wake. But it is sometimes necessary to be, as the blind son was, alone; that necessity is the tragedy that Fitzmaurice evokes in this little tour de force. It is a charming, rasping, frightening, moving little play, almost one of Fitzmaurice's best.

The Coming of Ewn Andzale is a one-act published in the issue for July–September, 1954, and as yet unproduced. Its theme, that one must compromise with one's hopes, is pertinent enough, but its manner is awkward. The play concerns a Big House family now in reduced circumstances. The mother, unable to bear the situation, writes a letter to herself about a man named Ewn Andzale who is coming to give them a fortune. Her daughter, noting that the man's name is an anagram for New Zealand, exposes the pitiful subterfuge; but the mother's brother actually does come from New Zealand to help them. He has not nearly as much money as the mother had imagined, but he has some. The point is clear and the characters tolerable, though this excursion into the life of the aristocracy was not really felicitous. Though Fitzmaurice purposely exaggerated the dialogue, it remains only stiffly gauche and coyly unreal. Probably this is his one really poor play.

The Terrible Baisht, or Ireland Must Have — If Not the Capital T. — At Any Rate a Bluebeard is a one-act published in the issue for October–December, 1954, and as yet unproduced. It is a realistic country farce such as Lady Gregory might have written in her early days. John Daly, a family grocer, has persuaded the villagers that a young man living in a nearby cave is the devil because he has a terrible carbuncle on his nose. After the villagers have persecuted the fellow, they find that he is supposed to be a seminarian, the canon's nephew. Frightened, they shower him with gifts, but as soon as he leaves town they learn that he was really only a tinker. The play is full of effective character vignettes and has a neat little plot that compares well with those of *Hyacinth Halvey* or *Spreading the News*. A charming piece, but a minor one.

The best published play of Fitzmaurice is *The Enchanted Land*, which appeared in the issue for January–March, 1957; it remains unproduced. It tells how Elaine, who lives under the sea, steals a magic ball of thread from Eithne, who was exiled there for loving Aeneas, the King of Ireland's son. With the ball, Elaine transforms herself into an earth woman and entices Aeneas away. She becomes Queen of Ireland and rules for eight years. When her thread runs out, she returns to her former state before her plots to save herself are completed. Eithne, who has escaped, does not, however, marry Aeneas, but says "No thanks, Aeneas. There was a time when sentimental twaddle used to move poor Eithne, but thank God! I have gained a little sense." She goes off to marry someone else. Elaine, the villainess, does not come off badly either: she has put some money by and plans to go to England and snare a king or a duke, for the English are not very bright.

This unique play is anti–Celtic twilight, anti-romantic, and anti–children's fairy tale, even though it contains qualities of each. The anti-romanticism may be seen in the unconventional dialogue, in the grotesque dance of the hags in Act II, in the hilarious gluttony of Elaine's foster-mother, in the vague stupidity of the hero ("Very appropriate — ah — 'pon my word — ah — "). Certainly it may be seen in the denouement in which romanticism is wittily set aside for practicality. It is as if the manner of Lewis Carroll had been amazingly wedded to the opinions of Emile Zola.

It is hard to sum Fitzmaurice up without sounding extravagant. He has written a body of plays nearly as large as O'Casey's and three times as large as Synge's. He has as unmistakably individual a voice as either, and his wry resignation is as fresh as his exuberant imagination. His plays are a fantastic, a brilliant, and an alternately joyous and grim body of work. There is no one like him in the modern drama.

Why, then, was he so long ignored? Why did the Abbey Theatre not encourage him? Perhaps it was partly a matter of luck; perhaps it was partly, as Austin Clarke thinks, the jealousy of Yeats. But, whatever the reason, it is clear that he was one of the masters; the theatre of Ireland and of the world can continue to ignore him only to its own impoverishment.

III THE POST-WAR SYNTHESIS

9

The Theatre Festival

THE Dublin Theatre Festival has received considerable criticism, but when we consider how the Abbey is still reorganizing itself, how the Gate is almost defunct, and how the Globe and the Pike have disappeared, then it seems clear that the Festival is now the most important theatrical force in the country. It generates more interest and discussion than any other theatrical event, it brings in the largest audience, it draws international attention, and, most important, it discovers new writers and encourages old ones. The Festival seems to have taken over the function, once the Abbey's and then the Gate's, of giving the vital impetus to Irish playwriting.

The Festival is the brainchild of Brendan Smith, a Dublin theatrical entrepreneur who was born in Essex in 1917 but has lived in Ireland since infancy. At present, in addition to being the director of the Festival, he —among other things—runs a theatrical academy and a modeling school, is a manager of the Queen's, a director of Radio Publicity, Ltd., and a director of Four Provinces Films.

The Festival grew out of the Irish Tostal, a now defunct national celebration which ran for a fortnight during the summer and consisted of various attractions in different cities including plays, curragh racing, folk dancing, and chess tournaments. For the fifth Tostal, in 1956, Smith staged a Cuchullain pageant as Dublin's main contribution. Then, according to him, at the end of the year:

I put to Bord Failte[1] a blueprint for a Dublin International Theatre Festival as a cultural and tourist promotion . . . The original idea was to have a festival that would be, roughly speaking, given over to about two-thirds Irish contributions — in terms of writing, acting, and directing — and one-third foreign contribution. That was the original intention. We found that it was very difficult to compete financially in the matter of bringing foreign companies to Dublin, and we also found, with no disrespect to visiting companies, that there was a great deal more interest among visitors in Irish productions. So that after the first year our policy changed to basing as much of the programme as possible on Irish writers, actors, directors, with the proviso that at least a couple of non-Irish writers and some visiting artists would be included. . . .[2]

🖙

The Festival's early years were rocky. In 1957, as a part of the Fifth Tostal, the Festival included the foreign imports of the Royal Ballet, Jean Vilar and members of his Theatre National Populaire playing Molière and Balzac, and Margaret Rutherford playing in *The Importance of Being Earnest*. The local offerings included *Juno* and *The Playboy* by the Abbey, Mac Liammóir in *The Old Lady Says "No!"* produced jointly by the Gate and the Longford Company at the Gaiety, seven Yeats plays done by the Globe in Dun Laoghaire, a traditional Irish Night's Entertainment produced by Gael Linn at the Damer Hall, the Dublin Grand Opera Society in three operas, Kenneth Reddin's *The Gilla Rua* produced by Fergus Cogley at the Studio Theatre Club, and Alan Simpson's production of Tennessee Williams's *The Rose Tattoo* at the Pike. There were also amateur performances of Colum's *The Land* and Ganly's *The Dear Queen* at the Pocket Theatre and of John O'Keefe's old *The Agreeable Surprise*, put on by an amateur group called the Irish Festival Players Club in a drawing room in Fitzwilliam Street.

The Irish part of the program, though sound, was more a tribute to the past than a hope for the future. The greatest excitement was generated by the arrest of Alan Simpson for the alleged immorality of his production of *The Rose Tattoo*. This event, which has been retold in Simpson's *Beckett, Behan — And a Theatre in Dublin* and in Krause's *Sean O'Casey: The Man and His Work*, was something of a *cause célèbre*. It gave the Festival some unfortunate publicity and reminded people that Ireland could still be hyperpious. Financially though, the Festival did not do badly: seventy per cent of its seats were sold; it sold £14,137 worth of tickets, spent £27,842, and lost £13,705. It had been guaranteed by Bord Failte and by the Guinness Brewery for losses up to

£14,000, and so the point was made that with a subsidy the effort was financially feasible.

The Festival plans for 1958, which was really to be the first Festival produced independently of the Tostal, were more elaborate, but the outcome was an even more calamitous fiasco. The main events were to be the world premiere of O'Casey's *The Drums of Father Ned*, the presentation of three mime plays by Beckett, and the premiere of *Bloomsday*, an adaptation by the Ulster writer Alan McClelland of *Ulysses*. The Archbishop of Dublin was naively asked to say a mass to inaugurate the Festival, and he, of course, refused a mass for a Festival featuring O'Casey and Joyce. This refusal threw several producers into a pious panic, and McClelland's play was tossed out. O'Casey was a knottier problem; one of the directors of the Globe which was to do his play wrote asking permission to make certain unnamed structural revisions. O'Casey naturally refused and withdrew his play, as was expected. He did not, however, withdraw it without some ferocious public snorts of contempt. Beckett then withdrew his mime plays as a sympathetic gesture for the insult to Joyce, and the upshot was that the Festival was first postponed and then abandoned.

The 1959 Festival was timid, but after the tremors of the first two years it is remarkable that it went on at all. The Liffey Theatre revived Synge's *Deirdre of the Sorrows* at the Eblana, the Globe revived Shaw's *Simpleton of the Unexpected Isles* at the Gaiety, with Anew McMaster, Jimmy O'Dea, and Milo O'Shea; the Longford Company revived Goldsmith's *The Good-Natured Man* at the Gate; the Lyric Players from Belfast did Yeats's *Oedipus at Colonus* and *Death of Cuchulain* at the Dagg Hall; the Gate revived Johnston's *Dreaming Dust* at the Gaiety; and Orion Productions revived MacDonagh's *Lady Spider* at the Gas Company in Dun Laoghaire. The only new Irish plays were the Abbey premiere of a trivial comedy by Anne Daly called *Leave It to the Doctor* and the Lantern's production of *Necropolis* by Roger McShane, the pseudonym of a Dublin architect. One imported show, *Landscape with Figures* at the Olympia, caused a minor fracas when the star Donald Wolfit disagreed in the press with the author Cecil Beaton about the play's merits. The most interesting production of the period appeared immediately after the Festival, when the Pike brought Dominic Behan's *Posterity Be Damned* to the Gaiety and immediately ran into trouble.

The 1960 Festival was excellent. Siobhan McKenna and Donal Donnelly did a beautiful *Playboy* at the Gaiety, where later Cyril Cusack premiered Macken's *Voices of Doolin*. Orion gave the premiere of Keane's *The Highest House on the Mountain* at the Gas Company, Simpson produced the lively Dublin Teddy-boy musical *The Scatterin'*, by the young Dublin sculptor James McKenna, and the Globe presented two sound premieres at the Eblana: the first was G. P. Gallivan's Parnell play, *Mourn the Ivy Leaf*, and the second was Hugh Leonard's *A Walk on the Water*. Mac Liammóir scored a personal triumph in his one-man show of readings from Wilde called *The Importance of Being Oscar*. The Abbey even rose to the occasion by reviving two of their best recent plays, MacMahon's *Song of the Anvil* and Behan's *Quare Fellow*. The Longford company did Wilde's *An Ideal Husband*, and the Lyric Players came again from Belfast with half a dozen short pieces by Yeats. The best foreign offering was the Old Vic's *Macbeth*.

The 1961 Festival was a bit overambitious. Both Brecht's *St. Joan of the Stockyards* with Siobhan McKenna, produced by the Gate at the Gaiety, and Cusack's Dublinization of Kafka's *The Trial*, called *The Temptation of Mr. O*, at the Olympia, had large casts and played over four hours. Both were excellently done, but about an hour too long. Hugh Leonard's Dublinization of *Peer Gynt*, called *The Passion of Peter Ginty* and produced at the Gate by Gemini Productions, was colorful if overlong. The best premieres were Keane's *No More in Dust* in Dun Laoghaire and *North City Traffic Straight Ahead* by the young Dublin electrician James Douglas at the Olympia. These two alone were sufficient justification for the Festival. The most notable foreign offering was a play about St. Teresa of Avila by Hugh Ross Williamson; it was too dull for even Sybil Thorndyke and Lewis Casson to redeem.

By 1962, the Festival had developed a pattern of two or three new plays by Irish writers, two or three well-staged classics, two or three foreign plays, two or three crowd-pleasers such as reviews or attempts at glossy musicals, and two or three fringe performances which might include readings, one-man shows, or plays in Irish. In 1962, there were three notable new plays. Hugh Leonard was represented again by his brilliant adaptation of Joyce, *Stephen D*. Seamus Byrne, after a six years' wait, finally had his imperfect but strong and thoughtful *Little City* done, and Patrick Galvin had his *And Him Stretched*. Both the Byrne and the Galvin suffered from being directed by the same producer, Barry Cassin, and neither was admired as much as it should have been. Another Irish piece was *Fursey*, a mediocre musical adapted from Murvyn Wall's novel *The Unfortunate Fursey*.

The Gate did a showy *Othello* at the Gaiety with Mac Liammóir as Iago, Eithne Dunne as Desdemona, and the American Negro actor William Marshall as Othello. It had been planned to have Anew McMaster in the lead, but that veteran actor unfortunately died during the year. Norah Lever staged a dull *Murder in the Cathedral* at St. Patrick's, and Eugene O'Neill was represented by the Abbey revival of *Long Day's Journey into Night* and the H. M. Tennant production of *A Touch of the Poet*. Saroyan's *The Cave Dwellers* also appeared.

The best new Irish plays of 1963 were Keane's *The Man from Clare* produced at the Abbey and two plays by the industrious Hugh Leonard —an adaptation of *Dubliners* called *Dublin One* and an original play called *The Poker Session*. Conor Farrington's *The Last P.M.* was presented by the Gate and generally panned until high praise from Frank O'Connor renewed people's interest. The annual musical was *Carrie*, from a story by James Douglas. The Joyce industry continued with *The Coach with the Six Insides*, an acting, miming, and dancing version of *Finnegans Wake* by the Jean Erdman Company from New York. One reviewer called it "stimulating but unsatisfying" — whatever that means. The Lantern staged Padraic Colum's poetic Noh play about Sir William Wilde, *Moytura*, and also Synge's rarely seen *Tinker's Wedding*. The foreign plays included a Genet, a Beckett, a Robert Bolt, a new Alun Owen, and an Irish translation of Wesker's *Roots*. How much the Festival had grown may be seen by Brendan Smith's remarks that it had cost £50,000 and that all but £17,000 had been recovered from ticket sales. About twenty-four hundred people had been attracted from abroad and about seventy thousand tickets had been sold.

An *Irish Times* editorial on the eve of the 1964 Festival well summed up its present accomplishment and future potentiality: "The Dublin Theatre Festival provides a mecca, and it is possible that it will perform in future the work for which Yeats and Lady Gregory founded the Abbey. Their dream may yet come true." There were four new Irish plays in 1964. One was *The King of the Castle* by Eugene McCabe. This play, mildly reminiscent of Sidney Howard's *They Knew What They Wanted*, was a powerful domestic tragedy that had won the 1963 Irish Life Drama award of £500. James Douglas's strong second play *The Ice Goddess* was stupidly panned, and Brian Friel's superb *Philadelphia, Here I Come!*, produced by the Gate, was only mildly liked, whereas Michael J. Molloy's new Abbey play, *The Wooing of Duvesa*, did not fare much better. There were two musicals. The home-grown one at the

Olympia was *Sir Buccaneer*, about Henry Morgan the pirate and with a book by G. P. Gallivan. No one was enthusiastic. The foreign musical was *Laurette*, based on the life of Laurette Taylor and starring Siobhan McKenna. Seamus Kelly summed it up as "alien corn." There were also a review, the usual Gaelic play, and a couple of translations.

The best new plays of the 1965 Festival were probably Hugh Leonard's *When the Saints Go Cycling In*, a loose adaptation of Flann O'-Brien's novel *The Dalkey Archive*, and, although less well received, Tom Coffey's *Gone Tomorrow* and G. P. Gallivan's *Campobasso*. The Abbey made a gesture toward the Yeats Centenary Year with a limp *Deirdre*, and the Dublin University Players did *The Resurrection* and, for the first time in Ireland, *Calvary*. The most notable foreign entry was an Alun Owen double bill called *The Game*.

The 1966 Festival produced four new plays: Louis MacNeice's *One for the Grave*, Hugh Leonard's *Mick and Mick*, Peter Luke's *Hadrian*, based on the works of Baron Corvo, and Eugene McCabe's new play *Breakdown*. From America came William Alfred's *Hogan's Goat*, O'Neill's *Hughie*, and Jack Aranson from San Francisco in his production of Sidney Michaels's *Dylan*.

❦

Perhaps it is incorrect to present the Festival as an unqualified success when so much criticism has been leveled at it. Of course, much criticism is leveled at anything in Dublin, often with some justice. The usual charges against the Festival are that there is favoritism in choosing plays, that good plays are frequently not chosen, that Brendan Smith is only a theatrical businessman with no sense of artistic merit, and that the Festival is really used as a tryout for plays which might be exported to London or New York.

The big money does not lie in Dublin, and perhaps some plays are chosen with an eye upon the bigger box office across the Irish sea. After all, the Festival, though partly subsidized, is a commercial venture. It must watch the box office — which is probably also the reason for each year's trivial reviews and mediocre musicals. Nevertheless, the Festival has subsidized a substantial number of new plays which would not otherwise have been produced. To my mind, the selection of plays can be defended merely by noting that the Festival has encouraged such excellent new talents as Keane, Douglas, Gallivan, Coffey, Farrington, Friel, Leonard, McKenna, and Kevin Casey as well as such older writers as Molloy, Macken, and Byrne.

A more frequent criticism is that the Festival causes much theatrical activity for two weeks and leaves the rest of the year a theatrical desert. This is to an extent true, but the fault is not only the Festival's. It would be more realistic to note that Dublin has lost several theatres in recent years. A much less refutable charge is that the mounting of fifteen or seventeen plays is too ambitious. There are not, it is truly said, enough good Irish actors to fill adequately the casts of that many plays. Consequently some plays suffer.

One charge comes more from participants than from observers of the Festival, and that charge is leveled against the quality of the criticism the plays get. On some evenings there will be as many as seven or eight plays opening, and when this happens the first-line critics usually go to the big production at the Gaiety while the newspapers call in their sports reporters and society editors to cover the rest. With one or two honorable exceptions, the journalistic criticism is stupid, though probably not more so than that in the New York papers. One fact militates against that poorness — a vocal public opinion which is almost impossible to avoid hearing. The opinions of typical playgoers wandering around the Festival Club sound a little sheep-like, but at least their "baas" are highly audible. Certainly, in the case of Farrington's *The Last P.M.*, Frank O'Connor alone managed to change the trend of opinion.

Festival workers have also commented on the savagery of journalistic criticism. An aggravated example might be noted in the years before the Festival when Cusack gave the premiere of *The Bishop's Bonfire* in 1955. The occasion brought over many English critics, among them Tynan and Hobson, who were generally enthusiastic about the play. The Irish brotherhood, led by Gabriel Fallon, raised such a howl of malediction that one would have thought they were discussing anti-Christ instead of O'Casey. In the 1964 Festival, Laurence Bourne, the director of Douglas's *The Ice Goddess* wrote to the press, "Two of the notices the play received were extremely savage and irresponsible. These critics discounted the play simply because they did not understand it." This is a deplorable but not unusual gambit for critics. Shaw, Beerbohm, and Nathan — much as I admire them — have a great deal to answer for.

At any rate, despite its undoubted flaws, some of them remediable and some not, the Festival is firmly established, and it seems to me the strongest sign of vitality in the Irish theatre.

⁂

The most produced, most commercially successful playwright of the Festival is Hugh Leonard, who was represented in 1966 with his seventh play and for his sixth year. Leonard is the pseudonym of John Keyes Byrne who was born on November 9, 1926. He lived with working-class foster parents in Dalkey, attended the national school there and then, on a scholarship, went to Presentation College in Dun Laoghaire. In 1945 he left school and worked in a film renters' office. He then joined the Civil Service and worked, as had Fitzmaurice, in the office of the Irish Land Commission. There he became interested in drama and did a great deal of amateur acting and producing. He wrote "a few abortive one-acters," and completed his first long play, *The Big Birthday*, in 1950. It was finally produced by the Abbey in January, 1956.

His second play, *A Leap in the Dark*, was also done by the Abbey, in January, 1957, and in March, 1958, his *Madigan's Lock* was done by the Globe. In 1959 Leonard left the Civil Service to write professionally, and in 1960 moved to Manchester and worked for two years as a contract writer with Granada Television. In the meantime, Gemini Productions had put on *The Passion of Peter Ginty*, his Irish adaptation of *Peer Gynt*, in the 1961 Festival, and in the next Festival Gemini did his superb dramatization of Joyce, *Stephen D*. This production was successfully repeated at the St. Martin's Theatre in London. In 1963, he was represented by two plays, *The Poker Session* and *Dublin One*, an adaptation of Joyce's short stories. Both productions were by Gemini, which also produced his adaptation of Labiche's *Célimare* under the title of *The Family Way* in August, 1964. In the 1965 Festival, Gemini produced his *When the Saints Go Cycling In*, from Flann O'Brien's novel *The Dalkey Archive*. Leonard writes that "Of the ten plays named, my own preference is for *The Passion of Peter Ginty* of which, unfortunately, I don't have a complete copy." [3] His new work includes three stage plays: *The Au Pair Man*, *Judas*, and *Mick and Mick*, the last produced for the 1966 Festival. His plays have been so successful that he is now able to spend only half of each year writing for films and television. "This," he writes, "buys time in which to spend the remaining six months working on stage plays." [4]

Only three of Leonard's plays have been published, and I have read only one other in manuscript. All are technically proficient, and one brilliantly so. The original plays, *A Walk on the Water* and *The Poker Session*, might be called psychological melodramas. Both are absorbing and a bit disappointing, perhaps because Leonard leads you to expect insight and gives you mainly dramatic tension.

A Walk on the Water takes place on the pier at Dun Laoghaire on a day in 1956 when Owen and his English wife Alma have come to Ireland for the funeral of his father. Owen left in 1945 with a feeling of hysterical betrayal when he learned that his father was remarrying. In 1945 he had been the center of a group of young people who met on the pier and had acted the role of Father Confessor to them, probing their weaknesses and deriving a vicarious thrill from their lives. When his own vulnerable spot is exposed, the others gloat over his weakness, and he retaliates by some savage remarks aimed at their most private insecurities. Now, years later, he has arranged a meeting on the pier, hoping to learn if his remarks affected their lives. At first it appears that he has had no effect, but then it accidentally spills out how each of his friends has had his life more or less blighted. One is now a drunkard, one a homosexual, another a puritanical bachelor, and, worst of all, one has caused his wife's death. The manner in which layers and layers of motivation are peeled away is deft, and so is the technique of sliding from a dialogue between Owen and Alma in 1956 to a dramatization of Owen's memory of 1945. Each of the seven roles gives an actor more than a stereotype to grapple with, but there is about the play the air of a technical exercise.

Stephen D, however, is one of the most impressive plays to appear in Dublin since the war. A few years ago this adaptation of Joyce's *Portrait of the Artist as a Young Man* and *Stephen Hero* might have been prosecuted like *The Rose Tattoo* or forced off like *The Ginger Man*. Its acceptance is certainly a symptom of a lessening parochialism. And, of course, in Ireland as elsewhere, when morality conflicts with business it is business that wins. This play did excellent business at the box office.

From the Catholic point of view, there is some justice to the charge that the play is blasphemous and immoral, for the theme of Joyce's novels and of Leonard's play is the revolt of the artist — a revolt which in Irish terms means a repudiation of what Leonard calls "the four great 'F's' of Ireland: faith, fatherland, family and friendship." The "F" most stressed in the play is faith, and this most exacerbates the feelings of devout Catholics. The most objectionable scene is at the end of Act I when

Stephen receives Holy Communion. It should be pointed out that he is in a state of grace at the moment, having repented for his earlier lust and having made his confession. Immediately after the Communion scene, however, the act closes with this abrupt and sardonic shift of tone:

(*The light changes, suddenly harsh.*)
STEPHEN: Chastity, having been found a great inconvenience, was quietly abandoned.
(*He lights a cigarette.*)

The other irritating scene took place when the prostitute removed her blouse. In another play, I doubt that this would have occasioned comment. Girls more scantily clad have appeared on the Dublin stage, and in the state-censored movies there is much that is more risqué and in shoddier taste.

The compression of the novels' details and the heightening of their dramatic effect is firm evidence of Leonard's craftsmanship. He presents salient dramatic scenes bearing on the theme and all linked by the narrator Stephen, who remembers them as he leaves Ireland for exile. The play would require imagination and skill from a director, for Leonard incorporates no stage directions in the text. The modern stage has been long aware, however, that it possesses a fluidity nearly as great as the film's. It is only recently, in the work of Leonard and Coffey and Douglas, that Irish playwrights have taken advantage of this freedom. In *Stephen D*, Leonard handles this free realism consummately.

The Poker Session is an original play about a man of good will, Billy Beavis, who has just returned home from a year in a lunatic asylum. He has been victimized by his family and friends, and, as the play unravels, it becomes increasingly clear that they were more responsible for his breakdown than he was. The play is a kind of detective story set on the night that Billy returns, and it slowly answers the three questions of, in Leonard's words, "Is Billy now sane? Why has Des, the missing guest, failed to show up? Who drove Billy into the asylum?"

There is a growing sympathy with Billy until we learn that what caused his insanity was not the treachery of his family or his girl, but that his friend Des had bluffed him in a poker game. This discovery answers the question of Billy's present sanity even more clearly than the revelation that he has murdered Des and is going to fix the blame on Teddy, a middle-aged hipster friend from the asylum. The pertinent point of the play is, then, that "It's the innocent who get punished . . . we all have it done to us, and we do it to other people."

This point is not sufficiently stressed at the end, for the gimmicky twists of the plot command too much attention. Indeed, because of the plot, the play at the end is reduced in stature from what should have been a serious work to what is little more than a crafty melodrama. Through much of the piece, Leonard seemed to aim higher.

Leonard is a thorough professional of much experience. This fact gives his work a slickness and command of technique greater than many of his Irish contemporaries, but it also implies a danger of falling into a pat commercialism. A psychological thriller like *The Poker Session* is good, taut theatre, as good as *Night Must Fall*, but so far Leonard's best work has been in adaptation. He is a writer in his prime, however, and with the technical weapons at his command he could go on to a series of equally deft but more penetrating original plays which would make these early ones look like exercises.

Certainly a long step in that direction is *Mick and Mick* (or, to give it its new title, *All the Nice People*), which was first presented by Gemini at the Olympia Theatre, Dublin, on October 10, as part of the 1966 Festival. Almost totally absent is the pat gimmickry of the earlier original work. This play is a rasping and yet partly loving indictment of middle-class Dublin seen through the eyes of a girl who has returned from working in England. If the play has a fault, it is that Leonard more persuasively documents the reasons for detesting the middle-class than the reasons for loving it. That fact may make the play rather more coldly caustic than is comfortable, but the quality of the indictment is first-rate. Here, for instance, is the heroine's brother-in-law:

You behold the sinking of the not-so-good ship Charlie Lambert. Every year he submerges a bit: he gets cleaner and tidier, he learns to mind his manners, his language, his personal habits, his job, his opinions and his good suit. His mind shrinks like a stomach that hasn't been fed. His wife, lovely girl, is buying him on a mortgage: twenty years or so and he's all hers: inside, outside, the lot: one owner, immaculate condition, any trial; needs a drop more oil than he used to, but the mileage is modest. And he'll end up like your grandfather inside; a mummified old nuisance, only he'll have nothing to show for it, no medals and no rebellions. It's the slobs who always go to the wall, Fran. You should know that. You're one.

⁂

G. P. Gallivan is about ten years older than the other writers discussed in this chapter. He was born on July 29, 1920, at Limerick and went to

Crescent College there. Out of school at eighteen and unable to get a job, he wrote a book he could not get published, emigrated in 1940 to England, worked there for five years, and married there in December, 1945. Back in Ireland for a vacation in 1946, he found a job with T.W.A. and has been working for that firm in Ireland ever since. His first play, produced in 1949, was the original version of his Parnell play *Mourn the Ivy Leaf*. This play and five others were produced in Limerick by the College Players when he was working for T.W.A. at Shannon. When *Decision at Easter* was put on at Limerick, Godfrey Quigley of the Globe Theatre journeyed out to see it, found faults with it, but accepted it for production.

After *Decision at Easter*, two more Irish historical plays, *Mourn the Ivy Leaf* and *The Stepping Stone*, were produced in Dublin. The latter play had earlier been produced for a seven-weeks' run in Cork by the Southern Theatre Group. Gallivan also wrote the book for the musical *Sir Buccaneer*, which appeared in the 1964 Festival. This play, about Morgan the pirate, was the only one that he did not rewrite considerably — and the only one that failed badly. Several of his plays have been done on radio and television, and he has two unproduced plays, *Colleen*, a comedy, and *A Beginning of Truth*, a drama. His *Campobasso* was performed at the 1965 Festival.

The Globe presentation of *Decision at Easter* took place on March 17, 1959. It is a realistic study of the leaders of Easter Week. The characters are not heroically exaggerated or sentimentally patriotic, but none is a really vivid stage creation. The play is well constructed, rising to moments of strength and tension, but in places it seems talky and slow. It is sound and competent, but not exciting.

Mourn the Ivy Leaf was done first by the Globe at the Eblana Theatre on September 12, 1960. A well-wrought, soundly built piece of realism, it shows what disastrous effects Kitty O'Shea had upon Parnell and poses as its theme the idea that, after Parnell agreed to support O'Shea as a liberal candidate rather than an Irish party one, he had in a sense betrayed the people. Gallivan suggests that without Parnell, Home Rule was a lost cause, but that he was now a tainted leader. His Parnell does not come across with great vividness. We hardly see in this Parnell the force and magnetism that made the Irish follow him so devotedly. The aloofness and reserve are there, and so is a scathing contempt for O'Shea; however, these qualities make the stage Parnell a trifle cold and unsympathetic. More successful is Gallivan's O'Shea, a foppish, unscrupulous, selfish creature who sometimes manages, nevertheless, to seem more endearing than Parnell himself. Kitty is little more than a foolish woman here, and the love scenes do not generate much intensity. The most intense passages concern the political maneuvering in the Galway by-election; Joe Biggar, who opposes Parnell, is one of the most substantial roles that Gallivan has drawn.

Gallivan's next historical play, *The Stepping Stone*, about Michael Collins, I have not read, but *Time and the Devil*, a revision of one of his amateur scripts, is for two acts a convincing and fluent realistic drama set in a fishing village on the southwest coast. In the third act Gallivan heaps incident on incident so fast that the play shoots off into melodrama. There is an apparent death at sea, an apparent ghost, the confession and madness of the uncle, the heroine's renunciation of the hero, and a good bit of offstage action. Still, in the earlier acts, there was some real character-drawing and honest observation.

Campobasso has interesting parallels to Irish history. Perhaps this is the most interesting fact about the play; in manuscript it seemed to me talky, repetitive, and without particular point. The play is set in an unspecified European country which has had a successful revolution against a foreign power; now the revolutionary forces have split. The party out of power is led by Mario Campobasso. The parallels to the Rising and the Civil War seem clear, and, since a point is made of the foreignness of Campobasso's name, there seems a hint that the part is meant to suggest De Valera.

As a political allegory, the play allows Gallivan to make some points about De Valera and the Civil War that he could hardly do overtly in his play about Collins. Although the events took place forty years ago, they still have some inflammatory vitality. To an un-Irish audience which would be primarily concerned with the tale of Campobasso rather than with the implied relevance to Irish history, the play might seem a bit pointless and rambling. Some of the roles are demanding ones for actors, but the play does not strike me as Gallivan's best.

His best is probably the unproduced *A Beginning of Truth*, set in the present and concerning contemporary Irish politics. A West Briton journalist now working in England returns to write a set of articles on the contemporary scene and strongly criticizes the political establishment as timid, ineffectual, church-ridden, and somewhat stupid. Michael Crotty, an old patriot, has himself long been a critic of government policy and is on the verge of resigning from the cabinet in protest against government policy. His son-in-law Tommy, a pushy but loyal party man, attempts to prevent his resignation. After some fierce clashes in which all become more than stereotypes of critic or reactionary, the play ends with Crotty still undecided.

The political argument, interesting as it is, embodies only part of Gallivan's theme. The rest is conveyed by several less indigenously Irish clashes. A "not over intelligent" playwright named Bill Regan has a play panned by the journalist and cannot face this beginning of truth, taking refuge in excuses and drink. One of Crotty's daughters, Monica, learns that the journalist had earlier had an affair with her younger sister, and her own squeamishness about sex is revealed. Tommy comes at least partly to grips with the fact that he has got ahead by being Crotty's son-in-law. Most of the characters are pushed into regarding themselves more clearly. Some cannot face the prospect and wince away from it. Others may come through the searing revelation somewhat changed.

The dialogue is smoother than that of the history plays, and many observations strike acutely home. The playwright's excuses — critics write only to show off their own cleverness, there was an organized clique of jealous actors who kept up a stream of derogatory comment during the show, etc. — are hit off with witty accuracy.

The play is not obviously theatrical and has some dull spots. Its curtains are fairly weak, its story line is not at all strong, and there is a tendency for politics to seem its real subject. Despite these faults, it is a thoughtful attempt to put on a stage intelligent conversation about real issues. It is also Gallivan's most complex attempt at character-drawing. If his subsequent plays improve on this one, he will be a very important playwright.

⚜

James Douglas was born in Bray on July 4, 1929. He went to the National School there until he was fifteen and then to the technical school in Bray for two years more. From age seventeen to age twenty-two he was an apprentice electrician, and three days a week he is still an electrician. His first produced play was *North City Traffic Straight Ahead*, which was directed by Alan Simpson for the 1961 Theatre Festival. At the 1963 Festival a musical named *Carrie* was based on a story of his, and at the 1964 Festival his *The Ice Goddess* was done at the Gate.

He has written four plays for television — *The Bomb, The Hollow*

Field, Babbi Joe, and an adaptation of *North City Traffic* — and they have played on the Continent and in Australia as well as in Ireland. He put in a stint of twenty-six weeks scriptwriting for *The Riordans,* a Telefis Éireann soap opera, and he vows never to tie himself down so again. He has recently finished a play titled *The Savages,* which traces the effect of the Congo police action upon Dubliners. His work is urban and modern as opposed to that of Molloy and Keane, whose work really harks back to the agrarian past of Ireland.

His *North City Traffic Straight Ahead* is a deceptive script to read, for much of its dialogue is of a bare-bones repetitiveness that seems copied from Anderson, whose *Winesburg, Ohio* is one of Douglas's favorite books, or from Hemingway in his more mannered moments. The dialogue appears on the page deceptively simple, even to the point of banality or parody. Indeed, the entire plot as well as the characterization seems hypersimple and a bit adolescent. Harry Hopkins is a middle-aged man who works nights in the United News office. He was brought up in a rigorously moral, stiffly lower-middle-class morality. He wooed the preacher's daughter but ran away with a circus because he loved a girl named Tilly more, was disillusioned by her, returned home to marry Emmy the preacher's daughter, and is now bitterly gnawing at himself and sardonic toward the world, his wife, and himself. He entertains a young co-worker Donal, a whore named Annie, and a woeful, friendly Jew named Mossie with the story of his life. His slatternly and pitiful wife Emmy frequently calls up, and his sardonic nature makes him lacerate both himself and her. During the play, Donal goes into the next room with Annie, and their laughter is overheard by Emmy on the phone. She rushes over to the office, and at the very end of the play it seems for a moment as if she and Harry will have some saving moment of human contact. That moment passes, however, and they are left still alone in separate worlds of anguish. The final words are "God help us all."

Despite its neo-realistic dialogue, this is not a realistic play. It is a simplified extract, a symbolic essence of life, rather than a full photograph. The play needs to be done with a strong hint of stylization. If so, its effect is not to amuse the audience at the cartoon of reality or to alienate it as Brecht does. The effect is rather to humanize the characters, to bring out the human relevance of their story and of the theme. Realistically, Harry is no more than a middle-aged simplification of Osborne's Jimmy Porter. Stylistically, he is modern man, even existential man, alone on his island, full of torment and anguish. Played in that fashion, some of the scenes are the most bleedingly human of any in the recent Irish drama.

The Bomb is a simple half-hour television play about two boys who decide to torment an eccentric old lady by tossing a home-made "bomb" fashioned from burning camera film into her room. When one boy slips and falls, the old lady brings him in, and he comes to lose his fear, to like and to feel sorry for her. It is a good play for three actors; its theme, about the necessity for humans' touching and understanding, resembles that of *North City Traffic*.

The Hollow Field is a long television script, first transmitted in February, 1965, over Telefís Éireann. At first, it seems quite like George Shiels's *The Fort Field* in its situation, which is the leveling of a fairy fort. In treatment, Shiels's play is fuller and more satisfying, for he has two hours and a half to work in, and the demands of television limit Douglas to an hour and a half. In theme, Douglas's play is more satisfying because it is subtler. Shiels's play had reason, or at least practicality, triumphing over ingrained superstition, and it ended with the leveling of the fairy mound. In Douglas's play, local superstition is too strong, and the play ends with the engineer erecting a barbed wire fence around the mound and not leveling it. In a sub-plot, the engineer turns away from the simple Irish girl who loves him and goes off in disgust with Ireland to France. However, Douglas's main scorn is directed at the engineer who did not have the courage to attack one of Ireland's "untouchables," and the field, surrounded by its ugly barricade, remains nicely symbolic of one of the anachronistic elements in Irish culture.

Superficially *The Ice Goddess* is in the simplified manner of *North City Traffic*; really it carries a weighty load of symbolism. Its story concerns an elderly woman, Mrs. Fury, who lives in a grand old house which dominates a little town — not necessarily an Irish town. Mrs. Fury keeps her house as a sort of museum, drawing the blinds to protect the furniture that her husband made. Her husband had become at the end of his life a wreck of a man, bent over and dribbling, and his son-in-law Leslie Phibbs had to break his back to fit him into the coffin. In the same way, a tree finally falls across the old house, breaking its back. Mrs. Fury's grandson Kevin had built himself a treehouse, which takes on a symbolic coloration of youth, innocence, a golden era, and which is also broken up in the storm. In many ways, the action shows that change and death are inevitable and that one cannot restrain either.

What most disrupts any static ideal state is man's own animal nature.

The point is made especially by the Gage family who live in a small modern villa near the big house and who are rooted in animal sensuality. Mrs. Gage, who can be touched by Kevin's innocent love, throws him viciously aside when her husband comes home. A girl and a schoolmate of Kevin try to pull his treehouse down, and at the end of the play they are going to have a child. An ideal state, then, is impossible to maintain, but when one ideal state is being destroyed another is rising to take its place. Kevin's father Leslie will now build a big new house, making it in his own image. This truth about change Kevin has learned from watching the thawing of his grandmother, the Ice Goddess, who is unable finally to maintain her house as her husband built it. The point is also well made in the last exchange of the play:

> JEAN: It'll be born. The baby'll be born. And be different. Be different from me. From Joe. Really, really different . . .
> KEVIN (*With immense compassion*): Will it, Jean? Will it?

The compassion stems from Kevin's realization that man has never-to-be-transcended limitations. The dialogue, the symbols, and the characterization are again a stylized essence, a parable stated almost with banality. Yet perhaps it is necessary for Douglas to stray so near the cliché when what he has to convey is emotionally complex. Like Arden in England, Douglas seems to occupy a halfway point between the drama of realistic comment and the unrealistic drama of the Absurd. Quite as much as Arden and rather more than Pinter, he repays his audience by moments of savage and poignant effect. No other of the young Irish dramatists, except Brian Friel, has so acutely portrayed anguish, loneliness, the sense of betrayal, and the sharp, smarting sorrow that comes with them.

❦

Brian Friel is a slim dark man with a rich Northern accent; he has made a name as a writer of short stories, many of which appeared in the United States in the *New Yorker*. He was born in the north, in Omagh, on either January 9 or 10 — he has two contradictory birth certificates — in 1929. His father was a schoolteacher, and Friel went to school in Omagh until 1939, when his family moved to Derry, where he still lives. He went to St. Columb's College from about 1940 to 1945, and then he went on to the famous seminary at Maynooth for two years and a half. Deciding against the priesthood, he entered a teachers' training college, qualified, and began working in a secondary school in 1950. He taught until 1960, when he was able to give it up and devote his full time to writing. He is married and has two children.

His first collection of stories was called *The Saucer of Larks*, and his second *The Gold in the Sea*. He has had five plays produced. His first, *The Francophile*, was put on by the Group Theatre in Belfast. His play about St. Columba, *The Enemy Within*, was done by the Abbey, and his *The Blind Mice* appeared in Dublin at the Eblana with Sam Thompson in the cast. His only published play, *Philadelphia, Here I Come!*, was one of the successes of the 1964 Theatre Festival and of the 1965–1966 season in New York. *The Loves of Cass McGuire* played briefly in New York in the 1966–1967 season.

Philadelphia, Here I Come! tells the story of a young man in a small village who reluctantly accepts a chance to go to America. He has a number of reasons for going, most of which come down to an inability to communicate. His phlegmatic, silent father exists across an impassable gulf from his son. Even when the boy Gar is in love with Kate Doogan and she returns his love, he is misled by her father into thinking that she prefers another man, and so he loses her. Gar's American aunt, Lizzy Sweeney, is unable to convey her anguished desire for a son. Gar's friends, "the boys," a group of middle-twentyish virgins all "acting the mick," find they must disguise or squelch their own sorrow at his leaving home. The maid of the house deeply wanted a grandniece to be named after her but could not communicate the fact.

It is not only in conveying information but also in conveying sympathy that the characters fail, and that is the tragedy of the play. That tragedy is pointed up by Madge, the maid, who remarks at the end of the play that when Gar is his father's age "he'll turn out just the same. And although I won't be here to see it, you'll find that he's learned nothin' in-between times. That's people for you."

The most striking technical device of the play is splitting Gar into a public and a private self, played by two actors. The private self speaks, of course, the character's thoughts. Friel handles this device with no Eugene O'Neill solemnity, but gets much humor and pathos from it. In places, the dialogue between Public and Private Gar outdoes in exuberance Lucky Jim himself, and is a delight to see. For instance:

PRIVATE: It's a great day, Gar, old Fox! And tomorrow — tomorrow will be better!

*(Public makes airplane wings of his arms and imitates the droning
of a plane.)*
Up in the big bugger of a jet, with its snout pointing straight for the
States, and its tail belching smoke over Ireland; and you sitting up
at the front *(Public acts this)* with your competent fingers poised
over the controls; and then away down below in the Atlantic you
see a bloody bugger of an Irish boat out fishing for bloody pollock
and —
(Public nose-dives, engines screaming, machine guns stuttering)
PUBLIC: Rat-tat-tat-tat-tat-tat-tat-tat-tat-tat.
PRIVATE: Abandon ship! Make for the life-boats! Send for Canon Mick
O'Byrne!
(Public gains altitude and nose-dives again.)

This is enormously playable theatre, but Friel gains as poignant effects
as well as funny ones from splitting Gar. For instance, when Public Gar
is bidding a brash and cruel farewell to Kate, Private Gar is doubled over
in mute anguish that speaks louder than many words. There are many
really almost show-stopping moments in the play. Lizzy Sweeney in
her one scene has a superb aria in which her feelings are more and more
remorselessly revealed. In sum, this is a brilliant and beautiful study of
isolation and its inevitably accompanying anguish. Well played, it should
leave its audience both charmed and bruised.

One of the Theatre Festival's healthiest symptoms is that a large number of its plays are written in a style of free realism. Of the writers discussed at length in this chapter, only Gallivan is a fourth-wall, photographic realist. Without leaping into total Expressionism, the others
manage to establish a plausible sense of the real while at the same time
dispensing with the confines of the box set. Douglas in *The Ice Goddess*,
Leonard in *Stephen D*, Coffey in *Gone Tomorrow*, and McKenna in
The Scatterin' — to pick only a few typical examples — all swing easily
back and forth to different areas of the stage which represent places
widely separated in space. The work of the Gate, of the Lyric Players
Theatre, of Johnston, of Yeats, of Clarke, perhaps of Fitzmaurice and
O'Casey, has had its effect on Irish writers and audiences. Both have become more sophisticated, and the promising young writers handle their
eclectic techniques as easily as their English and American counterparts
do. The Green Goddess of Realism, as O'Casey called it, is no longer
on its pedestal in Erin.

10

The Short Happy
World of Brendan Behan

BRENDAN BEHAN will not lack biographers. From his drunken appearance on B.B.C. television in 1956 until his death in 1964, he lived his life in the public eye. He made better newspaper copy than any poet since Dylan Thomas whom, in some ways, he resembled. Like Thomas, he fostered legends – some true, some false, some wildly exaggerated. He was capable of great kindness and outrageous cruelty, of great generosity and self-centered boorishness. He was often delightfully witty and often a sore trial to anyone who knew him. He was a man of rare talent, even though he squandered much of it.

He was born in 15 Russell Street, Dublin, on February 9, 1923, while his father was imprisoned in Kilmainham Jail for Republican activities. His mother's brother was Peadar Kearney, who wrote the Irish national anthem "The Soldier's Song," as well as many other popular ballads. An uncle by marriage was P. J. Bourke, who managed the Queen's Theatre and produced Irish melodramas by Boucicault and Whitbread and himself. One of Bourke's sons, Seamus de Burca, is also a dramatist whose work is discussed in a later chapter.

Behan's father Stephen Francis is a housepainter and has been, since 1948, president of the Irish National Painters Union. After he graduated from school and revolutionary activities, painting was also Brendan's profession. First, however, he had several notable brushes with authority. When he was sixteen, he was apprehended in Liverpool with a suitcase full of explosives that he had intended to use in blowing up a battleship. He was sentenced to three years in a Borstal prison, a British reform school for juvenile offenders. In 1944, after a wave of Republican violence, he was sentenced to fourteen years in Mountjoy, but was released in the general amnesty of 1946. He was arrested twice again, and the last time, in 1952, he was deported to France. When he made his way back to Dublin and half settled down, he acquired a local celebrity as a good minor poet in and major drinker of Irish. In February, 1955, he married Beatrice ffrench Salkeld, and in November, 1963, they had a daughter.

The first version of his play *The Quare Fellow* was a one-act in Irish called *The Twisting of Another Rope*, a wry play upon the title of Douglas Hyde's famous old one-act. Behan's little play was rejected by the Abbey, so he rewrote it in a three-act English version which the Abbey also rejected, as did most of the other Dublin managements. Finally Alan Simpson and Carolyn Swift accepted it for the Pike, their little theatre in Herbert Lane. After the Dublin production, Behan succeeded in getting Joan Littlewood to produce it at her Theatre Workshop in May, 1956, when he also made his celebrated television appearance. Six months after the London opening, Ernest Blythe accepted the play for the Abbey.

After the success of *The Quare Fellow*, Gael Linn, an Irish revival organization, commissioned Behan to do a play in Irish. The result, *An Gaill*, was put on in the Damer Hall, Dublin, in June, 1958. Joan Littlewood produced the expanded English version, *The Hostage*, in October, 1958, and later transferred the piece to the West End for a successful run. *The Hostage* was about the last serious writing Behan did. Various books continued to appear — *Brendan Behan's Island, Hold Your Hour and Have Another, The Scarperer*, and *Brendan Behan's New York* — and some were quite good, but there was little new work in them. There was also a projected play called *Richard's Cork Leg*, which was commissioned by the Dublin Theatre Festival but never written.

At the end of December, 1963, Behan was found lying injured in a Dublin street and taken to the hospital suffering from pneumonia and head injuries. On January 12, 1964, he left the hospital, but on March 10 he went back in suffering from liver and kidney complaints, diabetes, and jaundice, all of which were aggravated by drink. He went into a coma, and on March 20, at the age of forty-one, he died.

This bare account hardly suggests what a fascinating man Behan was, but there are already many such testimonials. My point is that he was also a fascinating artist.

※

Restraint and complexity are not the terms usually associated with Behan's plays. As the *New York Times* remarked, "His plays were looked upon as a shapeless collection of bright quips that could be given polish only by a talented director."[1] This view seems to me demonstrably incorrect, particularly in the case of *The Quare Fellow*. In it, Behan is the conscious and subtle artist, playing his tricks on the audience precisely in the way that, say, Bernard Shaw did. When people called Shaw's attitudes perverse, they really meant that he had tricked them consummately. His magnificent powers of comic persuasion had finagled them momentarily into believing something that their sober selves would probably reject. *The Quare Fellow* works the same kind of highly moral trick. The main difference between it and *Major Barbara* is that Behan's audience is less likely to become untricked when the show is over. In this play, Behan comes closer to convincing his audience permanently of the rightness of his theme than Shaw does in his.

An audience approaches this prison play with the conventional social attitude toward criminals, for the collective morality of an audience is a good deal more rigid than the individual morality of any of its members. Moreover, Behan's prisoners are such a scruffy, antisocial, and unrepentant group that there would seem an unbridgeable distance between them and the audience. Any appreciation of the play should begin by recognizing this difficult problem of arousing sympathy for characters whom most of the audience could only thoroughly deplore.

Quite early in the play Behan begins to work his trick. He first introduces bits of proof that his motley prisoners do have certain standards of morality. These proofs do not immediately deluge us; they are unobtrusively but insistently slipped in. The first comes in the form of a joke, when Dunlavin reacts unpredictably to the crime of a new prisoner: "oh, the dirty beast, look what the dirty man-beast is in for. 'Clare to God, putting the likes of that beside me. They must think this is the bloody sloblands." The spectacle of this hopelessly hardened old reprobate reacting with the finicky disgust of a pillar of the community cannot miss getting its laugh. But as the audience laughs at this unexpected incongruity, it has inadvertently swallowed a pleasant-tasting pill of morality. And once we have even half-unconsciously recognized a kind of morality that these wretched prisoners profess, we have begun to extend a sympathetic toleration.

This beginning of sympathy is enlarged in a dialogue that shortly follows. Prisoner A and Prisoner B and Dunlavin consider how it must feel to receive a last-minute reprieve. "It must be a great thing," says B, "to be told at the last minute that you're not going to be topped after all." Notice how easily the second personal pronoun is intruded. In the conversation that follows, with its simple and graphic detail evoking the feelings of the condemned prisoner, notice how the word "you" gains strength. "And after that, the tea is drunk and they offer you cigarettes. . . . And they ask you would you like another game of draughts, or would you sooner write a letter." Behan is with beautiful unobtrusiveness playing on the sympathetic identification of the audience, and the audience suddenly finds itself caught in a deeper emotion than it is usually prepared for at a simple evening's entertainment.

Also by the end of the play, our sympathies have been focused on one individual, the Quare Fellow, who has come to symbolize the ultimate injustice of the law toward humanity. As the politeness, the concern, the sympathy of both prisoners and warders go out to him, so do ours. We know little about him; he is a human being and that is enough. Behan does not even bring him onstage, as a writer of melodrama would, to jerk out the last tear. He is too reticent to make his point by an easy sentimentality. But he does make his point, which is our ever-growing conviction that, no matter what crime the Quare Fellow committed, the punishment is a greater crime.

The Quare Fellow is broader than a thesis play which arouses at best an intense intellectual conviction that one could get as well from a newspaper editorial. The play evokes a deep emotion, not an intellectual conviction. It makes us feel that capital punishment is wrong, but it never speaks out in open argument. If the play is done well, I should imagine that the most rabid believer in capital punishment would be as moved as the gentlest opponent.

The Quare Fellow is also broader than a thesis play because it never relies upon too simple emotions. Although part of Behan's trick is to awaken our sympathy, another part is not to awaken too much sympathy. Often gangsters in plays or films are glamorized, and the audience reacts sentimentally. Behan avoids such spurious overcharacterization; one of his best brakes against such sentimentality is the colorful and bawdy language which quite definitely keeps the prisoners from seeming noble victims of a malevolent society.

His tragi-comic effect emerges from one central incongruity which has partly to do with the language. Running through the play are constant reminders of the approaching execution, and as the play nears its end these reminders grow more insistent. Contrasted with this somberness is all of the superficial dialogue. Most of this talk, in its wild profanity, its banal triviality, its bawdy humor, and its raucous song seems supremely inappropriate for the central motif of the execution. But, despite the impending death, the jocose and sordid trivialities of daily existence in a prison go on. Such a perception of incongruity is basic to the tragi-comic structure of such masterpieces as Chekhov's *The Three Sisters* and O'Casey's *The Plough and the Stars*.

This tragic and comic pattern is most forcefully apparent at the end. The Quare Fellow, until his death, had come more and more to dominate the play. The mournful songs in English and Irish had contrasted brilliantly with the callous brutality of the preparations for the execution. The audience was painfully aware of the implied contrast, and moved by it. But after the Quare Fellow is executed and the prisoners have broken into their animal howl, all the mourning is abruptly dropped; we are back in the ordinary, daily world of the prison. Dunlavin and Neighbour callously discuss their bet. Prisoner B is told to chisel the Quare Fellow's number on the tombstone. Not his name, but his number. And not even his correct number, but one easier to carve. Then the prisoners filling in the grave squabble over the Quare Fellow's letters. And finally the scene is closed by the song which opened the play — only now the song is given an added verse with a bawdy meaning.

Behan has contrasted against the death every possible feeling that is callous and ignoble. To an audience still feeling the importance of the death, these violent contrasts offer a chilling shock. Yet the trivialities that follow the death do not trivialize the death, for the audience has been much too moved. Nor are the trivialities superficially sardonic. Rather, they make the death even more terrible because this is the immemorial way in which life treats death — by ignoring it. After the duel in *The Three Sisters*, poor old Chebutykin merely reads his newspaper and mumbles to himself. After the devastation in the Dublin tenement in *The Plough and the Stars*, Stoddart and Tinley sit down for a cup of tea. This is the inexplicable, the rare kind of emotion that the writer of tragi-comedy brings out of his bag of technical and moral tricks.

༖

The Hostage was one of the most total pieces of theatre to appear in London or New York since the war. The Joan Littlewood production was entirely in harmony with the exuberant, randy, free-wheeling spirit of the script. This rare and nearly perfect marriage of creator and inter-preter was an electrifying reminder of how vital the theatre at its best could be. Yet despite the almost universal delight that greeted the pro-duction, the script itself has come in for some cutting criticisms.

The chief criticism is that it was Miss Littlewood and her Theatre Workshop actors who made the play, with all the song, dancing, lights, color, commedia dell' arte quips, and vitality that they brought to it. Proponents of this view usually point out how thin and flat the script is when stripped of everything players and producer brought to it.

I think it really does not detract from the genius of Joan Littlewood to say that such criticism could come only from people who know little about the theatre. The production of a play is not the work of an individual talent, but the fusion of many talents. The professional pro-duction can combine all these disparate efforts in some competent fash-ion. Often the professional production can rise above competence to ex-cellence, and sometimes to brilliance. Such was the case when Clurman and Strasberg came to the plays of Odets in the 1930's and when Kazan came to the plays of Miller and Williams in the 1950's. When the the-atrically untutored intellectual saw Lee J. Cobb's performance in *Death of a Salesman*, he was, like everyone else in the audience, immensely stirred. When, later, he turned to the play script hoping to relive that profound emotional experience, he found something much thinner and more naive than the play on the stage. So he damned the play script.

Much the same thing happened to *The Hostage*. It is certainly true that some of the production's best efforts are barely visible in the script. The words of the final song are a case in point:

> The bells of hell
> Go ting-aling-a-ling
> For you but not for me,
> Oh death, where is thy sting-aling-a-ling?
> Or grave thy victory?

The words alone only palely suggest the electrifying effect they produced on the stage. But that is usually all that words and plot and characters in a script can ever do. Some few great plays do have almost as persuasive a life on the page as does a novel, but still the effect of a Shaw or an Ibsen when staged halfway well is much, much greater than the effect of the play in the study.

Despite this, I think just, apologia, *The Hostage* is not so deeply moving nor so fine as *The Quare Fellow*. However, the final version of the play, even if it be a collaboration between Behan and the Littlewood company, is written down with considerable craft. Structurally, it is both sound and conventional. Its first act makes the exposition, establishes the situation, and starts the plot moving. The second act does not contain great plot development or complicated intrigue, but it has a growing tension as Leslie the hostage and his unwilling captors grow aware of the implications of the situation — mainly, that is, that Leslie will be shot. The third act increases the tension, comes to a strong climax in the raid and in Leslie's accidental death, and then surprisingly rises to a denouement even more moving and exciting than the climax. This denouement is the most interesting, effective, and theatrical structural device. In *The Beggar's Opera*, John Gay had arbitrarily reprieved Macheath on the gallows; in *The Hostage*, Behan goes a step farther by arbitrarily retrieving Leslie from death to lead the cast in the mordantly accusing final song.

The play's structure is not its most interesting aspect, but I have harped on the matter to stress that the structure really is there and that the play does not basically rest upon its decoration of songs, dances, minor characters, and vulgar drolleries.

The characters are little more than two-dimensional stereotypes, although they have their theatrical vitality. Much of that vitality comes from their novelty rather than their thickness. Like the characters of *The Beggar's Opera*, the denizens of Behan's Dublin doss house are seedy opponents of established society and have a peculiar society of their own with its own morality. All of them are outsiders: members of an illegal army, prostitutes, homosexuals, eccentrics, and bums. Their caustic disenchantment, so vividly expressed in dialogue and songs and dances, establishes the whole tone of mordant vitality.

The dialogue, curiously enough, is not often witty and is sometimes flat. Even Monsewer's superb "The Captains and the Kings" has two verses so weak that they are seldom sung. Many of the quips are more surprising than pointed, like the designation of Macmillan as "that multiracial coon" or the song of Rio Rita, Princess Grace, and Mr. Mulleady:

> We're here because we're queer,
> Because we're queer because we're here.

Despite such weakness, the dialogue is some of the finest since the early O'Casey. It has no literary fullness like the dialogue of Synge, Fitzmaurice, or Molloy, but it does have a glib, conversational breeziness. Just as much as the comic dialogue of a Coward, Behrman, or Barry, it demands a certain style; when the actors can provide it the whole play is lifted.

Behan creates a unique world in *The Hostage*, better in ways than the prison world of *The Quare Fellow*. Some critics have pointed out that certain characters and incidents are unrealistic, but I think that they are deliberately so and that the play has about the same connection with reality as do O'Casey's later satires, fantasies, and pastorals. It comments on reality by heightening it and seeing it through a unique, sometimes bleary, often humorous, and finally sad imagination. No matter how much help he had in refashioning the play, this point of view is indisputably Behan's own.

Although this is both an angrier and a happier play than *The Quare Fellow*, its characters are not unfeeling Jonsonian monsters. They detest both the inhumanity of established society and that of the rebel army. And, amazingly enough, Behan makes us believe, at least momentarily, in their view. He has worked his trick again and worked it more startlingly than in *The Quare Fellow*, for he hurls his accusation of inhumanity pointblank at his audience. That moment at the end of *The Hostage* is one of Behan's triumphs and a great moment of the modern theatre.

Three other Behan plays have been staged. All were originally one-acts written for Radio Éireann. *The Big House* is a lovely, boozy farce about how the Dublin jackeen, Chuckles Genockey, is left in charge of a Big House and how he totally sacks it in the absence of the owners. It is an example, I suppose, of the Irish getting a little of their own back. *Moving Out* and *The Garden Party*, are brief, funny farces based on the Behan family's experiences on being moved from a tenement to a new corporation house. All three play beautifully.

The charge of slapdash technique has been leveled at Behan's undramatic work also; and is well on its way to becoming the chief cliché invoked about the man's work. His longest book, *Borstal Boy*, after an eloquently bawdy mélange that closely examined the author's early days in prison, then telescoped months into a few pages and wound up hastily, as if the author had had enough of it. *Hold Your Hour and Have Another*, *Brendan Behan's Island*, and *Brendan Behan's New York* have been with some justice dismissed as mildly pleasant grabbags of fugitive pieces; the short novel *The Scarperer* did not raise much dust; *Confessions of an Irish Rebel* came out of a tape recorder. However, as little critical attention has been given these books and as Behan is such an important figure, we might glance at a couple of the best.

Brendan Behan's Island is a mixture of disparate material, but would be worth its price merely for the inclusion of *The Big House*. The Behan world is seen more clearly, however, in *Hold Your Hour*, a collection of short articles that first appeared in the *Irish Press*. Most of the pieces are anecdotes and scenes. There is no connecting thread, and the book is not one to be dashed through but rather to be lingered over and dipped into. What gives unity to the disparate scenes is the personality of the narrator "Brending Behing," as the inimitable Mrs. Brennan calls him. It is a book of pub conversation that reports what Brending and his friends Crippen, Mrs. Brennan, and Maria Concepta said to one another. It is a world bounded by the Hammond Lane Foundry and Mountjoy Prison and peopled by Granny Nutty, Jimmie the Sport, Chuckles Cleary, Mister Moo, the Rasher, Hot Malt, Whacker Kinsella, and a German grocer called Frankenstein for short. It is a leisurely rambling world of talk, bits of song, wit, and stupendous non sequiturs. It discourses of the poet Yeets, of James Joyce and his book *Useless*, of Eveleen Warr, of racing, politics, and drinking, of legendary heroes like Fill Mac Coon and Hanna Bow Lane who went around with her head tucked underneath her arm. It is a world in which the English language suddenly takes on a drunken vitality. A pub full of weeping widows is a boo-hoozer, and for these women the obituary column is the boo-hoo's Who. It is a world in which one may recover one's perspiscasity at the zooahlogical moment and be nonplussed by a man with a face like a plateful of mortal sins. It is a world not much like Alice's, but nevertheless a kind of Wonderland.

This same world we find in *The Scarperer*. This little novel has an ingenious story, although Behan hardly gives it the loving development that an Eric Ambler would. There is hardly a person in it who is not a "character," but each is sketched in with the lightest of strokes. There is exaggeration, but no thickness. Behan has no Micawbers. We see his people in a flash, as one of a crowd of equally engaging eccentrics. It is as if Behan took for granted our previous acquaintance with Tralee Trembles, Pig's Eye O'Donnell, The Goofy One, and Pierre le Fou, and did not have to go through the laborious business of characterization.

This might be a prime drawback in another writer, but Behan avoids trouble by the whole tone of his story. That tone is conveyed mainly by the racy dialogue which makes up the great bulk of the novel and which actually suggests a kind of characterization. This is not usually dialogue's main purpose, but it does prove that Behan was the master of a certain inimitable idiom. His is not language taken down verbatim from the North Side of Dublin slums, any more than O'Casey's was solely that. It is heightened speech, depending much on slang, but not the flat, pallid slang of an O'Neill play. It is a yet alive slang — colorful, clear, funny, and quite sufficient to make a work by Behan as recognizable as one by Synge or Lady Gregory or O'Casey.

Probably what this discussion about dialogue boils down to is that Behan did create, after all, one superb character. He does not overtly appear, but it is through his eyes that we see this strange, brave new world. He is as fine a character as Shaw's "G.B.S." and his name was "Brending Behing." Long may he live.

11

The Hidden Ireland of John B. Keane

I AM GOING to visit John B. Keane next week."
"Ah," said my companion, "you mean the man who is larger than life."
Even though the comment was meant to be satirical, probably Keane appears that way to Dubliners. He is a Kerryman and easily the most popular Irish dramatist of the last five years. His popularity with audiences, though, does not impress the Irish critics, who praise him with faint damns. He is sometimes accused of being a latterday Boucicault whose plays are faultily constructed and harmed by large injections of melodrama. However, Dublin critics are little more aware of what life is like in Clare and Kerry than New York critics are familiar with life in Nebraska and Georgia. Keane is not really larger than life, but life itself in Kerry is larger than life in Dublin.

He lives in Listowel, a small farm town which the local bookseller described as full of boredom — which was hardly my impression. The town has a large square with a handsome Church of Ireland in its center; but that church has only a handful of parishioners; most of the people are Catholic. The Feale River runs past, between the Greyhound racecourse and the remains of a castle. The streets are long, a bit winding, and usually busy. A man leads a pack of greyhounds by; a donkey and cart clumps past; a lorry rumbles around the corner. To walk with Keane through the streets is an experience, and you get the feeling that it would be impossible for him to go anywhere in town quickly. He walks out of his pub, meets a man and stops to talk, moves on, is hailed and stops to talk, strolls on a few paces, calls to a passing tramp and stops to talk, wanders on a bit further, and a little girl tugs at his hand crying, "John!"

And what dazzling talk it is — leisurely, gay, gossipy, full of anecdote, jokes, and wild whimsy. Consider Roger Trueblue, for instance, the hero of Patricia Lynch's *The Man with the Red Face* and the original of Danger Mullaly in Keane's *Many Young Men of Twenty*. He is a short, stout, balding, red-faced man with a fancy that is dazzlingly inventive. His imitations of the call of the whale and the mongoose should doubtless be recorded for posterity. "P-tweet, p-tweet, p-tweet, hronk-hronk!" is an approximation of the whale; the mongoose is indescribable.

In Keane's pub, I met an old farmer named Canavan, the father of twenty-one children. He is a ripe natural actor who climaxed a story of how he lost his eye in a fight at a wake by pulling his glass eye out of its socket and dashing it to the floor. "And there," he said, kicking it across the room, "there it is!" Later Keane posed him the hypothetical problem of what remedy a long-married couple should use to have children. Canavan thoughtfully cross-examined Keane to find out more about their age and condition. Then he recommended that the husband should take two brown stones, tie them in a handkerchief, and put it secretly beneath his wife's pillow. Then, during intercourse, the husband should reach under the pillow and give the handkerchief a lusty shake. That, he averred, was infallible.

Obviously this is not the Ireland of modern Dublin with its new skyline of skyscrapers and television antennas. And it is not the technicolored Ireland of a film like *The Quiet Man*. It is a hidden Ireland — truer, bigger, richer, and we may find it honestly portrayed in Keane's plays.

❦

Keane was born on July 21, 1928, in Listowel. The "B" in his name is for Brendan, the name he took at Confirmation. His mother was the daughter of a small farmer, and his father was a schoolteacher. He himself went to the Listowel National School and from there to the local secondary school, St. Michael's College. From St. Michael's, he "was expelled several times — for smoking, speechmaking, ballad-writing and play-acting." After school, he became a fowl-buyer and then a chemist's apprentice. Early in January of 1952, he emigrated to England; his portrait of this trip on the mail boat from Dun Laoghaire is one of the saddest passages in his autobiography. Keane has strong roots in Kerry, and his time in England was largely a Purgatory. Nevertheless he did a great deal of apprentice writing in the two years before he made his way back to Ireland. Early in 1955, he married, and he and his wife bought the pub he still runs.

A pub is open long hours every day, and for the first two years the pub took all of Keane's time. When he began writing again, he could only find time after twelve at night when his customers had all departed. Finally he had a light radio play named *Barbara Shearing* accepted by Radio Éireann. Then one night he saw the Listowel Drama Group in a production of Joseph Tomelty's *All Souls' Night*. "When I came home that night," he writes, "I was impatient and full of ideas. . . . I started to write and six hours later, or precisely at 6:30 a.m., I had written the first scene of *Sive*." [1] The finished script was rejected by the Abbey but accepted by Micheál Ó h Aodha for Radio Éireann and also by the Listowel Drama Group, which won the All-Ireland Amateur Drama Finals with it and played it over Radio Éireann and in the Abbey. In Ireland it is probably the most performed play of recent years. Since *Sive*, Keane has poured out a continuous stream of work. *The Highest House on the Mountain* was first presented by Orion Productions at the Gas Company Theatre in Dun Laoghaire, and was the longest running show of the 1960 Theatre Festival. *Sharon's Grave* was first produced by the Southern Theatre Group in Cork on February 1, 1960. In 1961, the Southern Theatre Group produced Keane's musical *Many Young Men of Twenty*, playing it first in Cork and later at the Olympia Theatre in Dublin. *No More in Dust* was produced at the Gas Company for the 1961 Festival. The Southern Theatre Group produced *The Man from Clare* on July 1, 1962, in Cork, and in the fall of 1962 Keane had his first Abbey production with *Hut 42*. On July 17, 1963, the Southern Theatre Group first did *The Year of the Hiker*, and on November 2, 1965, *The Field* was first presented at the Olympia Theatre, Dublin. *The Rose of Tralee*, another musical, appeared in 1966. Keane has also published a volume of poems titled *The Street*, an autobiography titled *Self-portrait*, and a collection of newspaper essays called *Strong Tea*.

᪥

The popularity of *Sive* seems at first difficult to explain. The play is not original in its situation, theme, or realistic manner. The problem of a young girl forced into a marriage with an older farmer by her grasping relatives has been used and reused in Irish plays. Carroll's *Things That Are Caesar's* is basically the same situation, and D'Alton's *Lovers Meeting* is even closer. Micheál Ó h Aodha noted several other weaknesses: "the faulty curtain lines, the contrived letter scene, the melodramatic ending and a tendency to substitute shocks for strength." [2] These are well-taken criticisms. All of the curtains, save the last, dribble away; and much of the last act depends upon the ancient device of the undelivered letter. There is, in other words, nothing in the plot that other authors could not have done more felicitously.

Some of these flaws, however, loom larger in retrospect than they do in the playing. In a really good production, the charge of melodrama seems an academic quibble, for the piece hovers close to tragedy in its grip upon the audience. James N. Healy of the Southern Theatre Group remarked: "*Sive* is the greatest play I have ever encountered for audience participation — on the stage one could feel the reactions of the people in front to what was going on on the stage in quite an extraordinary way. I have played the part of the matchmaker well over a hundred times now, and this feeling persists with every performance." [3] The reasons for the play's theatrical strength seem to me the meticulously faithful realism, the firm character-drawing, the brutally observed theme, and the emotionally effective songs of the two wandering tinkers.

Shiels, D'Alton, Murray, Robinson, and MacNamara were all excellent realistic playwrights, but their realism hardly ever caught an audience up with a shock of recognition. Keane, however, has focused his vision with a harder clarity upon the minutiae of everyday life. Superficially, this clarity can be seen in his diction. Words like "Bogdeal, doodeen, bocock, muller, lurgadawn, tathaire" appear frequently enough to suggest that these characters are not far removed from a time when Irish was spoken. The diction is only one of several qualities which suggest a whole culture and complex of ideas. This authentic sense of place comes out even in the "business" which Keane gives his characters. When, for instance, Mena makes bread, she does it with an evocative accuracy:

Mena kneads the dough vigorously and smooths it out in the shape of a circle. She takes a knife from the lower part of the cupboard and makes a Cross across the top of the loaf. Taking a fist of flour in her hand she goes to the hearth and sprinkles the bottom of the pot with it. She returns to the table, takes the dough in her hands and places it in the pot.

She catches hold of the tongs and pushing the pot nearer the fire, arranges the coals around the pot. She takes a cloth from the cupboard and cleans the table, returning the saucer to the flour bag, and the jug to the dresser. She returns the cloth to the lower part of the dresser.

This is simple enough; any playwright could observe as precisely. But not many since Tom Robertson have, and it is the kind of activity that works superbly on the stage in convincing an audience of a story's reality. Such observation is the glory of and the chief reason for realism.

Most of the characters are drawn with a similar fidelity, heightened by just a touch of grotesqueness. In many realistic plays, the minor characters at the edge of the picture fade off vaguely. They are only stereotypes, there for the purposes of the plot. The edges of Keane's photograph are never fuzzy. Sean Dota, the obscene and senile old farmer who hopes to marry Sive, is a small part, and so is Liam Scuab the boy who loves her, and so is Carthalawn the simpleton poet son of the tinker — yet each is defined with a convincing individuality. If there is any deficiency in the character-drawing, it is in Sive herself, for she does not really hold her own with Mena or the matchmaker or the tinkers.

The strongest quality of the play is the cold accuracy with which Keane paints the lust for money. This is the basic theme of innumerable Irish plays, but it has rarely been put with such cold clarity since William Boyle's most venomous play *The Building Fund* or since Carroll's *Things That Are Caesar's*. Keane's characters have a Jonsonian rapacity. Sive's Aunt Mena and the matchmaker Thomasheen Sean Rua are almost monsters of greed, but yet never unbelievable. There is one ghastly scene in which they turn upon Sive's grandmother Nanna, who opposes the marriage to Sean Dota; it is so intensely black that one thinks of Bosola tormenting the Duchess of Malfi. It is too long to quote, but here is one speech from it by the matchmaker:

Sure the County Home is filled to the jaws with the likes of her. You will see the crowds of them sticking their heads out of the windows watching the visitors coming and going and they hoping that someone will come to take them away out of it. 'Tis the sport of Cork to see the way they do be haggling and scraping over the few potatoes and the forkfull of meat. (*He looks solemnly at Mena.*) Ah, but sure the hardest of all, God pity us, is that they will stop the oul' women of smoking. An oul' lady from the other side of the mountain that used to have a liking for her pipe of tobaccy went out of her mind after three days. She would be heard screeching in the other world. They had a piece of sacking over her mouth to keep her quiet but sure that was no good but as little.

She started scraping herself till the flesh hung from her in gibbles and the blood used to be coursin' down out of her in streams. 'Twas a madness for the pipe, you see! By Gor! in the long run they tied her up with ropes and still 'twas of no good. She used to get fits of rolling her eyes around in her head like marbles and she would start holding her breath till her face was the colour of a raven's hide. (*Then, sanctimoniously.*) She was a terrible sight when she died. They buried her in the middle of the night with not a living Christian in the world of her own people to say a prayer for her. . . .

One of the most deadening qualities of realism is its lack of the theatrical elements of song, spectacle, color, dance, and music. Keane avoids this pitfall by means of the traveling tinkers, Pats Bocock and Carthalawn. These characters emerge naturally from his landscape, but in the play they function in about the same way that the Greek chorus did — that is, they help arouse emotion by theatrical rather than literary means. Carthalawn's songs are stinging commentaries upon the action and immensely effective. The song at the end of the play, for instance, does not have great effect as a poem on a page, but when sung to Keane's tune it creates a conclusion of haunting intensity:

> Oh, come all good men and true,
> A sad tale I'll tell to you,
> All of a maiden young, who died this day.
> Oh, they murdered lovely Sive,
> She would not be a bride,
> And they laid her dead, to bury in the clay.

Sharon's Grave is subtitled "A Folk Play" and diverges from photographic realism by many touches of heightened imagination which might loosely be described as poetic. However, the main divergence from realism is a pervasive grotesquerie. It is a startling play to come out of Ireland, for it dramatizes the intensity of the sexual drive. The point is made most strongly by the macabre Dinzie Conlee, a wizened hunchback who cannot use his legs and who gets around by riding on the back of his powerful brother Jack. Dinzie's warped body is an externalization of his warped mind. He is obsessed to the point of insanity with the idea of sex. Despite moments of plaintive sanity, he is generally as venomous and diabolic a character as the English-speaking stage has seen since the Jacobean dramatists. Frustrated by his inability to drive his cousin Trassie out of her home so that he may have it and then attract a wife, he becomes craftily sadistic. At the wake for Trassie's father, mounted on his brother Jack and wielding a whip, he drives the schoolteacher and two gossipy neighbors from the room. In a terrible scene in the last act, when Jack is fighting outside with a wandering thatcher who loves Trassie, Dinzie crawls across the floor grasping a knife to kill the girl. These events must sound like an outlandish recital of horrors, but in the play there is a hypnotic plausibility about them.

Trassie's brother Neelus is so obsessed by sex that he has been driven truly mad. However, if Dinzie's obsession is diabolic, Neelus's is angelically simple and harmless. He spends his time peering into Sharon's Grave, a deep hole near the cliffs where the water is always wild even when the sea is calm. According to local legend, there was once a beautiful princess named Sharon who was about to be married, but her ugly and hunchbacked handmaiden Shiofra was jealous. As Sharon was riding to the wedding, Shiofra whispered an incantation into the ear of the horse which then leapt into the hole. Sharon tried to save herself by grabbing at Shiofra, and they both fell in. Sharon obviously embodies the beauty of sex, and Shiofra the hideousness which drags the beauty down.

In the same way that Shiofra destroyed Sharon, Dinzie tries to destroy Neelus. He pays Pats Bo Bwee, a local witch doctor, to assert that Neelus is mad so that Dinzie may put him in an asylum and drive Trassie away. At the end of the play, to save Trassie, Neelus picks up Dinzie, runs off to Sharon's Grave, and jumps in with him.

Trassie and Peadar, the thatcher, stand for a healthy sexual urge, but their desire has an intensity rare in Irish drama. There is a kind of pagan acceptance of sex in this play, and in truth it is not a particularly Christian play. Its symbolism, its imagery, its evocation of folk superstitions all look back to the pre-Christian past. And despite its ferocity, there is little violent or uncontrolled about its technique. *Sharon's Grave* will probably not be one of Keane's most popular plays in Ireland, but it proves even more than *Sive* that his is an eminently individual voice.

✤

The Highest House on the Mountain is patently a Keane play; it is set in a farmhouse kitchen in the southwest of Ireland, and again depicts a number of characters grotesquely warped by the demon of sex. Yet the play seems poorer than the two previous ones and gives the impression of hastier writing. The firmly established sense of place is less evident here, the dialogue seems closer to what George Shiels might have written, and the grotesque characters seem more types than individuals.

Still, the view of life that emerges is an arresting one. The only character who has not been in some way blighted by sex is the younger brother Connie Bannon, a thoroughly opportunistic villain. The father, Mikey Bannon, has long been a widower and has sublimated his sexual desires in a passion for food. His younger brother, Sonny, having innocently frightened a woman years before, has an almost pathological timidity toward women. Patrick, the son who returns from England, has been jilted by an English girl and is a confirmed drunkard. The woman whom he brings home as his wife has been a prostitute. By these examples, Keane seems to say that being scarred by sex is unavoidable. Even Connie, to whom sex is unimportant, is finally killed by a group of angry neighbors for having seduced a local girl. Perhaps Keane is using sex as a symbol for the entire human state; it is as impossible to avoid the consequences of being a sexual animal in his play, as it is impossible to avoid some of the unfortunate consequences of being a man.

If this were Keane's sole insight into man's state, his plays would be enormously depressing. However, there seems to be a final affirmation in this play. Two characters, Sonny and Julia, achieve happiness by going away to live in Sonny's house, the highest house on the mountain. The highest house apparently means the best existence to be achieved on earth. That existence seems to be characterized by selflessness, a simpler and more generous living of life that only comes after the soul has been tempered. The play really dramatizes the combat between man's spirit and his animal body. It is a harrowing combat, and spirit wins by the narrowest of margins. But it does win.

꿍

Like Behan's *The Hostage*, Keane's *Many Young Men of Twenty* is not his best drama, but it is his best piece of theatre. It is a play with music, and the tunes Keane composed for it give the piece a buoyant lift. One goes about humming them for days afterward.

No other of Keane's plays so reflects his attachment to his country. It is a poignant lament over the seemingly prosaic theme of emigration. The rural areas see an annual pilgrimage of thousands of young Irishmen to the cities, to America, or, most often, to Britain. In cold statistics, this situation would scarcely seem a promising theme for drama, but in *The Wood of the Whispering* and other plays Michael J. Molloy had already proven how poignantly dramatic it could be. Certainly little else in his own experience has given Keane so much personal anguish as his own exile in England, and this play is a bitterly moving plaint directed against the circumstances that force many young men of twenty to leave their country. The emigration problem is dramatized in many ways in the play, but nowhere more effectively than in Dawheen Timmineen Din who is summed up by the inimitable Danger Mullaly as: "Mountainy farmer, chickens twenty, cows six, dogs two, wife one. Misery. . . . Sons numerous. Daughters too. All departed. House of grumblin'. House of arguein'. Dawheen Timmineen Din!" Every year Dawheen brings one or two of his children down to the village to send off to England. He cautions them, on the one hand, to beware of "doxies with dyed heads cockin' their dresses high in the air, an' exposin' fair amounts o' thigh to entice the innocent young gorsoons"; but, on the other hand, he reminds them to send home a fiver a week. Both sons, especially Dinny, the younger, are distraught at leaving, and when they come back for a visit a year later Dinny is considerably changed for the worse.

The play is more than a lament; it is also a biting condemnation of the conditions that cause emigration. It criticizes greed for money, religious prudery, and the time-serving, pork-barreling, hypocritical politician. This seems a scattering of shots, but each is on target. At the end of the play, most of the sympathetic characters pack up and march off to the boat. Only Peg Finnerty, the barmaid ostracized because of her illegitimate child, and Maurice Browne, the unfrocked schoolmaster, stay to make a fight of it in Ireland. The play offers no solution to a complex problem, but its indictment is blisteringly accurate.

The characterization is excellent, particularly the tattered old vendor of holy pictures, Danger Mullaly, who is one of the most actable characters in the recent Irish drama. Here is his first speech on entering the pub in the morning:

(*To no one in particular*) "Oh, rise up, Mikey Houlihan, that brave and dauntless boy . . ." Mikey Houlihan! Mikey Boloney! Shot by accident for Ireland. Twenty-four of his relations drawing State pensions and twenty-four more in Government jobs, and here am I, Danger Mullaly, with my box full of holy pictures an' short fourpence on the price o' the pint. (*Changes his tone to intimacy.*) 'Tis frightful quiet, Peg Finnerty, for a mornin' before the train. 'Tis frightful quiet, Tom Hannigan. (*Puts his box on the table*.) That's the lookin' they have at me! You'd swear I was the solicitor that advised Pontius Pilate . . . (*Changes tone*) Tom Hannigan, as sure as there's brown bastards in China, I'll pay you the extra fourpence . . . here's a shillin' on the table, a silver shillin', made an' manufactured by tradesmen that had a feelin' for beauty . . . proposed, passed and seconded herewith . . . one pint of Guinness for a sick man . . . balance to be paid in due course on the word of Danger Mullaly, guilty but insane. . . .

Danger would be an actor's dream, for Keane has given him a superabundance of extended and magnificent speeches. His speech that begins, "Hang the poor! Damn the poor!" is too long to quote, but it has a fervor comparable to some great speeches from Shaw. Such rhetoric, when allied to vivid dances, songs, and jokes, makes this play a triumphant piece of theatre, fit to rank with *The Hostage*.

🙹

No More in Dust is unpublished, and my remarks are therefore based on my memory of the 1961 Theatre Festival production. The play is set in Dublin and tells of the plight of two country girls sent by their families to the city to make a living. The play might have been called *Many Young Women of Twenty*, for Keane criticizes the parents who push such young girls away from home and throw them on their own resources in the city. The two girls, living in their seedy Leeson Street flat, seem the best women Keane has drawn. One falls in love with and then is deserted by a Kerryman, and this is the main action of the play. A couple of scenes are enlivened by two Beatnik types from Trinity College, and Keane gets considerable sad strength from his stricken heroine. It is not one of Keane's best, but it is both funny and moving.

The Man from Clare is also minor Keane, but its theme is quite relevant to Ireland and has not, to my knowledge, been treated by any other playwright. Padraic O'Dea has been for years a great football player from the town of Cuas in County Clare. Football has been such an absorbing passion that Padraic has really remained a boy in a man's body. After his body lets him down in the big annual match against Bealabawn, he begins to grow toward maturity. The deification of sport, like the passions for drinking and betting, is a major social problem in Ireland, perhaps arising from an economic system that still keeps many people from marrying until rather late. Basically, however, the play is about maturity and should be relevant anywhere. The characters lack the fascinating grotesquerie of those in the first plays, but they are quietly believable. The play has much less vitality than the first two plays or the musical, though it is a sound and persuasive job.

Hut 42, first produced at the Abbey on November 12, 1962, is a drama of Irish laborers in England. About the same comment can be made of it as of *The Man from Clare*: it is minor Keane, but has a relevant theme treated from an original angle. It has also the usual Keane excellencies — some finely theatrical songs, strong characterizations, and trenchant speeches. However, the quality that makes it memorable among a host of other minor realistic plays is its intensity of feeling. No modern Irishman has written more bitterly or more movingly about exile than Keane, and some of that writing appears in *Hut 42*.

Keane's best recent work is *The Year of the Hiker*, which is a kind of rural *Home is the Hero*. The Hiker Lacey is an almost legendary character who deserted his wife and family twenty years ago to go on his wanderings, and who now, a subdued and battered old man, returns home to die. His children regard his return with disgust, irritation, and aversion. Their father seems to them a dirty, stupid, and repulsive stranger.

There are several recurring motifs in Irish drama — greed for land and money, the made marriage, emigration, criticism of the clergy, and criticism of the father. In innumerable plays, ever since Christy Mahon attacked his da with a loy, this criticism of the father appears. Sometimes the father is a wastrel like Captain Boyle or a criminal like Macken's Paddo Reilly or obsessed with money and social status like D'Alton's Tom Mannion or obsessed with religion like Gerard Healy's "Thy Dear Father" or an old political man who has debased his ideals like Macken's Dacey Adam in *Twilight of a Warrior*. Or sometimes, as in Murphy's *The Country Boy*, the father is the voice of an unyielding past. In that play and in Keane's, there is a reconciliation with the father. In *The Country Boy*, the father compromises with the present, but in *The Year of the Hiker* the father throws himself for mercy upon the present. The play seems particularly valuable because of the struggle in the minds of the children. Simey Lacey, the younger son, is on his way to becoming a successful veterinarian, and the Hiker is a reminder of a past that a successful bourgeois would like to forget. He can never forgive his father, but he can never forget him either. The older son, Joe, beats the father when he comes home, but is finally able to extend sympathy and even love. Whether consciously or not, Keane seems to me to have written for

his own countrymen a parable that cuts deeply into the national consciousness.

⌘

I do not know *The Roses of Tralee*, but Keane's most recent drama,
however, is the powerful and popular *The Field*, which was first produced at the Olympia Theatre, Dublin, by Gemini Productions on November 1, 1965. It might profitably be compared to George Shiels's *The
Rugged Path* and its sequel *The Summit*. The themes and situations of
both the Keane and Shiels plays are similar — a dispute over land and
money initiates the action, and there follows a murder by a bullying
Irishman who intimidates his neighbors against informing. The endings
and the tones of the plays differ strongly, though. In Shiels, the neighbors do inform and justice is done even though a dour criticism of the
Irish character lingers after. In Keane, the neighbors do not inform, justice is not done, and the criticism of the Irish character is savage.

But Keane is also understanding; his anger does not turn his characters
into monsters. The countrymen who wander into Mick Flanagan's pub
are real people — easy, gregarious, droll, and all the more frightening and
believable because of their anachronistic reaction to the modern world.
This is a depressing play, but an honest one. For instance, when the priest
and the Garda sergeant are attacking the murderer, "The Bull" McCabe,
at the end of the play, "The Bull" replies:

I'm no bigger a twister than the two of you. Your Bishop spoke about
Christ last Sunday. Well, Christ had no Guards uniform and He had no
white collar around His neck. But He picked a gang of small farmers and
poachers. They had no outfits, no hangers or black clothes to protect
them. They had their cross, like all poor people, and that held them together. If a poor man does something wrong he gets a Guard's baton on
the poll and he's lugged up to the Barracks. But, if 'tis the doctor or the
school master or the lawman, they say 'tis tough and there's a way out
and the law is law no more. . . . There's two laws. There's a law for
them that's priests and doctors and lawmen. But there's no law for us.
. . . When you'll be gone, Father, to be a Canon somewhere, and the
Sergeant gets a wallet of notes and is going to be a Superintendent,
Tadhg's children will be milkin' cows and keepin' donkeys away from
our ditches. That's what we have to think about and if there's no grass,
there's the end of me and mine.

In other words, two moralities govern people's lives; the practical real
morality of ordinary people governed by self-interest and self-preserva-

tion is more basic and powerful than legislated codes or ten commandments. This is an unusual view for the stage, a fact that gives a startling persuasiveness to the play.

❦

Although I am not sure how meaningful it is, Keane's plays might be divided into three groups: first, the folk or country plays like *Sive, Sharon's Grave*, and *The Year of the Hiker*, which most show the influence of Molloy; second, plays of modern life like *No More in Dust, Hut 42*, or *The Man from Clare*; third, the musicals like *Many Young Men of Twenty* and *The Roses of Tralee*. This may be an arbitrary division; for Keane is still young and developing. This much, however, is certain: the songs, the colorful vigor of characters and dialogue, the bold symbolism in some plays, and the boldly treated themes in all strain the boundaries of realism to bursting. The Dublin critics have often charged that Keane's plays are melodramatic. They are, for life in Kerry is still melodramatic. Melodrama is their value and their strength.

The Outsiders

O UTSIDERS" sounds like a term of faint or no praise. By it I mean only that the writers discussed here have stood a bit outside the literary and theatrical establishments. They have not been notably connected with a particular theatre. Some of them have not written many plays, and some have not had very good luck. All, however, have done some first-rate work, and any history of modern Irish drama would be incomplete without an account of them.

Seamus de Burca is the Irish pen name of Jimmy Bourke, who belongs to one of Ireland's distinguished families. His uncle Peadar Kearney, whose biography he wrote, is the author of the national anthem, and his cousins are the Behan brothers. His father, P. J. Bourke, was manager at one time of the Queen's Theatre and a writer of Boucicaultian melodramas. P. J. Bourke also started the flourishing play-costuming business which his sons now run in conjunction with a myriad of other theatrical enterprises throughout the country.

Seamus de Burca himself was born on March 16, 1912. He attended King's Inn Street Convent and after that the St. Peter's National School at Phibsboro until he was fourteen. He then went to work in the Queen's as property man, scene-painter, and film projectionist. While running the film projector, he worked his way through the plays of Shakespeare. "I wasn't," he remarked, "in an operating box, I was in Paradise."

From his youth he was steeped in the theatre and has worked consistently at playwriting. Much of his early work is negligible, and he has been a long time in the ripening. Even yet he has little reputation as a playwright in Dublin, despite the fine character-drawing in his recent work. The reason may partly be that the Bourke name has for two generations been closely wedded to popular entertainment — first to the Queen's, Boucicault, and Whitbread, and then to variety and the management of ballrooms and cinemas. Possibly the reason may partly be that Dublin does not yet realize the great difference between his early work and his late.

The Boys and Girls Are Gone was his first really good play. Originally performed in 1950 under the title of *Margaret Nowlan*, it was revived at the Gate on April 25, 1961. It has been popular among amateurs, for the author in the second edition remarked that the piece had sold two thousand copies. The time of the play is 1910, the place is a townland near Drogheda, the situation is the familiar one of the made marriage, and the dominating motive is greed for money and land. This situation and this motive have been staples of Irish realistic drama from William Boyle to John B. Keane, but Bourke infuses some vitality into them mainly through the strongly drawn widow Margaret Nowlan. Her greed and snobbishness have driven one daughter away to a life of hard labor and poverty in America, but she is well repaid now when her youngest son runs away to England with the girl of his choice. She is a hard woman, but not a monster, and the role offers some good opportunities.

On October 30, 1944, his play *Knocknagow; or, The Homes of Tipperary* was produced at the Olympia, directed by his brother Lorcan and having in the cast such well-known actors as Maureen Delany, W. O'Gorman, John Stephenson, and Jack Cruise. The play dramatized Kickham's novel and harked back in its manner to Boucicault. Like the plays of Boucicault, *Knocknagow* really belongs more in the theatre than in the pages of a book. It is hardly literature, though it has enough theatrical vitality to entertain its audience as much as did the plays of the dapper Dion himself. *Knocknagow* is an anachronism in the modern Irish drama, but a pleasant one.

Limpid River was produced at the Gate on June 11, 1956, later made into a novel, and still later revised as a play. It is set in the Dublin of 1919, and is a lovingly re-created family play which opens shortly after the death of Dolphin Jordan's wife Josephine, a local singer. The plot is ambling, but that probably is one excellence of the piece which so finely catches the atmosphere of middle-class Dublin. The characters are minutely observed, warmly human, and highly playable. Particularly delightful is the deceased wife's stepmother, Mrs. Dillon from the country, a cheery and indomitable old soul who has been to America twice, is working on her third husband, and carries her own mattress about on her travels. There is also the ripely comic part of a Queen's Theatre actor of the old school, E. J. Mackey. Mackey is an elderly sponger with a vast capacity for drink and a dash and swagger that almost overcome his hopelessly seedy appearance. It is a show-stopping part, and Bourke gives him some superb arias. Here he is on acting:

The Abbey has done the legitimate stage a lot of harm. They have pinched some of our best actors and turned them into drawing room puppets. What they call natural acting — as if any actor was natural! If they were, they wouldn't be on the stage. Just imagine talking on the stage as you and I are talking now — ridiculous! (*He is actually bellowing his head off.*) The fellow up there in the gods must hear you — no use in playing to the critic in the first row of the stalls.

And here he is on Synge's *Playboy* and other matters:

Could you compare it to a full blooded melodrama like *The Face at the Window* or *The Strangler of Paris*? An audience must be shown the ship tossing on the waves — there is no use in just telling them that someone was drowned. I knew a fellow who used to plunge into a tank of water night after night in *The Colleen Bawn* to save the heroine. He was only an amateur, mind you, but it was his glory to deputise for the actor playing Myles. Nowadays we have to pay amateurs — it is the curse of the profession. . . .

The Howards was first performed at the Gate on February 16, 1959, under the title of *Mrs. Howard's Husband*. Margaret Howard is, as Behan put it in his introduction, "a bit of a bitch." She is Margaret Nowlan grown twice as ruthless and amoral. She believes in appearances as did Margaret, but is a thorough trickster of a businesswoman who has even arranged to burn her factory down and then to wangle more than its worth from the insurance company. She is the kind of cold, hard character you expect to find in a play like *The Miser* or *Volpone*. She has driven her husband away to sea; she has inherited all her father's money, pays her older sister to come in as a scullery maid and offers her stale bread to take home; she countenances her older daughter's running away from her family and taking up with a well-to-do man, but snobbishly refuses to let the younger daughter marry a poor man.

Predictably, Mr. Howard is pallid beside her, and Bourke does not make him more sympathetic by having him get two sailor friends to beat up his daughter's lover instead of doing it himself. But some of the minor characters are excellent. The brainless shopgirl Dolores, the bitchy older daughter Madeleine, and Mrs. Howard's sister Gretta O'Neill are as memorable a trio of minor female characters as are likely to be found in any recent Irish play. Consider, for instance, the startling effect of this dialogue between Mrs. Howard, Gretta, and Madeleine:

> MISS O'NEILL: It's a quare house you have, Margaret . . . not that I'd be sayin' anything. I beg your pardon, ma'am. I must learn to know me place, mustn't I? Still if anyone did hear me calling you by your Christian name . . . we ARE old friends, aren't we? We might even have gone to the same school.
>
> MADELEINE (*Bursts out of the door back. Shouts*): O'Neill, where the hell did you get yourself to . . .?
>
> MISS O'NEILL: I'm doing it as quickly as I can, dearie.
>
> MADELEINE (*Seeing her mother, hesitates*): Hello, ma. Be careful with that petticoat . . . Christ, look what you're doing. You bloody old cow . . .
>
> MRS. HOWARD (*Rises authoritatively*): Madeleine, behave yourself.
>
> MADELEINE: Mother, will you sit there and hear that cow speak to me like that.
>
> MRS. HOWARD (*To audience*): Christ preserve my patience!

It is not only the savagery of Madeleine that makes the scene strong, but also the implication about how conventional values have been totally upended. This is one of the most vicious family plays to come out of Ireland, and all the more startling because it lacks melodramatic horrors. Indeed, it is a curiously entertaining play, through which jokes, songs, and wry asides to the audience are liberally sprinkled. To that extent, it seems rather like Brendan Behan's own technique, but it is more re-strained and more horrible in tone.

In her short introduction to *The Boys and Girls Are Gone*, Lady Longford wrote, "Seamus de Burca is a man of the theatre, if ever there was one. He has lived in the theatre and knows it inside out. So it follows that he has an ear for dialogue and an eye for good scenes, and knows how to give opportunities to actors." In *Limpid River* and *The Howards*, he is more than a man of the theatre; he is an artist.

⚜

With equal justice, Gerard Healy could be called a man of the theatre. When he died on March 9, 1963, at the age of forty-five, he was in London, playing the role of the Jesuit in Leonard's *Stephen D.* He was born in Dublin, educated at the Synge Street Christian Brothers School, and worked for a time after school in a Dublin drapery store. He joined the Edwards–Mac Liammóir company as assistant stage manager and toured with the group to the Balkans and to Egypt. While with the Gate, he met his wife, the good actress Eithne Dunne, and played in several of the theatre's productions before moving to the Abbey for five years. For the Abbey he wrote *Thy Dear Father*, which has been several times revived. His other play, *The Black Stranger*, he produced for the short-lived Players' Theatre, which he helped to found in 1945. Illness removed him temporarily from the stage, and he wrote radio notes for the *Irish Times*, became a member of the Radio Éireann Repertory Company, and wrote many radio scripts and documentaries. He was also one of Austin Clarke's verse-speaking team on Radio Éireann. When asked why he did not write more plays, he replied, "I cannot satisfy myself . . . Playwriting is an art. I'm afraid my work is purely ephemeral."

Thy Dear Father, first presented at the Abbey on August 30, 1943, is worth mentioning for its criticism of hyper-religiosity. The dead father of the Dooley family was fanatically religious, and his contributions to charity have put the family grocery so far in debt that the younger son Jack cannot save it. The whole family has been affected by the father. The mother is a nagging critic of Jack and devoted to the externals of religion. The older girl is a nun, the older boy a priest, and the younger girl so foolishly religious that she wants to found an order of nuns. His milieu has so convinced Jack of his guilt and sinfulness that the loss of the grocery is the final push over the brink into madness.

Healy is not condemning religion, but rather the abuse of it. The older brother and his friend Father Tahaney are sensible priests who see the harm that has been done and who try to combat it. The play has some tense moments — as when Jack violently repulses his fiancée, calling her a whore and fleeing from the temptation of sex. It also has some limp ones: Jack's growth to madness is more theatrically than psychologically persuasive. The play is not drawn in great depth, but it grapples honestly with a still delicate problem. It is the kind of play which, though not memorable in itself, says clearly something that should be said.

The Black Stranger was first put on by the Players' Theatre at the Opera House, Cork, on February 26, 1945, and then at the Gate in Dublin on March 6, 1945. The piece is set during the potato famine, and is the story of the suffering and destruction of two families. Like *Thy*

Dear Father, it is not at all experimental, but a leanly written, tightly structured piece of realism. In several places — particularly the death of the mother and the revelation of Bridie's prostitution in order to gain food — it is especially moving. The first-act curtain with Sean the Fool prophesying is a bit contrived, but most of the play seems persuasively real. For instance, here is the ending, when Bart returns home after having meant to sail for America with the last of the family:

BRIDIE: So you didn't go after all, Bart?
BART: No.
BRIDIE: Why not?
BART: I don't know. I just came back.

This ending, so underplayed and stripped of "theatre," is most canny; by this time the pageant of suffering has so worn down the audience that very little emotion other than a bleak and gutted sadness could be drawn from them. The simplicity of the ending, so typical of Healy's two plays, shows what force can be derived sometimes from flat statement.

Maurice Meldon died at an even earlier age than Gerard Healy, at thirty-two following a fall from his bicycle in a traffic accident. However, many canny Dubliners already regarded him as "the most exciting new voice in the Irish theatre." Born in Dublin, he was educated at St. Mary's College in Dundalk, and became a civil servant attached to the Department of Defence. He was married and had two children.

He first came to notice when his play *Song of the Parakeet* won a Radio Éireann competition in 1950. In 1951 the Abbey produced his *House under Green Shadows*, and the *Evening Herald* selected it as the best play of the year. *The Halcyon Horseman* was accepted but never produced by the Abbey; Hugh Leonard described it as "a satirical romp among the Fianna." Meldon's last productions were by the 37 Theatre Club which did *Aisling* and *The Purple Path to the Poppy Field*. His last play, *No Moon for the Hunter*, a version of the Diarmuid and Grania story, was rejected by the Abbey. Leonard thought him "probably our most neglected author." Although apparently not embittered by many rebuffs, he was not writing at all at the end of his life on November 12, 1958.

Three of Meldon's plays have been published. *House under Green Shadows* is another play depicting the decline of the Big Houses. Tullakeeven House in 1949 is a decrepit country residence peopled by the elderly Edward Carten and his sister Florence. Even by selling property bit by bit, Edward has been unable to arrest the creeping decay. That decay is apparent also in his and his sister's character. They have both regressed from the cultivated ideals of their ancestors. Edward is trying to send Florence to an insane asylum, and Florence is trying to bring on a heart attack for Edward. There are some intense passages between them, but the other characters are only stock types and much of the exposition is stilted and stagey. Despite two interesting main roles, the piece is a rather awkward and overwrought melodrama.

Aisling, which means the vision, is subtitled "A Dream Analysis"; it is a wryly Expressionistic treatment of recent Irish history, reminiscent of *The Old Lady Says "No!"* in technique. It is the kind of play that the recent Abbey would not and probably could not do. The Gate in its heyday might have taken it on, but in 1953, on April 4, it was produced by Barry Cassin and Nora Lever at the 37 Theatre Club. In a prefatory note, Meldon confesses his indebtedness to "Shaw, O'Casey, Synge, Johnston, Gregory, Chekhov, Ibsen, Strindberg, O'Neill, and Longford," but actually the play is no eclectic ragbag. Captain Boyle of *Juno* appears briefly, and there are passages in the style of the early Yeats as well as reminiscences of Lady Gregory and Synge; but in general Meldon has assimilated his influences, and the play is clearly in his voice.

The first act is a stylized parable taking place during the Troubles. A British general auctions off a young girl named Caithlin Maeve Emer Grania Ni Houlihan to the highest bidder. Some gunmen attempt to rescue her, one is killed, and in the hurlyburly she escapes. The satiric point is unmistakable and is particularly stressed in the scene between the clergyman and the general. The clergyman protests selling the girl, but when the general mentions "that a sizeable contribution to your Church Fund might help to redress the sordid element in the transaction" the clergyman is all acquiescence.

In Act II, depicting the Civil War and afterwards, the girl is on the road, where she meets a young man, Donal Ryan, who has left his farm because "there came rumours of the fighting in the town and that the queen of Ireland was set free at last, but that she was in hiding in the Hills or wandering the roads in fear because the Saxon yeomanry were out in hot pursuit of her." Not finding the queen, he has begun to doubt; the girl restores his faith by speaking of her people and their land:

227

Four green fields they had, each of them stretching out as far as the eye could see and well beyond. And all around, you'd hear the whisperings of the sea on grey shore and golden sand . . . Out of the long grass of the meadows, into the bright blue sky of the morning, the larks would go soaring up and up.

Donal then goes off and is shot, and the girl next meets the best character of the play, a flamboyant poet named Padraigeen Mullarkey, who falls in love with her. We then see some of the soldiers of Act I who have now retired and returned to Ireland to buy up some estates. Finally Padraigeen and Caithlin flee from the parish priest who wants someone to make an honest woman of the girl. That act ends with the pair retreating into the past; and the last act is taken up with scenes from her past.

The first scene is laid in an O'Caseyish pub; in the next Yeatsian scene Padraigeen plays Cuchullain and Caithlin Emer; in the next, best scene he plays Diarmuid and she Grania; in the final scene he is Ailill and she Maeve. Then the play returns to the present; Caithlin is again auctioned off, this time by her present guardians, the local County Council. When Padraigeen is outbid, Caithlin says, "A brave man might snatch me away out of this — the way brave men did before," and Padraigeen replies in a speech of superb sadness:

When we're young, talk is cheap. But, I haven't the build of a hero nor even the mental approach of a doer of deeds. Fighting is only for strong men or for fools. Myself, I'm no fool . . . No, that isn't the journey for me . . . D'you know what I'll do? I'll go on my way out of this and my heart will be pierced with the sorrow of parting from you. It's a sorrow I'll keep to the grave. In the morning I'll feel it. At noon and at night it'll haunt me. I'll waste to a shadow with thinking of you. And I'll not know a joy but the breeding of sorrowful thoughts and telling the tale of my woe to the world till the last breath of life is knocking in pain to be free.

He leaves, the auction continues, and the play ends. *Aisling* is without a doubt one of the most moving, experimental, and accomplished plays to come out of Ireland. There has been nothing like it since Denis Johnston was a young man. It is as theatrical a mixture of satire and poignance and fantasy as one can find outside of O'Casey.

The Purple Path to the Poppy Field, subtitled "A New Legend," was first produced at the 37 Theatre Club on September 24, 1953. It is a longish one-act in eight scenes which, despite an auctorial disclaimer, is a trenchant symbolic satire on many of the evils of modern Ireland.

The scene takes place on a sparsely populated island, most of whose people are old or dying. The people are superstitious in the extreme, their island depends upon poteen for its economy, and it has little touch with the outside world. Its only young people are a boy and a girl, and the boy is usually ignored as negligible. However, when by accident he is blown up by one of his dead brother's hand grenades, his death is the occasion of wild rejoicing and of his canonization as a hero — even though his death means the decimation of the race.

The theme of this snarling little parable is that the Irish have had a mad regard for tradition, sometimes even a violent and stupid tradition. Perhaps the black satire might be summed up by this prayer of the villagers:

> DATHI: . . . But we who honor the Daghda know how futile are the works of mortal men and we recall a tale was told of fools who thought to raise a tower against the sky in ancient Babylon . . . Now, let us pray: O Lord, Prince of the Universe and the Sun, we give thee thanks —
> VOICES: We give thee thanks —
> DATHI: For making us what we are —
> VOICES: For making us what we are —
> DATHI: For giving us our immortal past —
> VOICES: For giving us our immortal past —
> DATHI: For providing the present in which to contemplate it —
> VOICES: For providing the present in which to contemplate it —
> DATHI: And for withholding the future for the enlargement of that contemplation.

In Meldon, the Irish theatre lost the boldest experimental talent it had seen in twenty years; it lost a symbolist, a satirist, and an allegorist, a tragi-comic writer capable of wit and poignance, a potential master.

※

At least passing notice should be given to Seamus O'Neill's *The Secret of the Island*, a realistic detective story and one of the few tolerable recent plays originally written in Gaelic. The County Waterford plays of James Cheasty are also of some interest. The best is *The Lost Years*, a strong study of the farming middle class. His other work, such as *A Stranger Came* and *Francey*, seem only pale variations of *Juno and the Paycock*. They show no progression, and their imitativeness hardly fulfills the promise of his occasional real strength.

※

J. P. Donleavy is no Irishman, and his play *The Ginger Man* ran only three nights in Dublin; no account of the Irish drama would be complete without him, however. He is an American who went to Trinity College on the G.I. bill and wrote one of the brashest and vulgarest novels about modern Ireland. That novel, *The Ginger Man*, on which the play is based, is the story of Sebastian Dangerfield, a young American also struggling through Trinity. Both novel and play have some striking resemblances to John Osborne's *Look Back in Anger*. In both the hero is an irritated young man whose tirades against the world seem out of proportion to his own injuries. Both heroes are married, each has a disreputable chum, and each seduces an acquaintance of his wife. And both plays have an indisputable vigor of language.

The play Donleavy extracted from the novel has not suffered in the transformation. It is faithful to the original and strong in its own right. Part of the strength comes from the shock value of its content, but part from how it is said. Although there are no extended tirades as in Osborne, there is some magnificently racy speech — so much that one may almost pick at random. Here, for instance, is Dangerfield's unwillingly celibate friend O'Keefe on an unsuccessful seduction:

Even this winter down in Connemara visiting the old folks, my retarded cousin who looked like a cow wouldn't even come across. I'd wait for her to go out and get the milk at night and go with her. At the end of the field I'd try to nudge her into the ditch. I'd get her all breathless and saying she'd do anything if I'd take her to the States and marry her. I tried that for three nights running, standing out there in the rain up to our ankles in mud and cow flop, me trying to get her in the ditch, knock her down, but she was too strong. So I told her she was a zombie and I wouldn't take her to East Jesus. Have to get them a visa before you can touch an arm.

Predictably, the play ran into opposition in Dublin. The reviews ranged from the mildly appreciative comment of the *Irish Times* to the outraged note in the *Irish Independent* that it was "one of the most nauseating plays ever to appear on a Dublin stage," accompanied by the curt suggestion that it be instantly withdrawn. Dublin has no official theatre censorship, but it can exert a great deal of unofficial pressure. In this case, Archbishop McQuaid sent his secretary to Louis Elliman, manager of the Gaiety, and the play was removed.

One cannot entirely defend the morality of *The Ginger Man* — and I am not talking about the language or about Dangerfield's seduction of the memorable Miss Frost. I refer rather to his long scream of anguish because he is a man; it is this spinelessness that hurts both book and play. Of course that issue was never the point in Dublin.

Still, Dangerfield is such a vigorous character and the whole play is so theatrical that it almost overcomes the built-in danger of the hero's puerility. When plays of such abounding talent are rushed off a stage, it is difficult for a free and vigorous drama to grow. With all its faults of philosophic adolescence, *The Ginger Man* has force and insight and passion. O'Keefe and Dangerfield in their savage love affair with Ireland sound, as did Swift and Joyce, an authentic note of exacerbation; and Donleavy gets Dublin just as excellently as do Michael Campbell and Honor Tracy in their fiction.

IV THE OLD MAN SAYS "YES!"

12

In Sean O'Casey's Golden Days

Ah, them were th' golden days with an arm round a waist,
When everything shone so shy an' gay;
When a man had heart to toss the girl as well as time to toss th' hay —
Oh, them were th' days when life had something fine to say!
                    Codger Sleehaun in *The Bishop's Bonfire*

IT IS a quaint irony that the commanding figure in the Irish
drama of the last forty years has been Sean O'Casey, for the
man hardly set foot in the country during all that time. He
did, from his nest in Devon, send a steady stream of crusty advice and
caustic criticism flowing across the Irish Sea, but such criticism — no
matter how apt — from a vigorously anti-clerical Communist was hardly
what his countrymen would relish.

However, there were the early plays — *The Shadow of a Gunman*,
Juno and the Paycock, and *The Plough and the Stars*. They were an ir-
refutable fact. They tenaciously retained their popularity, and each succeeding year made them look more and more like unqualified masterpieces and classics of the Irish drama. Perhaps, then, the only ploy the
Irish had was to disassociate the early work from the aging dramatist, and
that was precisely what they did. They reiterated *ad nauseam* that
O'Casey knew nothing about the new Ireland, that he was growing splenetic, eccentric, and senile, and that each new play was a frightful falling
off from the previous one. And it was not only sycophantic journalists
and intellectual clerics who raised their voices, but also many of O'Casey's
distinguished colleagues: Liam O'Flaherty, Daniel Corkery, F. R. Hig-

gins, T. C. Murray, Brinsley MacNamara, Austin Clarke, Denis Johnston, Sean O'Faolain, and Seamus Byrne all keened a woeful chorus or two.

Naturally, with such opposition O'Casey's later plays fared poorly in Ireland, and most were never even staged. The Abbey's belated staging of *The Silver Tassie* in 1935 caused a resounding furor in the Catholic press and occasioned Brinsley MacNamara's violent resignation from the Abbey Board. Shelagh Richards's production of *Red Roses for Me* a decade later ignited the peculiar psychological reaction and voluble aesthetic dismay of Gabriel Fallon, a journalist. The Cyril Cusack premiere of *The Bishop's Bonfire* in 1955 charmed visiting English critics, but only added oil to the flaming ire of their Irish counterparts. The shabby treatment of *The Drums of Father Ned* caused O'Casey to ban further professional productions of his plays in Ireland and even to ask his publishers to send no more of his books there for review. There were many complaints about the ban (which since O'Casey's death has been relaxed), but the old man's desire to avoid further vehement harassment from across the Irish Sea is understandable. The wisdom of his course is probably proved by the Irish review of *Behind the Green Curtains*, his last volume of plays. Apparently one review copy slipped through to the *Kilkenny Magazine*. The editor, with exquisite inappropriateness, sent it off to Gabriel Fallon, who charged that O'Casey was an egotistic pornographer attempting to incite Ireland to civil war!

In less rabid moments, the Irish critics contend that the later plays are the formless dodderings of a senile old man who had long ago lost touch with both Ireland and the theatre. As so many of the later plays have already proved themselves in the theatre, this view seems too perverse to refute. It is, however, important to decide why the later plays are good, and that brings up the question of whether they have some definite form. O'Casey thought they did, and remarked: "if critics . . . were lads of judgment and sense, they would never have criticized the play, THE BISHOP'S BONFIRE, by comparing it with the earlier plays; for this play is of another method and manner, a different genre. They should have compared it with the play that went before which is of the same method, manner, and the same genre: the play called *Cock-a-Doodle Dandy*." [1] The question of genre is often an academic quibble and probably responsible for most of the erudite nonsense written about drama since Aristotle. But in this case the question seems hardly academic; and so I shall try to demonstrate the soundness of the later plays by showing that their form has been the historical one for a particular dramatic genre.

🖰

By now it seems clearly established that O'Casey's early masterpieces are not the shapeless confusions that the Irish critics of the 1920's thought, but the culmination of the form of tragi-comedy. The form of *The Plough* is essentially that of *The Cherry Orchard, The Lower Depths, Heartbreak House, The Iceman Cometh*, and many other masterpieces of the modern drama. Tragi-comedy, however, has been a slow-developing form that underwent many transformations before its modern emergence in the plays of Chekhov, Gorky, and O'Casey.

It is essential for our argument to note that one important step in the development of the form was the pastoral tragi-comedy of the sixteenth and seventeenth centuries in Italy, Spain, France, and England. The nondramatic tradition of the pastoral goes back much farther, to the idyls of Theocritus, Bion, and Moschus; and its development may be traced through Vergil, Dante, Petrarch, Boccaccio, Mantuanus, Spenser, Sidney, Milton, Pope, and probably up to Robert Frost in our own day. The pastoral tradition in the drama was formed largely by two plays, Tasso's *Aminta* (1581) and Guarini's *Pastor Fido* (1590). In Renaissance England, the pastoral was more influential in nondramatic works like Spenser's *Shepherd's Calendar* and Sidney's *Arcadia*, but there were a few pastoral tragi-comedies, and many other plays were somewhat influenced by the form.[2] Peele, Lyly, and Samuel Daniel did notable work in the dramatic pastoral, paving the way for the masterpieces of Jonson, Fletcher, and Thomas Randolph. The pastoral tragi-comedy could not, however, compete with the vitality of the romantic drama, and by the middle of the seventeenth century, pastoral tragi-comedy had almost ceased to be written. In nondramatic forms, especially lyric poetry, the pastoral has been continuously influential. In our day, this influence has been brilliantly, if not always convincingly, traced in William Empson's *Some Versions of Pastoral*. It is my point that the later plays of O'Casey are also, in Empson's loose use of the phrase, versions of pastoral; and, indeed, they are probably closer versions than most of the material discussed in Empson's book.

From Tasso, Guarini, and their chief English imitators, we may distinguish several characteristics of pastoral drama that seem fairly constant. First, it represents a Golden Age. This Golden Age has given the pastoral both its significance and its reputation for frivolity. Arcadia is a rural Utopia, a Garden of Eden, a Watteau landscape in which idealized swains, dainty shepherdesses, and improbably fleecy sheep love, loll, and gambol through meadows whose green never fades, and by the marges of purling brooks never sullied by mud. This never-never land is usually regarded as either charming or silly, depending on one's cast of mind. But both idealist and realist probably have at the back of their minds a picture of the ladies of the French court toying with their garlanded shepherd's crooks as the nation leapt toward revolution. There is a real tendency to take the pastoral as perhaps delightful, but never revealing — to take it as entertainment rather than as art. However, C. G. Thayer soundly remarks that the Pastoral

. . . very often involves something much more serious than shearing clean sheep to the sound of well-tuned oaten reeds in or near a bower of roses. If an ideal world is essentially unreal (as it is certainly unrealistic), this by no means deprives it of significance for the lives of real men in a real world. Colin Clout is a shepherd, and as such he is a singer; but his songs are about politics, religion, and art, as well as about sheep and unrequited love.[3]

It is not a hackneyed and outworn literary form which probably never had much to say. "Rather," remarks Walter W. Greg, "is its importance to be sought in the fact that the form is the expression of instincts and impulses deep-rooted in the nature of humanity."[4] The ideal world of the pastoral is always an implicit and sometimes an overt criticism of reality, and this contrast gives it relevance and strength.

This contrast between a Golden Age and the modern reality forms the basic conflict of the later O'Casey plays. Unlike earlier writers of pastoral, O'Casey never brings his Golden Age entirely onstage. It is in the process either of dying or of being born. The O'Caseyan Golden Age is a vision of rural Ireland filled with golden lads and lasses full of vigor and love and life. This world comes into conflict with the debased present, the world of business, of hypocrisy, of religiosity. In some plays the Golden Age triumphs; in most it is defeated. In either case, the pastoral still, as Thayer remarked, "at its best, is superbly adapted by its stylized form to lead symbolically to the heart of human experience."[5]

Other characteristics of the pastoral tragi-comedy appear in O'Casey's late plays. The pastoral has a complicated love intrigue with several intertangled plots and at least two or three pairs of lovers. O'Casey had been accustomed to a complex plot in his early plays, but it is only in the late work that he really portrays more than one pair of lovers in a play.

Partly through the influence of Ovid, the pastoral was early in its career affected by the mythological and the supernatural. We see in O'Casey's later plays many instances of Irish myth, shadows of Greek myth, and examples of magic, including the usual pastoral devices of the transformation and the echo scene.

Chief among the characters of the pastoral are the chaste and coy nymph, the amorous nymph, the amorous or the sullen swain, the old shepherd or adviser, the satyr or villain, the country bumpkin or clown, and the magician or witch. Examples of each appear in O'Casey.

And, finally, there are so many parallels of diction and situation that I have not bothered to list the more tenuous.

卵

In *Purple Dust*, O'Casey depicts the efforts of two comic Englishmen to renovate a decrepit Tudor mansion and revive the pastoral life in the modern Irish countryside. The play does not attack the notion of a Golden Age but frivolous attempts to re-create one. O'Casey is saying that a Golden Age depends not upon shepherd's crooks and picturesque surroundings, but upon the honest hearts of honest men. Stokes and Poges are not honest men but businessmen; the real world for them is the world of finance. Poges is always ready to interrupt his make-believe idyl by a snappish call to his London broker. Because Stokes and Poges are not good and honest men, their view of the pastoral is foppish and absurd, and the tone of the play is broad farce.

We see immediately that this version of pastoral is silly when, early in Act I, Stokes, Poges, their mistresses, and two servants bolt onto the stage in a ridiculous parody of a country dance. Each is costumed in mock-pastoral fashion, and, as they dance, they sing an inane mock-pastoral ditty that goes in part:

> Rural scenes are now our joy;
> Farmer's boy,
> Milkmaid coy,
> Each like a newly-painted toy
> In the bosky countrie!

The body of the play shows, in a series of zany farcical situations, how the attempt to create a false pastoral is foiled — how the Englishmen are

239

frustrated, blarneyed, and cozened by the Irish, routed by cows and horses, and even defeated by the weather. Although the Irish clearly see the absurdity of Stokes and Poges, Ireland comes in for a few blistering criticisms. Canon Chreehewel tries to maintain his idea of a Golden Age by opposing dance halls, short skirts, and courting. However, as he remarks to Poges, "like Eden, sir, we've a snake in our garden too!" The snake is Jack O'Killigain, the foreman stonemason in charge of renovating the mansion. In O'Killigain and in Philib O'Dempsey, one of the workmen, O'Casey depicts his golden lads. O'Killigain has been wounded fighting for an ideal world in Spain, and O'Dempsey has visions of a Celtic Golden Age peopled with Irish heroes of legend and history. O'Casey makes it clear, however, that these two are a distinct minority in modern Ireland. Their visions are seen by most people "only as a little cloud o' purple dust blown before the wind." What is life in modern Ireland, O'Dempsey asks, "but a bitther noise of cadgin' mercy from heaven, an' a sour handlin' o' life for a cushion'd seat in a corner?" Still, the Golden Age wins a partial victory, for O'Dempsey gallops away with Poges's mistress, and O'Killigain carries the other away to his little house on the hill. Despite the gaiety and high spirits of the play, the theme is a sobering one. O'Casey's golden lads are rare figures in the modern world, and his golden lasses are a bit tarnished.

The play contains the principal pastoral elements. Its love plot, with two triangles, is sufficiently complicated. O'Killigain and O'Dempsey are the swains, Souhaun and Avril have some coy nymph scenes, and Stokes and Poges are the superannuated satyrs. There are rustic clowns and a good deal of song and poetry, some of it mock-serious and some of it quite charming. Hints of magic also appear. The Postmaster is a straightforward comic figure if we note only his dialogue, but the stage direction suggests something of the faun about him:

The room becomes darker. He [Poges] has hardly been writing a minute, when a curious face appears round the corner of the entrance leading to the hall. It is the stout little face of a little man dressed in neat black clothes covered with a saturated fawn-coloured mackintosh. Big spectacles cover his eyes. A huge fiery-red beard spreads over his chest like a breastplate, reaching to his belly, and extending out from his body like a fan turned downwards.

And later an even more magical figure appears: "He is dressed from head to foot in gleaming black oilskins, hooded over his head, just giving a glimpse of a blue mask, all illumined by the rays of flickering lightning, so that The Figure seems to look like the spirit of the turbulent waters of the river." This ominous figure can be taken realistically as a man, possibly a policeman, sent to warn the characters that the river is rising. He frightens them by his mere appearance, however, and the scene's foreboding tone suggests that something more than an ordinary man is meant here. It seems more than coincidental that river gods are frequent figures in pastoral literature. One speaks the prologue to *Pastor Fido*, and another is prominent in the best English pastoral tragi-comedy, Fletcher's *The Faithful Shepherdess*. O'Casey's meaning comes even clearer when we consider the flickering lightning that surrounds the Figure, for that lightning is alluded to again in O'Killigain's song as he rows away from the flooding house with Avril:

> Then away, love, away,
> Far away O!
> Where th' lightning of life flashes vivid we go,
> With a will an' a way, away O!

The Figure, then, embodies a Golden Age more vital, more hardy than the Walt Disney Arcadia imagined by Stokes and Poges. So in *Purple Dust*, O'Casey refuted the notion of the pastoral as a life of empty leisure, and developed at some length his own idea of the good life. In later plays, he developed that idea still further.

֍

Oak Leaves and Lavender is concerned mainly with the Second World War and thematically set apart from the other late plays. Even in it, however, we see a hint of O'Casey's preoccupation with the Golden Age — in the Prologue of Ghostly Dancers who symbolize the tradition of strength and civilization which is tested in the body of the play.

With *Cock-a-Doodle Dandy*, O'Casey returned fully to the pastoral. Indeed, many elements in the play remain enigmatic until we note their presence in earlier pastoral literature. One puzzling element is the suggestion of the Robin Hood legend in the characters of Marion the maid and Robin Adair the messenger. Of course, the many plays and poems about Robin Hood have a setting akin to the pastoral, but there seems small reason for the legend to be transposed to an Irish countryside which has more than its own share of native legends.

There are, however, two points — one tenuous, the other quite suggestive — which connect the Robin Hood story with the dramatic pastoral. The most pastoral of Shakespeare's plays is *As You Like It*, which is based partly on the old "Tale of Gamelyn," which is one of the Robin Hood cycle. The Robin Hood story is alluded to early in the play when Charles the wrestler remarks of the exiled Duke: "They say he is already in the forest of Arden, and a many merry men with him; and there they live like the old Robin Hood of England: they say many young gentlemen flock to him every day, and fleet the time carelessly, as they did in the golden age." Even more suggestive is Ben Jonson's delightful uncompleted play, *The Sad Shepherd*. Jonson fuses the Robin Hood legend with the traditional pastoral background. Robin, Marion, and the merry men appear with shepherds, shepherdesses, swineherds, a witch, and a Robin Goodfellow in the character of Puck-Hairy. The plots of the Jonson and O'Casey plays are, in a general sense, similar, both being chiefly concerned with false and true love. O'Casey's foolish satyr, Michael Marthraun, has cozened a young nymph, Lorna, into marrying him; Jonson's foolish satyr, Lorel, has captured a young nymph in a tree and attempts to woo her. Maudlin, the witch in Jonson, tries to destroy the ideal world, just as Michael Marthraun and Sailor Mahan do in O'Casey. In Jonson's play, however, it is the forces of evil that have supernatural powers, whereas in O'Casey's it is the forces of good. Jonson's witch Maudlin has a son named Lorel, which certainly resembles the name of O'Casey's witch, Loreleen. Maudlin and Loreleen are both able to take other shapes. Maudlin transforms herself into a beautiful girl and a crow. Loreleen, already a beautiful girl, is transformed into a cock, and perhaps also into a wild duck and a top hat.

The general similarity of the plots clarifies another puzzle in O'Casey's play. He has three heroines — Lorna, Loreleen, and Marion — which seems an inordinate number until we consider that one quality of the pastoral is its tragi-comic insistence on a number of plots. Jonson's play also boasts three heroines — Earine, Douce, and Marion.

The notable magical element in both plays emphasizes birds and bird songs. In Jonson, the presence of magical birds is sinister; in O'Casey, the magical bird is the symbol of life, vitality, and the Golden Age. In Act II, Scene 8 of Jonson's play, the sage Alken has a long speech about the sinister doings of witches. Part of it mentions "the shreikes of luckless Owles" and "croaking Night-Crowes in the aire" and "Blew firedrakes in the skie" and "giddie Flitter-mice, with lether wings." In Scene I of O'Casey's play, the false sage Shanaar has a similar long speech describing the doings of such demon birds as the cuckoo and the corncrake. Indeed, throughout O'Casey's play, we hear birdcalls and the beating of wings; and, of course, both Jonson's Maudlin and O'Casey's Loreleen are transformed into birds.[6]

The golden lads and tarnished lasses of *Cock-a-Doodle Dandy* have considerable fight in them; for a while the magical figure of the cock scatters all the crawthumpers before him, but finally the pastoral figures go down in defeat. The priest, Father Domineer, kills one of the peasant workmen. Loreleen is roughed up, and finally the three heroines go off to London, Robin Adair following. In this world, the pastoral is fighting a losing battle; the world is already a kind of Wasteland. Michael Marthraun's house is black, and the grass around is burnt yellow. One character calls it "this god-forsaken hole," and another says to Loreleen, "It isn't here you should be, lost among th' rough stones, th' twisty grass, an' th' moody misery of th' brown bog." As in *Purple Dust*, the golden lads and lasses retain their own indomitability, but in this play no healing river overwhelms the Wasteland world.

O'Casey's one-act *Time to Go* in its short space beautifully exemplifies the basic themes and the pastoral indebtedness of the later plays. Written in the fullness of O'Casey's later manner, it first establishes a realistic basis, and then works another of his magical transformations. Into this play stride the Widow Machree and Kelly from the Isle of Mananaun. At first they seem ordinary realistic characters, but then they begin to transform the landscape with typical O'Caseyan bolts of magic. The widow thinks she has sold a cow to Kelly for more than its worth, but Kelly feels that he has not paid enough for it. These attitudes are opposed to those of the hard-fisted, money-grubbing businessmen, farmers, and offstage priests, and the Civic Guards are called in to arrest the widow and Kelly for a breach of the peace. The shopkeeper and the pubkeeper are satiric portraits of the Irish small businessman, but they are not unrealistically exaggerated. The widow and Kelly, however, are fantastic figures who stand for the honesty, the openness, the grandness of an age which in Ireland has passed.

There are many instances of magic in the play. It first appears in hints, as in the offstage song "Jingle Coins." Later the song is heard more loudly, accompanied by a drum and a trumpet, and two barren trees onstage "suddenly flush with blossom, foliage, and illuminated fruit."

For a moment there appears a vision of the rich and vital pastoral world in the middle of this bleak wasteland, but the vision soon fades, and the characters return to their bartering and money-grubbing.[7]

There are one or two other reminiscences of the pastoral. Perhaps the most notable is the young couple attempting to find traces of Ireland's Golden Age who are cheated by the pubkeeper. The distinction between modern Ireland and its Golden Age is well drawn in this exchange:

> YOUNG WOMAN (*Rapidly*): A lovely crypt with groined arches, supported by lovely semi-columns, decorated with lovely foliage an' faces.
>
> BULL: D'ye tell me that, now? Well, if what it is is what yous want, it's more'n fifteen miles farther on. But th' whole thing's lost, man, in thickets, brambles, an' briars.

And in metaphorical thickets, brambles, and briars, O'Casey leaves the shopkeepers of the play. Kelly and the widow have vanished; it is time for what they stand for to go. In the lyric madness of its dialogue, this play yields to none of the longer later plays. It is a *Cock* or a *Father Ned* in miniature, and a lusty miniature it is.

⚓

The Bishop's Bonfire is subtitled "A Sad Play within the Tune of a Polka," and it and *Behind the Green Curtains* are the most pessimistic of the later plays. Although *The Bishop's Bonfire* contains much comedy, farce, and even slapstick, most of it is in a muted tone. It is a lament for the passing of the Golden Age, for in it the pastoral world is almost extinguished.

The landscape is even more blighted than that of *Cock-a-Doodle Dandy*. Councillor Reiligan has cows and hayfields, but they are thin and unproductive. Manus, one of the defeated swains, says that the town of Ballyoonagh is "where the rust of hell is on everything." Father Boheroe, the curate who tries to lead the people to a fuller life, remarks that Ballyoonagh has "Just a little life. No colour, no thought; lean cattle, thin milk; worn-out meadows giving dusty hay." This blighted pastoral land becomes a recurring leitmotif, and perhaps the point is best summed up by the old shepherd, Codger Sleehaun:

Meadows a medley of maywood an' of dock, with rushes creepin' in from the brook's bank. Grass that's tired of life before it's quarter grown. He calls his cattle cattle! The best of them crosseyed with the strain of spillin' out a few hundred gallons a year; spillin' out what all know is an illusion of what it ought to be; with every passerby turnin' his head aside so's not to see the tormented look on their gobs, an' they complainin' silently to God against the dawn's lift-up of another day.

O'Casey implies that the vitality has gone out of the land because love has gone out of the people, driven away by a narrow and officious Church. The presence of the Church in the play is pervasive and deadly. The main action is the preparation for the coming of the bishop, and the bonfire which touches off the celebration is one on which "piles of bad books an' evil pictures . . . are going to go away in flames." The bonfire really celebrates the victory of the loveless life and the defeat of the Golden Days. When the Prodical says that "the Bishop'll bring a few golden days to Ballyoonagh," the Codger retorts mournfully, "Ay, golden days of penance an' prayer . . . but not for me. Me golden days is over."

In this play, the pastoral figures are either beaten down or sent into exile, leaving the blighted wasteland to the businessman and the priest. The Codger, who is reminiscent of Jonson's Alken and of the old sage in *As You Like It*, is the most indomitable figure, but he is almost ninety years old. His wife is dead, his children are gone to America, and, in the last act, with beautiful appropriateness, he loses his job. He throws down his hammer, saw, and hayfork, and goes off with his scythe in its sheath.

The swains and nymphs of this play are more beaten down than their earlier counterparts. Manus is a spoiled priest, and Foorawn has taken a vow of chastity. Though they still love each other, the loveless religion of Councillor Reiligan and Canon Burren defeats them. In the last act, Manus, before leaving Ballyoonagh, steals some money that Foorawn has collected for the foreign missions. When she surprises him in the act, they quarrel, and he shoots her. She dies after writing a letter absolving him of guilt; he slinks away into the darkness.

The situation of the swain wounding the nymph is not unusual in the dramatic pastoral. In *Pastor Fido*, Silvio wounds Dorinda with an arrow, having mistaken her for a wolf. In Daniel's *Hymen's Triumph*, Montanus stabs Silvia, who is disguised as a boy. A still closer parallel occurs in Thomas Randolph's charming *Amyntas*. There, the shepherd Damon strikes and wounds the shepherdess Amarillis who loves him. He then leaves her, and to plead Damon's cause she writes a letter in her own blood to Laurinda, a nymph wavering between love for Damon and love for Alexis. The situation is not quite the same, but the basic elements of the wounded nymph who writes a letter in behalf of her swain appear in both plays.

The vow of chastity is also often found in the dramatic pastoral. This "extravagant virginity," as Greg calls it, is akin to that "ferocious chastity" that O'Casey saw in modern Ireland. This excessive chastity is also to be seen in Tasso, Guarini, and many English plays. There is the somewhat absurd nymph Nerina in Joseph Rutter's *The Shepherd's Holiday*, and the quality is prominent in Fletcher's *The Faithful Shepherdess*. Certainly there is a general resemblance between Fletcher's scenes of Clorin and the Satyr and O'Casey's scene between Foorawn and Codger. Clorin and Foorawn have both taken vows of virginity; the Satyr and Codger are both the rough but benevolent servants of the nymphs.

Despite the defeat of the good life, *The Bishop's Bonfire* is not a dreary play. Its final effect is melancholy, but it contains good doses of comedy and farce, several songs, a joyous dance, and a vividly playful prose. This is no place to dwell on the qualities of O'Casey's later dialogue, even though lyric language was one of the glories of the pastoral. It should be noted, though, that the color of O'Casey's language is a great antidote to melancholy. By "color" I mean both a general vividness and the actual use of colors. O'Casey had an acute visual sense which is even more apparent in the later pastorals than in the early tragi-comedies. It is as if the more his own eyesight failed in later years, the more his memory of color sharpened. This play abounds in references to color, both in the dialogue and in the careful stage directions. In his first stage direction, O'Casey remarks that the day on which the play occurs is one "when nature gives a last rally and sings a song of colour before winter brings death to flower and field." In other words, he is relating color to the pastoral landscape. Act I, the most pastoral in tone, has the most references to color. In Act III, when the pastoral world is defeated, the use of color is simpler and more somber. Instead of the vivid palette of Act I, he uses chiefly dark and light, and the play ends in a darkness alleviated only by the glow of the bonfire.

The play contains the major qualities of the pastoral — the complicated love plots, the swains and nymphs, the old shepherd and the satyrs, a delightful assembly of clowns, buffoons, rustics, and, in the character of the Prodical, a fine Jaques figure. It has a touch of the supernatural also, though the magic is largely on the side of death and confined to the statue of St. Tremolo blowing a blast on his "buckineeno" whenever he spies someone slipping into sin.

Bird imagery also abounds. At the end of Act I, the Codger identifies the lark singing in the meadow with the pastoral life: "The lark's a bonnie bird; our Lady's hen singin' near all the year round. But for all her singin', the lark has her troubles like the rest of us, a lot of sorra." Then he sings to his bonnie bird a verse of "My Bonnie Lies over the Ocean." The last act is closed by him and the Prodical singing the same song as they fade away into the darkness.

The play's tone might be summed up by the Codger's remark: "We're all in a mournful mood, merrily mournful all." It is a tone hardly unusual for the pastoral. The same remark might justly be applied to *As You Like It*, which balances its rollicking Touchstone with its melancholy Jaques.

❦

The Drums of Father Ned is a triumphant play, as gay as *The Bishop's Bonfire* was sad. It is as if some of O'Casey's own hardy spirit, which had been muted in *The Bishop's Bonfire*, blazed out to make what is in every sense a brilliant play. The story again concerns the clash between the loveless present and the vital pastoral past. The play is in a Prologue, called a Prerumble, and three acts. The Prerumble occurs during the Troubles, and shows how the older generation has just about completely destroyed the Golden Age. A contingent of Black and Tans is burning the town of Doonavale, and the only things that stand out from the flames are a church spire and a Celtic cross. The cross we may take as a symbol of the Golden Age, which is in this play conceived wholly in terms of Irish mythology. The cross, writes O'Casey in his stage direction, "dazzling in its whiteness, stands quietly, but a little crookedly, its symbol silent now, and near forgotten." Lest that point be missed, O'Casey underscores it by a passage in which the Black and Tan officer promises not to destroy the town's round tower, another symbol of the past, if Binnington and McGilligan will reconcile their differences. "Not for a hundhred round towers," says McGilligan. "Not for a hundhred more," says Binnington. So O'Casey makes it explicit that the businessmen, as much as the Black and Tans, are contributing to the destruction of the Golden Age. This Prerumble is fiercely biting and eminently theatrical. Its color, its offstage chorus of song, and the bitter irony of its dialogue combine to make it one of the most effective scenes in O'Casey's later plays.

The rest of the play takes place in the present. Binnington and McGilligan are successful businessmen who still loathe each other but work together because "Business is business." They are in close league with the old priest, Father Fillifogue, who deplores dancing, courting, and wearing blue jeans. The young people, led by the young priest Father Ned, are feverishly preparing for a Tostal festival which is really an attempt to revive the Golden Age. "WE *were* DEAD *and are* ALIVE AGAIN!" cries one of their posters, and the Tostal is clearly meant to resurrect the pastoral life. The young people, for instance, are preparing gaily-colored window boxes full of flowers to decorate the town, and the spirit of an Irish Golden Age is constantly intruded by many references to Irish mythology. At the beginning of Act III the young people are gilding shields on which are painted the faces of Irish heroes. The most prominent hero is the god of youth, Angus, on whose shield is significantly painted "a gaily-plumaged bird — green breast, black satiny head, wings tipped with crimson and gold."

The play ends on a triumphant burst of color, song, and drum rolls. The older generation has been defeated, their hypocrisy revealed, and the vigorous young people are busily creating a brave new world. The conclusion of the last act, with its magnificent use of music, sound, and color, must rank with the beautiful third-act transformation scene of *Red Roses for Me* and the unforgettable second act of *The Silver Tassie*. It proves what theatre can really be when all of its resources are used by a master.

The basic ingredients of the pastoral are again present. There are two pairs of young lovers. There is a delicious comic satyr and a coy-nymph scene in Act II. There are clowns and rustics aplenty, among whom must be especially singled out the belligerent Oscar McGunty with his dynamic conclusion to all arguments: "An' that's the climmax of McGunty!"

Although much of it occurs offstage, the play abounds in magic. The magical atmosphere centers on Father Ned, who never appears but whose presence is pervasive and wonderful. As Bernadette remarks, "he might be anywhere, though some may think he's nowhere; again he may be everywhere; but he's always with th' drums." Father Ned appears to Skerighan as a vision of "fierce green eyes shinin' lak umeralds on fire in a white face that was careerin' aboot though stayin' stull as an evenin' star, starin' up from doon in th' valley below."

Another instance of magic is the voice of the Echo which comments sometimes ironically, sometimes emphatically upon the dialogue. The Echo scene is so usual a device of the pastoral that Butler ridiculed it in *Hudibras*. Greg calls the Echo scene "one of those toys which, as old as the Greek Anthology, and cultivated in Latin by Tebaldeo, and in Italian by Paliziaro, owed, not indeed their introduction, but certainly their great popularity, in pastoral, to Guarini." [8] Some notable instances of the scene appear in *Pastor Fido*, of course, and also in Randolph's *Amyntas* and in Sidney's *Arcadia*. Each time its use resembles O'Casey's.

All in all, *The Drums of Father Ned* is one of the gayest plays that O'Casey ever wrote. It could have been subtitled *The Old Man Says "Yes!"* It was a remarkable performance to come from an old man. It was a remarkable performance to come from any man.

⚜

O'Casey's last volume of plays contains a short full-length play, *Behind the Green Curtains*, and two one-acts, *Figuro in the Night* and *The Moon Shines on Kylenamoe*, all of which are in his pastoral manner, even though they are widely different in tone. *The Moon Shines* is a pastoral farce which is pure entertainment and pure delight; the other two are more serious. *Behind the Green Curtains* is in the mood of *The Bishop's Bonfire*, but bleaker and more savage in its indictment. *Figuro* is in the mood of *Father Ned*, a paean, a shout in the street.

Behind the Green Curtains has, appropriately, fewer reminiscences of pastoral than the other late plays; its view of Ireland is the furthest removed from the Golden Age. Earlier, O'Casey had treated his powers of darkness with a relatively light hand. Stokes and Poges, Michael Marthraun and Sailor Mahan, Binnington and McGilligan and Father Fillifogue were prime repositories of sham and pomposity but delightful characters. Only occasionally, as when Father Domineer kills the lorry driver in *Cock-a-Doodle Dandy*, or when Rankin spits in Keelin's face in *The Bishop's Bonfire*, does O'Casey condemn with heat. In *Green Curtains*, however, the condemnation has grown almost Swiftean. Christy Kornavaun, the spokesman for organized religion, is a totally loathsome character. He heads a sort of religious storm troop that pries into everyone's personal and public life. Noneen calls him "a gabby slug," and Reena calls him a "bordher-line lunatic" and "a mouldy crumb of life."

When Kornavaun cannot frighten the artists and writers into follow-

249

ing the Church's line by his threats, he sets his thugs on them. After No-neen repulses his advances, he has his thugs carry her off to a house where two women strip off her clothes, put a nightdress on her, and tie her to a telegraph pole where she stays all night. This incident happened in Ireland, but the situation of the nymph tied to a tree by a satyr also appears in Act III of Tasso's *Aminta*. The situation occurs again, possibly borrowed from Tasso, in Jonathan Sidnam's English translation of Bon-arelli's *Filli di Sciro*. And in Lyly's semi-pastoral *Galathea* a nymph is to be tied to a tree by the seashore to be carried off by the monster Agar.

The basic ingredients of the pastoral are evident, though dimly. There are two complicated love triangles. There is a satyr and nymph scene in which the repulsed Kornavaun significantly calls Noneen an "Arcadian slut." There is a touch of magic when a peal of ominous thunder fades into the ringing of a doorbell. And perhaps there is a faint parody of the Golden Age in the rosettes which the repentant artists must wear as members of the Brothers Repentant.

The first act is grandly theatrical; the drunken entrance of the two old trulls, Angela and Lizzie, at the end is a show-stopper. The conclusions of the last two acts are difficult. The second ends melodramatically and the third romantically, and melodrama and romance are among the most difficult effects to attain in our basically realistic theatre. Much of Act III is intensely difficult, because it has a long muted love scene between Reena and Chatastray and because its ending requires a delicate inter-play of comedy topped off with an almost swashbuckling romantic verve. The play is a demanding one for both actors and audience, and it is not one of O'Casey's best. Still, if produced well, it could achieve some rare effects.

Figuro in the Night is an appropriate play to close on, for it is not a keen but a last hurrah. Like the last scene in *Father Ned*, it shows a tri-umphant transformation of the dead world into the live one of the Gold-en Age. The play has two scenes. The first shows us a drab suburban street near Dublin. In one house a young girl is mourning for her absent beau. Then an Old Man and an Old Woman enter, and they stand for what "the ferocious chastity" of Ireland does to people. After some fine satiric dialogue, they totter off on their lonely, separate ways.

The second scene is a total contrast. The houses are now gaily painted. A great half moon fills the sky. "The bare trees of the former scene are full of foliage, and many-coloured fruits, shining like lighted globes, hang from some of them. Birds sing cheerily, and in the distance we hear the faint, pleasant lowing of cattle, gentle baaing of sheep, and the chal-lenging crow of the cock." The Golden Age has returned with a bang, for in the center of Dublin a statue has appeared, "the figuro of the laddo weaving a fountain outa him in a way that was a menace to morality; with thousands of women, old, middle-aged, and young sthruggling to get a close-up view."

Magical transformations occur. Women attack the Civic Guards; Kathleen ni Houlihan throws herself upon one guard, and they vanish in a puff of smoke above Nelson's Pillar. Caws from an invisible crow are heard. The Catholic bishops join in community singing. A bird-like lad dressed like a green crow enters, and the play ends as a group of youths and girls, brightly dressed, enter into a gay dance. A similar orgy con-cludes Paliziano's mythological drama *Favola d'Orfeo* of 1471, and Greg's criticism of that play could justly be applied to O'Casey's:

Lyrical beauty rather than dramatic power was . . . Paliziano's aim and achievement. The want of characterization in the hero, the insignifi-cance of the part allotted to Euridice, the total inadequacy of the tragic climax, measure the author's powers as a dramatist. It is the lyrical pas-sages — Aristeo's song, Orfeo's impassioned pleading, the bacchanalian dance chorus — that supply the firm supports of art upon which rests the slight fabric of the play.[9]

Gabriel Fallon calls the play "a priapic extravaganza" that has afforded O'Casey "still another outlet for an obsession with sex." To a less fanatical critic, O'Casey would not seem obsessed with sex but with love, which is the central quality in his Golden Age. Sex is one facet of love, and the sex which explodes in *Figuro* is not the prying, peeping leer of a pornog-rapher but the joyous shout of a man in love with life.

From this résumé, the pastoral resemblances are probably evident. There are the pairs of lovers, pervasive lyricism, magic, and some fine clowns. The play is not major, but if produced with spirit it should prove to have put the pastoral tradition to one of its liveliest uses.

❦

To sum up: O'Casey has not written pure pastorals, but used the tech-nique for his own purposes. For him, the Golden Age is a vision of the good life set in a rural Ireland filled with golden lads and lasses who hear the voice of the past and who are not afraid to love and be free. The con-flict of this vision with the debased reality of the present is at the center of all of these late plays. Such a use of the pastoral is quite traditional, even though O'Casey's version is pervaded by his own personality. As Greg remarks, "What does appear to be a constant element in the pastoral as known to literature is the recognition of a contrast, implicit or expressed, between pastoral life and some more complex type of civilization." [10] By seizing on that contrast, O'Casey has asserted that the pastoral tradition is not dead, but may give point and vigor to the drama of today. The validity of this assertion seems brilliantly proved by his late plays. By their vitality and superb theatricality, these plays and not the early masterpieces may ultimately prove to be O'Casey's great contribution to the theatre. They certainly suggest why he has remained the commanding figure in the last forty years of Irish drama.

Since this chapter was first drafted, O'Casey has died, and I am tempted to add one last note.

O'Casey was sometimes thought to be a cranky, splenetic, combative old man, both hating his exile and hating Ireland. I personally did not find this so. He seemed to me at peace with the world — if at war with its stupidities and cruelties. A wise, witty, lovable man, a gay companion and a good friend, with his fires not out but banked and giving a serene glow. It is hardly odd that plays of a Golden Age should have been written by a man who was living one.

Cheerio, Titan!

NOTES, BIBLIOGRAPHY,
AND INDEX

Notes

CHAPTER 1. THE ABBEY: SHADOW OR SUBSTANCE OF A THEATRE?

1. From a letter to Robert Hogan dated September 26, 1962.
2. From a letter to Robert Hogan dated February 22, 1962.
3. Iain Shaw, "*Juno* and *The Plough*," *Encore*, II (July–August, 1964), 52.
4. Reprinted in Walkley's *Drama and Life* (London: Methuen, 1907), p. 311.
5. Joseph Holloway, the Dublin diarist and a friend of Fay who had followed his career from the first, thought that in later life Fay's reading of verse became monotonous because of the even and drawn-out stress that the actor gave nearly every word. Holloway attributed this change to an overdose of Shakespeare, the pernicious effect of the melodramas that Fay played in after leaving the Abbey, and a pomposity which overtook Fay in his last years.
6. Andrew J. Stewart, "The Acting of the Abbey Theatre," *Theatre Arts*, XVII (March, 1933), 245.
7. Andrew E. Malone, "The Decline of the Irish Drama," *The Nineteenth Century*, XCVII (April, 1925), 588.
8. George Jean Nathan, "Erin Go Blah," *Newsweek*, X (December 27, 1937), 24.
9. Sean O'Faolain, *She Had To Do Something* (London: Jonathan Cape, 1938), pp. 11–12.
10. Holloway's journal, *Impressions of a Dublin Playgoer*, is in the National Library of Ireland. This extract is from the entry of January 20, 1925. See also *Joseph Holloway's Abbey Theatre*, an extract from the years 1899–1926, ed. Robert Hogan and Michael J. O'Neill (Carbondale: Southern Illinois University Press, 1967).
11. Denis Donoghue, "Dublin Letter," *The Hudson Review*, XIII (Winter, 1960–1961), 583.
12. *Early and Often*, a kind of Dublin *Last Hurrah*, and *I Know Where I'm Going*, a charming but unpublished light comedy.
13. Dorothy Macardle, "Experiment in Ireland," *Theatre Arts*, XVIII (February, 1934), 126–127.
14. Lennox Robinson, *Ireland's Abbey Theatre* (London: Sidgwick & Jackson, 1951), p. 152.
15. Ernest Blythe, *The Abbey Theatre* (Dublin: The National Theatre Society, Ltd., [1963]), [p. 18].
16. John Synge, "Letters of John Millington Synge: From Material Supplied by Max Meyerfield," *Yale Review*, XIII (July, 1924), 703.

17. Henry Hewes, "Broadway Postscript," *Saturday Review*, XL (May 18, 1957), 34.

18. Seamus Kelly, "Where Motley Is Worn," *The Spectator*, CXCVI (April 20, 1956), 540.

19. Ulick O'Connor, "Dublin's Dilemma," *Theatre Arts*, XL (July, 1956), 65 & 96.

20. Joseph Holloway, October 12, 1925.

21. Paul Smith, "Dublin's Lusty Theatre," *Holiday*, XXXIII (April, 1963), 157.

22. Donat O'Donnell, "The Abbey: Phoenix Infrequent," *Commonweal*, LVII (January 30, 1953), 424.

23. Quoted in Kelly's article "Where Motley Is Worn," p. 540.

24. Blythe, [p. 6].

25. *Ibid.*, [p. 7].

26. *Ibid.*, [p. 26].

27. At this writing, the Abbey in its new theatre has just produced or announced for production the following works: an enthusiastically received revival of Boucicault's *The Shaughraun*, directed by Hugh Hunt and featuring Cyril Cusack; P. J. O'Connor's applauded adaptation of Patrick Kavanagh's novel *Tarry Flynn*; the first Irish production of Brian Friel's *The Loves of Cass Maguire*; the first Abbey productions of Donagh MacDonagh's *Lady Spider* and O'Casey's *Red Roses for Me*; a season of new plays by George Fitzmaurice; a Gaelic play by Seamus O'Neill, John O'Donovan's *Dean Swift Programme*, and new plays by the young writers Maurice Davin Power and James McKenna. The prospects, as Honor Tracy put it, are pleasing.

CHAPTER 2. THE ABBEY DRAMATISTS, 1926–1945

1. Peter Kavanagh, *The Story of the Abbey Theatre* (New York: Devin-Adair, 1950), p. 181.

2. J. D. Riley, "On Teresa Deevy's Plays," *Irish Writing*, No. 32 (Autumn, 1955), 30.

3. Jack MacGowran, "Preface," *In Sand*, by Jack B. Yeats (Dublin: The Dolmen Press, 1964), p. 5.

CHAPTER 3. PAUL VINCENT CARROLL: THE REBEL
AS PRODIGAL SON

1. The first quote is from "The Substance of Paul Vincent Carroll," New York *Times* (January 30, 1938), Section X, p. 1. The second is from "Reforming a Reformer," New York *Times* (February 13, 1935), Section II, p. 3.

2. "The Substance of Paul Vincent Carroll."

3. *Ibid.*

4. *Ibid.*

5. *Ibid.*

6. Kavanagh, p. 166.

7. Carroll also acknowledges a debt to T. C. Murray whom in some ways he resembles and to whom he sent several early scripts for criticism.

8. "Irish Eyes Are Smiling," New York *Times* (April 17, 1938), Section X, p. 1.

9. Winifred Bannister, *James Bridie and His Theatre* (London: Rockliff, 1955), p. 207.

10. *Ibid.*, p. 230.

11. "Reforming a Reformer."

CHAPTER 4. THE ABBEY DRAMATISTS, 1946–1965

1. In a letter of November 16, 1965, to Robert Hogan, Byrne pointed out that "Behan's QUARE FELLOW was written about seven years after HEADSTONE. In fact, Seamus Kelly, Dublin's top theatre critic, described HEADSTONE as the 'blue-print' adopted by

Behan for QUARE FELLOW; and without suggesting plagiarism, Behan did fairly obviously 'use' HEADSTONE, even to adopting the 'running commentary' which I gave Jakey, in Act 3 on the activities of the prisoners locking the warders into the cells. Dublin saw many similarities!"

2. In a letter of October 21, 1965, to Robert Hogan, O'Donovan wrote, "when I discovered at rehearsal that several lines had been cut by his [Ernest Blythe's] order without reference to me, and indeed in spite of his verbal undertaking not to change the text, I sprang up from my seat in the theatre and emphasised an apostrophe to the heavens with a blow of my fist on the back of an iron seat that broke it (the iron seat, not my fist)."

3. *Ibid.*

4. From a letter to Robert Hogan dated September 1, 1965.

5. The Oireachtas is a national festival of Gaelic culture which offers awards for literary, dramatic, and musical works in Gaelic. It sponsors, among other activities, an annual drama contest.

CHAPTER 5. MICHAEL MOLLOY'S DYING IRELAND

1. From a letter to Robert Hogan dated November 11, 1965.

2. *Ibid.*

3. *Ibid.*

4. From a letter to Robert Hogan dated July 5, 1965.

5. *Ibid.*

CHAPTER 6. AT THE GATE THEATRE

1. Micheál Mac Liammóir, "Preface," *The Mantle of Harlequin*, by Hilton Edwards (Dublin: Progress House, 1958), p. xv.

2. Hilton Edwards, *The Mantle of Harlequin*, p. 3.

3. From a letter to Robert Hogan dated November 27, 1964.

4. From a letter to Robert Hogan dated December 27, 1964.

5. In a letter to Robert Hogan dated December 13, 1965, Lady Longford remarked, "I think you over-rate my plays, especially the one about Sarsfield, but naturally I'm not protesting."

CHAPTER 7. THE ADULT THEATRE OF DENIS JOHNSTON

1. From a letter to Robert Hogan dated November 6, 1965.

2. Denis Johnston, *The Old Lady Says "No!" & Other Plays* (Boston: Atlantic-Little, Brown, 1960), p. 10.

3. Many of its references are glossed in Curtis Canfield's anthology, *Plays of Changing Ireland*.

4. One character is a belligerently lowbrow playwright named Seamus O'Cooney, who wears his hat in the house, punctuates his boorish criticism with "bloodys," and is obviously a satiric portrait of O'Casey in the first days of his fame.

5. From a letter to Robert Hogan dated November 6, 1965.

6. *Ibid.*

7. I have not discussed Johnston's fine one-act *A Fourth for Bridge*, a war play with nothing particularly Irish about it. Nor have I discussed his work for radio and television, for none has been published. His most recently produced television play, *The Glass Murder*, was first transmitted over Telefís Éireann on February 24, 1963.

CHAPTER 8. THE EXPERIMENTAL THEATRE OF THE POETS

1. Vivian Mercier, "In Defense of Yeats as a Dramatist," *Modern Drama*, VIII (September, 1965), pp. 164 & 165.

2. John T. Unterecker, "The Shaping Force in Yeats's Plays," *Modern Drama*, VII (December, 1964), p. 345.

3. Joseph Holloway, October 31, 1904.

4. *Ibid.*, November 5, 1908.

5. *Ibid.*, May 27, 1915.

6. Donagh MacDonagh, quoted in the Introduction to *Four Modern Verse Plays*, ed. E. Martin Browne (Harmondsworth, Middlesex: Penguin, 1957), p. 13.

7. See, for instance, "Playwrights and the Stationary Carrot," in *Theatre Arts*, XLVI (February, 1962), 21–22.

8. Micheál Ó h Aodha, "The Radio Plays of Padraic Fallon," *Plays and Players* (Dublin: Progress House, 1961), p. 64.

9. *Ibid.*, p. 59.

APPENDIX II. THE GENIUS OF GEORGE FITZMAURICE

1. To Liam Miller of the Dolmen Press, I am indebted for making available to me all of Fitzmaurice's plays and for allowing me to read Howard K. Slaughter's unpublished monograph on Fitzmaurice. Most of the biographical information here is taken from Slaughter who has uncovered more about Fitzmaurice's life than anyone else.

CHAPTER 9. THE THEATRE FESTIVAL

1. The Irish Tourist Board.

2. Veronica Kelly, "Talking to Brendan Smith," *Irish Times* (September 23, 1964), p. 10.

3. From a letter to Robert Hogan dated September 18, 1965.

4. *Ibid.*

CHAPTER 10. THE SHORT HAPPY WORLD OF BRENDAN BEHAN

1. An obituary in the New York *Times*, March 21, 1964, p. 25.

CHAPTER 11. THE HIDDEN IRELAND OF JOHN B. KEANE

1. John B. Keane, *Self-Portrait* (Cork: The Mercier Press, 1964), p. 87.

2. Micheál Ó h Aodha, "Foreword," *Sive* (Dublin: Progress House, 1959), p. 6.

3. James N. Healy, "Foreword," *Sharon's Grave* (Dublin: Progress House, 1960), p. vii.

CHAPTER 12. IN SEAN O'CASEY'S GOLDEN DAYS

1. Sean O'Casey, *The Green Crow* (New York: George Braziller, 1956), p. 138.

2. The definitive account of the form is Walter W. Greg's *Pastoral Poetry and Pastoral Drama* (New York: Russell & Russell, 1959), a volume indispensable in writing this chapter.

3. C. G. Thayer, *Ben Jonson: Studies in the Plays* (Norman: University of Oklahoma Press, 1963), p. 249.

4. Greg, p. 2.

5. Thayer, p. 250.

6. This bird symbolism is hardly unusual. For one somewhat tongue-in-cheek account of it, see Patricia Abel and Robert Hogan, "The Cock and the Singing Birds," in *A D. H. Lawrence Miscellany* (Carbondale: Southern Illinois University Press, 1959), pp. 204–214.

7. Similar transformations occur in Act III of *Red Roses for Me* and in the second scene of *Figuro in the Night*.

8. Greg, p. 199.

9. *Ibid.*, p. 164.

10. *Ibid.*, p. 4.

Bibliography

For reasons of space, this bibliography is highly selective. Mainly, it lists published work which is fairly available: criticism, history, and memoirs; anthologies of plays; individual plays of individual authors; and some critical essays about individual authors. The dramatic criticism I have limited to what seems the most significant or the most available. However, the serious student should consult the files of the *Irish Times*, *The Dublin Magazine*, *The Bell*, and *Irish Writing*.

A. CRITICISM, HISTORY, MEMOIRS, ETC.

Blythe, Ernest. *The Abbey Theatre*. Dublin: The National Theatre Society, Ltd. [1963].

Edwards, Hilton. *The Mantle of Harlequin*. Dublin: Progress House, 1958.

Fay, Gerard. *The Abbey Theatre, Cradle of Genius*. London: Hollis & Carter, 1958.

Gregory, Lady Augusta. *Lady Gregory's Journals*, ed. Lennox Robinson. New York: Macmillan, 1947.

Hobson, Bulmer, ed. *The Gate Theatre, Dublin*. Dublin: The Gate Theatre, 1934.

Holloway, Joseph. *Joseph Holloway's Abbey Theatre*, eds. Robert Hogan and Michael J. O'Neill. Carbondale: Southern Illinois University Press, 1967.

Kavanagh, Peter. *The Story of the Abbey Theatre*. New York: Devin-Adair, 1950.

Kennedy, David. "The Drama in Ulster," *The Arts in Ulster: A Symposium*, ed. Sam Hanna Bell *et al*. London: Harrap, 1951, 47–68.

Longford Productions: Dublin Gate Souvenir, 1939. Dublin: Corrigan & Wilson [1939].

McCann, Sean, ed. *The Story of the Abbey*. London: New English Library, 1967.

Mac Liammóir, Micheál. *All for Hecuba*. Dublin: Progress House, 1961.

———. *Theatre in Ireland*, 2nd ed. Dublin: Cultural Relations Committee of Ireland, 1964.

MacNamara, Brinsley. *Abbey Plays, 1899–1948*. Dublin: At the Sign of the Three Candles, [1949].

O'Mahony, Mathew J. *Guide to Anglo-Irish Plays*. Dublin: Progress House, 1960.

Robinson, Lennox. *Ireland's Abbey Theatre*. London: Sidgwick & Jackson, 1951.

———, ed. *The Irish Theatre*. London: Macmillan, 1939.

Simpson, Alan. *Beckett and Behan and a Theatre in Dublin*. London: Routledge & Kegan Paul, 1962.

Young, Derek, ed. *Stagecast: Irish Stage and Screen Directory*. Dublin: Stagecast, published annually from 1962. (Contains among other things a valuable although incomplete record of stage and television productions during the year.)

B. ANTHOLOGIES

Barnet, Sylvan *et al.* *The Genius of the Irish Theatre*. New York: New American Library, 1960. (Contains Shaw's *John Bull's Other Island*, Lady Gregory's *The Canavans*, Synge's *Deirdre of the Sorrows*, W. B. Yeats's *The Words upon the Window-Pane*, Jack Yeats's *La La Noo*, O'Connor's *In the Train*, O'Casey's *Purple Dust*, introductory notes, and essays by Beerbohm, W. B. Yeats, Joyce, O'Connor, and O'Casey.)

Browne, E. Martin. *Three Irish Plays*. Baltimore: Penguin Books, 1958. (Contains Johnston's *The Moon in the Yellow River*, Joseph O'Conor's *The Iron Harp*, and Donagh MacDonagh's *Step-in-the-Hollow*.)

Canfield, Curtis. *Plays of Changing Ireland*. New York: Macmillan, 1936. (Contains Yeats's *The Words upon the Window-Pane*, Johnston's *The Old Lady Says "No!"*, Robinson's *Church Street*, Lord Longford's *Yahoo*, Shiels's *The New Gossoon*, Lady Longford's *Mr. Jiggins of Jigginstown*, Mary Manning's *Youth's the Season . . . ?*, Rutherford Mayne's *Bridge Head*, also copious notes, biographies, and play lists. An invaluable collection of plays of the early thirties.)

Hogan, Robert. *Seven Irish Plays, 1946–1964*. Minneapolis: University of Minnesota Press, 1967. (Contains Molloy's *The Visiting House*, Byrne's *Design for a Headstone*, MacMahon's *Song of the Anvil*, O'Donovan's *Copperfaced Jack*, Keane's *Sharon's Grave* and *Many Young Men of Twenty*, and Douglas's *The Ice Goddess*, also introduction, notes on individual authors, and glossary of Irish terms.)

Nathan, George Jean. *Five Irish Plays*. New York: Modern Library, 1941. (Contains Synge's *Playboy* and *Riders to the Sea*, Lady Gregory's *Spreading the News*, O'Casey's *Juno*, and Carroll's *Shadow and Substance*.)

C. INDIVIDUAL AUTHORS

The entry for each author is arranged in roughly the following fashion: his plays, his nondramatic works, and critical works about him.

Brendan Behan

The Quare Fellow. New York: Grove Press, 1957.

The Hostage. London: Methuen, 1962. (The final version.)

Two Short Plays: Moving Out & The Garden Party, ed. Robert Hogan. Dixon, California: Proscenium Press, 1967.

Borstal Boy [autobiography]. New York: Alfred A. Knopf, 1959.

Brendan Behan's Island: An Irish Sketchbook [miscellany]. New York: Bernard Geis, 1962. (Contains the short play *The Big House*.)

Hold Your Hour and Have Another [sketches]. Boston: Little, Brown, 1964.

Brendan Behan's New York [miscellany]. New York: Bernard Geis, 1964.

The Scarperer [novel]. Garden City, New York: Doubleday, 1964.

Confessions of an Irish Rebel [autobiography]. London: Hutchinson, 1965.

Behan, Dominic. *My Brother Brendan*. London: Leslie Frewin, 1965.

De Burca, Seamus. "The Essential Brendan Behan," *Modern Drama*, VIII (February, 1966), 374–381.

Kiely, Benedict. "That Old Triangle: A Memory of Brendan Behan," *The Hollins Critic*, II (February, 1965).

Jeffs, Rae. *Brendan Behan, Man and Showman*. London: Hutchinson, 1966.

McCann, Sean, ed. *The World of Brendan Behan*. London: The New English Library, Ltd., 1965. (A collection of essays by Irish friends and acquaintances — Keane, Mac Liammóir, etc.)

BIBLIOGRAPHY

Dominic Behan

Tell Dublin I Miss Her [autobiography]. New York: Putnam's, 1962. (Published in England as *Teems of Times and Happy Returns*.)
My Brother Brendan. London: Leslie Frewin, 1965.

George A. Birmingham (Pseudonym of Canon J. Owen Hannay)

General John Regan. London: Allen & Unwin, 1933.

Seamus Byrne

Design for a Headstone. Dublin: Progress House, 1956. (Also in Hogan's *Seven Irish Plays*.)
"Oh! Most Wise Judge! [story]," *Irish Writing*, II (June, 1947), 52–60.
Ó h Aodha, Micheál. "Design for a Headstone," *Plays and Places*. Dublin: Progress House, 1961, 39–44.

Frank Carney

Bolt from the Blue. Dublin: James Duffy, 1950.
The Righteous Are Bold. Dublin: James Duffy, 1959.

Paul Vincent Carroll

Shadow and Substance. New York: Random House, 1937.
Plays for My Children. New York: Julien Messner, 1939.
Three Plays. London: Macmillan, 1944. (Contains *The White Steed*, *Things That Are Caesar's*, and *The Strings, My Lord, Are False*.)
The Old Foolishness. London. Samuel French, 1944.
The Conspirators. London: Samuel French, 1947. (Also called *Coggerers*.)
Green Cars Go East. London: Samuel French, 1947.
Interlude. London: Samuel French, 1947.
The Wise Have Not Spoken. London: Samuel French, 1947; New York: Dramatists Play Service, 1954.
Irish Stories and Plays. New York: Devin-Adair, 1958. (Contains some short stories, short plays, and the long play *The Devil Came from Dublin*.)
Farewell to Greatness!, ed. Robert Hogan. Dixon, California: Proscenium Press, 1966.
"The Substance of Paul Vincent Carroll [article]," New York *Times*, January 30, 1938, Section 10, p. 1.
"Irish Eyes Are Smiling [article]," New York *Times*, April 17, 1938, Section 10, pp. 1–2.
"Reforming a Reformer [article]," New York *Times*, February 13, 1955, Section 2, pp. 1–3.
"The Rebel Mind [article]," New York *Times*, January 24, 1960, Section 2, p. 3.
Coleman, Sister Anne Gertrude, "Paul Vincent Carroll's View of Irish Life," *Catholic World*, CXCII (November, 1960), 87–93.
Pallette, Drew B. "Paul Vincent Carroll — Since The White Steed," *Modern Drama*, VII (February, 1965), 375–381.

James Cheasty

A Stranger Came. Dublin: Progress House, 1956.
The Lost Years. Dublin: Progress House, 1958.
Francey. Dublin: Progress House, 1962.

Austin Clarke

Collected Plays. Dublin: The Dolmen Press, 1963.
Bright Temptation [novel]. Chester Springs, Pennsylvania: Dufour, 1932.

The Singing Men at Cashel [novel]. London: Allen & Unwin, 1936.
The Collected Poems of Austin Clarke. London: Allen & Unwin, [1936].
Later Poems. Dublin: The Dolmen Press, 1961.
Twice Round the Back Church [autobiography]. London: Routledge & Kegan Paul, 1962.
Harmon, Maurice. "The Later Poetry of Austin Clarke," *The Celtic Cross*, ed. Ray B. Browne *et al.* Lafayette, Indiana: Purdue University Studies, 1964, 39–55.
Mercier, Vivian. "Austin Clarke – The Poet in the Theatre," *Chimera*, V (Spring, 1947), 25–36.
Saul, George Brandon. "The Poetry of Austin Clarke," *The Celtic Cross*, 26–38.

Robert Collis

Marrowbone Lane. Monkstown, Dublin: The Runa Press, 1943.

Padraic Colum

Mogu, the Wanderer. Boston: Little, Brown, 1917.
Balloon. New York: Macmillan, 1929.
Moytura. Dublin: The Dolmen Press, 1963.
Three Plays. Dublin: Allen Figgis, 1963. (Contains his early plays *The Land, The Fiddler's House*, and *Thomas Muskerry*.)

Myles na gCopaleen (Pseudonym of Brian O'Nolan)

Faustus Kelly. Dublin: Cahill & Co., 1943.

Louis D'Alton

Two Irish Plays. London: Macmillan, 1938. (Contains *The Man in the Cloak* and *The Mousetrap*.)
To-morrow Never Comes. Dublin: James Duffy, 1945.
The Devil a Saint Would Be. London: Samuel French, 1952.
This Other Eden. Dublin: P. J. Bourke, 1954.
They Got What They Wanted. Dundalk, Ireland: Dundalgan Press, 1962.
The Money Doesn't Matter. Dublin: P. J. Bourke, 1963.
Lovers Meeting. Dublin: P. J. Bourke, 1964.
Cafflin' Johnny. Dublin & Dixon, California: P. J. Bourke & Proscenium Press, 1967.
Death Is So Fair [novel]. London: Heinemann, 1936.

Seamus de Burca (Pseudonym of James A. Bourke)

Find the Island. Dublin: P. J. Bourke, [1950?].
Family Album. Dublin: P. J. Bourke, 1952.
The Howards. Dublin: P. J. Bourke, [1960].
The Boys and Girls Are Gone, 2nd ed. Dublin: P. J. Bourke, 1961.
Thomas Davis. Dublin: P. J. Bourke, 1962.
Limpid River in *First Stage: A Quarterly of New Drama*, V (Spring, 1966), 30–55.
Knocknagow, or The Homes of Tipperary [dramatization of Kickham's novel]. Dublin: P. J. Bourke, 1945.
Phil Lahy [one-act adaptation of Kickham's *Knocknagow*]. Dublin: P. J. Bourke, [1953].
ed., *Arrah-na-Pogue, or The Wicklow Wedding* by Dion Boucicault. Dublin: P. J. Bourke, n.d.
The Soldier's Song: The Story of Peadar O Cearnaigh [biography]. Dublin: P. J. Bourke, 1957.
Limpid River [novel]. Dublin: P. J. Bourke, 1962.

BIBLIOGRAPHY

Teresa Deevy

Three Plays. London: Macmillan, 1939. (Contains *Katie Roche, The King of Spain's Daughter*, and *The Wild Goose.*)
The King of Spain's Daughter and Other One-Act Plays. Dublin: New Frontier Press, 1948. (Contains also *In Search of Valour* and *Strange Birth.*)
"Going Beyond Alma's Glory," *Irish Writing*, No. 17 (December, 1951), 21–32.
Riley, J. D. "On Teresa Deevy's Plays," *Irish Writing*, No. 32 (Autumn, 1955).

J. P. Donleavy

What They Did in Dublin with The Ginger Man. London: MacGibbon & Kee, 1961. (Contains the text of the play and a long introduction.)
Fairy Tales of New York. Harmondsworth, Middlesex: Penguin, [1961].
The Ginger Man [novel]. Paris: The Olympia Press, 1955.
A Singular Man [novel]. Boston: Atlantic–Little, Brown, 1963.
Meet My Maker the Mad Molecule [novel]. Boston: Atlantic–Little, Brown, 1964.
Moore, John Rees. "Hard Times and the Noble Savage: J. P. Donleavy's *A Singular Man*," *The Hollins Critic*, I (February, 1964).

James Douglas

The Bomb. Dixon, California: Proscenium Press, 1966.
The Ice Goddess in Hogan's *Seven Irish Plays, 1946–1964.*
"P. J. [story]," *The Kilkenny Magazine*, No. 5 (Autumn–Winter, 1961), 30–33.

Sean Dowling

The Bird in the Net. Dublin: James Duffy, 1961.

St. John Ervine

Mixed Marriage. Dublin: Maunsel, 1911.
Four Irish Plays. London & Dublin: Maunsel, 1914. (Contains *Mixed Marriage, The Magnanimous Lover, The Critics*, and *The Orangeman.*)
Jane Clegg. London: Sidgwick & Jackson, 1914.
John Ferguson. New York: Macmillan, 1920.
The Ship. London: Allen & Unwin, 1922.
The Lady of Belmont. London: Allen & Unwin, 1923.
Four One-Act Plays. London: Allen & Unwin, 1928. (Contains *The Magnanimous Lover, Progress, Ole George Comes to Tea*, and *She Was No Lady.*)
The First Mrs. Fraser. London: Chatto & Windus, 1929.
Anthony and Anna. London: Allen & Unwin, 1936.
Boyd's Shop. London: Allen & Unwin, 1936.
People of Our Class. London: Allen & Unwin, 1936.
Robert's Wife. London: Allen & Unwin, 1938.
Friends and Relations. London: Allen & Unwin, 1947.
Private Enterprise. London: Allen & Unwin, [1948].
The Christies. London: Allen & Unwin, 1949.
My Brother Tom. London: Allen & Unwin, 1952.
The Organised Theatre [criticism]. London: Allen & Unwin, 1924.
How to Write a Play [criticism]. London: Allen & Unwin, 1928.
The Theatre in My Time [criticism]. London: Rich & Cowan, 1933.
Oscar Wilde [biography]. London: Allen & Unwin, 1951.
Bernard Shaw: His Life, Work and Friends [biography]. London: Constable, 1956.

Padraic Fallon

Ó h Aodha, Micheál. "The Radio Plays of Padraic Fallon," *Plays and Places*. Dublin: Progress House, 1961, 57–73.

Conor Farrington

"The Ghostly Garden [one-act play]," *Prizewinning Plays of 1964*. Dublin: Progress House, 1965.
"Playwrights and the Stationary Carrot [article]," *Theatre Arts*, XLVI (February, 1962), 21–22.
"Tar [story]," *The Dublin Magazine*, IV (Spring, 1965), 52–56.

George Fitzmaurice

Five Plays. Dublin: Maunsel, 1914.
The Plays of George Fitzmaurice, Vol. I. Dublin: The Dolmen Press, 1967.
Clarke, Austin. "The Dramatic Fantasies of George Fitzmaurice," *The Dublin Magazine*, XV (April–June, 1940), 9–14.
Kennedy, Maurice. "George Fitzmaurice: Sketch for a Portrait," *Irish Writing*, No. 15 (June, 1951), 38–46.
Miller, Liam. "George Fitzmaurice: A Bibliographical Note," *Irish Writing*, No. 15 (June, 1951), 47–48.
Riley, J. D. "The Plays of George Fitzmaurice," *The Dublin Magazine*, XXXI (January–March, 1955), 5–19.
Wardle, Irving. "Reputations – XV: George Fitzmaurice," *The London Magazine*, IV (February, 1965), 68–74.

Dick Forbes

Nedser and Nuala. Dublin: P. J. Bourke, 1954.

Brian Friel

Philadelphia, Here I Come! New York: Farrar, Straus & Giroux, 1966.
The Loves of Cass McGuire. New York: Farrar, 1967.
The Saucer of Larks [stories]. Garden City, New York: Doubleday, 1962.
The Gold in the Sea [stories]. Garden City, New York: Doubleday, 1966.

G. P. Gallivan

Decision at Easter. Dublin: Progress House, 1960.
Mourn the Ivy Leaf. Dublin: Progress House, 1965.

Lady Gregory

Guari, or My First Play. London: E. Matthews & Marrot, 1930; Dublin: The Cuala Press, 1931.
Irish Folk-History Plays. 2 vols. London & New York: Putnam's, 1912.
New Comedies. London & New York: Putnam's, 1913.
The Golden Apple. London: John Murray, 1916.
The Jester. London & New York: Putnam's, 1919.
The Dragon. Dublin: The Talbot Press, 1920; London: Putnam's, 1920.
The Image and Other Plays. London & New York: Putnam's, 1920.
Seven Short Plays. London & New York: Putnam's, 1923.
Three Wonder Plays. London & New York: Putnam's, 1923.
The Story Brought by Brigit. London & New York: Putnam's, 1924.
Three Last Plays. London & New York: Putnam's, 1928.
Our Irish Theatre [memoir]. New York: Putnam's, 1914.
Lady Gregory's Journals, ed. Lennox Robinson. New York: Macmillan, 1947.

BIBLIOGRAPHY

Coxhead, Elizabeth. *Lady Gregory.* New York: Harcourt, Brace, 1961.
——. *J. M. Synge and Lady Gregory.* New York: London House, 1962.
Robinson, Lennox. "Lady Gregory," in *The Irish Theatre,* ed. Robinson. London: Macmillan, 1939, 55–64.

Gerard Healy

The Black Stranger. Dublin: James Duffy, 1950.
Thy Dear Father. Dublin: P. J. Bourke, 1957.

W. D. Heppenstall

Two on a String. Birr: The Midland Tribune, n.d.

Denis Johnston

The Old Lady Says "No!" and Other Plays. Boston: Atlantic–Little, Brown, 1960. (Contains also *The Scythe and the Sunset, A Fourth for Bridge, The Moon in the Yellow River, The Dreaming Dust,* and *Strange Occurrence on Ireland's Eye,* as well as valuable introductions by the author.)
Storm Song and A Bride for the Unicorn: Two Plays. London: Jonathan Cape, 1935.
Blind Man's Buff [after Ernst Toller]. London: Jonathan Cape, 1938.
The Golden Cuckoo and Other Plays. London: Jonathan Cape, 1954.
Nine Rivers from Jordan [war memoir]. London: Derek Verschoyle, 1953.
"What Has Happened to the Irish," *Theatre Arts,* XLIII (July, 1959), 11–12.
"That's Show Business," *Theatre Arts,* XLIV (February, 1960), 82–83.
"The College Theatre — Why?," *Theatre Arts,* XLIV (August, 1960), 12–15.
"Sean O'Casey," *The Nation,* CXCIX (October 5, 1964), 198.

John B. Keane

Sive. Dublin: Progress House, 1959.
Sharon's Grave. Dublin: Progress House, 1960. (Also in Hogan's *Seven Irish Plays, 1946–1964.*)
The Highest House on the Mountain. Dublin: Progress House, 1961.
Many Young Men of Twenty. Dublin: Progress House, 1961. (Also in Hogan's *Seven Irish Plays, 1946–1964.*)
The Man from Clare. Cork: The Mercier Press, 1962.
The Year of the Hiker. Cork: The Mercier Press, 1962.
The Field. Cork: The Mercier Press, 1967.
The Street and Other Poems. Dublin: Progress House, 1961.
Strong Tea [essays]. Cork: The Mercier Press, 1963.
Self Portrait [autobiography]. Cork: The Mercier Press, 1964.
Letters of a Successful T.D. Cork: The Mercier Press, 1967.

Hugh Leonard (Pseudonym of John Keyes Byrne)

Stephen D. London: Evans Brothers, 1963.
The Poker Session. London: Evans Brothers, 1964.
Mick and Mick [new title, *All the Nice People*] in *Plays and Players,* XIV (December, 1966), 31–46.
(Also many reviews in the English magazine *Plays and Players.*)

The Earl of Longford (Edward Arthur Henry Pakenham)

Yahoo. Dublin: Hodges, Figgis, [1934]. (Also in Canfield's *Plays of Changing Ireland.*)
Armlet of Jade. Dublin: Hodges, Figgis, 1935.
Ascendancy. Dublin: Hodges, Figgis, [1935].
The Vineyard. Dublin: Hodges, Figgis, [1943].

Trans. *The Oresteia*, by Aeschylus. Dublin: Hodges, Figgis, 1933.
Trans. *The School for Wives*, by Molière. Dublin: Hodges, Figgis, 1948.
Poems from the Irish. Dublin: Hodges, Figgis, 1944; Oxford: B. H. Blackwell, 1944.
More Poems from the Irish. Dublin: Hodges, Figgis, 1945; Oxford: B. H. Blackwell, 1945.
The Dove in the Castle, A Collection of Poems from the Irish. Dublin: Hodges, Figgis, 1946; Oxford: B. H. Blackwell, 1946.

Christine, Countess Longford

Mr. Jiggins of Jigginstown in *Plays of Changing Ireland*, ed. Curtis Canfield. New York: Macmillan, 1936.
Lord Edward. Dublin: Hodges, Figgis, [1941].
The United Brothers. Dublin: Hodges, Figgis, 1942.
Patrick Sarsfield. Dublin: Hodges, Figgis, 1943.
The Earl of Straw. Dublin: Hodges, Figgis, [1945].
The Hill of Quirke. Dublin: P. J. Bourke, 1958.
Mr. Supple, or Time Will Tell. Dublin: P. J. Bourke, n.d.
Tankardstown. Dublin: P. J. Bourke, n.d.
Vespasian and Some of His Contemporaries [nonfiction]. Dublin: Hodges, Figgis, 1928.
Making Conversation. London: L. Stein & V. Gollancz, 1931.
Country Places. London: Victor Gollancz, 1932.
Mr. Jiggins of Jigginstown [novel]. London: Victor Gollancz, 1933.
Printed Cotton. London: Methuen, 1935.
A Biography of Dublin. London: Methuen, 1936.
(Also in recent years many book reviews in the *Irish Times*.)

John McCann

Twenty Years A-Wooing. Dublin: James Duffy, 1954.
Early and Often. Dublin: P. J. Bourke, 1956.

Donagh MacDonagh

Happy as Larry, in *Modern Verse Plays*, ed. E. Martin Browne. Harmondsworth, Middlesex: Penguin Books, 1958.
Step-in-the-Hollow in *Three Irish Plays*, ed. E. Martin Browne. Harmondsworth, Middlesex: Penguin Books, 1959.
The Hungry Grass [poems]. London: Faber, 1947.
New York Theatre Critics Reviews, 1950, ed. Rachel W. Coffin, XI (week of January 9, 1950), 394–396.

Roger McHugh

Trial at Green Street Courthouse. Dublin: Browne & Nolan, n.d.

Walter Macken

Mungo's Mansion. London: Macmillan, 1946.
Vacant Possession. London: Macmillan, 1948.
Home Is the Hero. London: Macmillan, 1953.
Twilight of a Warrior. London: Macmillan, 1956.
Quench the Moon [novel]. New York: The Viking Press, 1948.
I Am Alone [novel]. London: Macmillan, 1949.
Rain on the Wind [novel]. London: Macmillan, 1950.
The Bogman [novel]. London: Macmillan, 1952.
Sunset on the Window-Panes [novel]. London: Macmillan, 1954.

BIBLIOGRAPHY

The Green Hills and Other Stories. London: Macmillan, 1956.
Sullivan [novel]. London: Macmillan, 1957.
Seek the Fair Land [novel]. London: Macmillan, 1959.
The Silent People [novel]. London: Macmillan, 1962.
God Made Sunday and Other Stories. London: Macmillan, 1962.
The Scorching Wind [novel]. London: Macmillan, 1964.
New York Theatre Critics Reviews, 1954, ed. Rachel W. Coffin, XV (week of September 27, 1954), 307–310.

Micheál Mac Liammóir

Ill Met by Moonlight. Dublin: James Duffy, 1954.
Where Stars Walk. Dublin: Progress House, 1962.
The Importance of Being Oscar. Dublin: The Dolmen Press, 1963.
Put Money in Thy Purse [memoir]. London: Methuen, 1952.
All for Hecuba [autobiography]. Dublin: Progress House, 1961.
Theatre in Ireland, 2nd ed. Dublin: Cultural Relations Committee of Ireland, 1964.

Bryan MacMahon

Song of the Anvil in *Seven Irish Plays, 1946–1964*, ed. Robert Hogan. Minneapolis: University of Minnesota Press, 1967.
The Lion Tamer and Other Stories. New York: Dutton, 1949.
Jack O'Moora and the King of Ireland's Son. New York: Dutton, 1950.
Children of the Rainbow. New York: Dutton, 1952.
The Red Petticoat and Other Stories. New York: Dutton, 1955.
The Honey Spike. New York: Dutton, 1967.

Brinsley MacNamara (Pseudonym of John Weldon)

Look at the Heffernans! Dublin: The Talbot Press, [1929].
Margaret Gillan. London: Allen & Unwin, 1934.
Marks and Mabel. Dublin: James Duffy, 1945.
The Glorious Uncertainty. Dublin: P. J. Bourke, 1957.
The Valley of the Squinting Windows [novel]. Dublin & London: Maunsel, 1918.
The Clanking of Chains. Dublin & London: Maunsel, 1920.
The Mirror in the Dusk. Dublin & London: Maunsel & Roberts, 1921.
The Smiling Faces and Other Stories. London: Mandrake Press, 1929.
The Various Lives of Marcus Igoe. London: Sampson Low, 1929.
Return to Ebontheever. London: Jonathan Cape, 1930.
Othello's Daughter. London: Mellifont Press, [1942].
Some Curious People. Dublin: The Talbot Press, 1945.
Michael Caravan. Dublin: The Talbot Press, 1946.
Abbey Plays, 1899–1948. Dublin: At the Sign of the Three Candles, [1949].
The Whole Story of the X.Y.Z. Belfast: Carter, 1951.

Mary Manning (Mrs. Mark De Wolfe Howe, Jr.)

Youth's the Season...? in *Plays of Changing Ireland*, ed. Curtis Canfield. New York: Macmillan, 1936.
Passages from Finnegans Wake by James Joyce. Cambridge, Massachusetts: Harvard University Press, 1957. (Also published as *The Voices of Shem*.)
Mount Venus [novel]. Boston: Houghton Mifflin, 1938.
Lovely People [novel]. Boston: Houghton Mifflin, 1953.

Rutherford Mayne (Pseudonym of Samuel John Waddell)

The Drone. Dublin: Maunsel, 1909.
The Troth. Dublin: Maunsel, 1909.

Bridge Head. London: Constable, 1939. (Also in Canfield's *Plays of Changing Ireland.*)

The Turn of the Road. Dublin: James Duffy, 1950.

Peter. Dublin: James Duffy, 1964.

Maurice Meldon

Aisling. Dublin: Progress House, 1959.

House under Green Shadows. Dublin: Progress House, 1962.

Purple Path to the Poppy Field in *New World Writing, Fifth Mentor Selection.* New York: New American Library, 1954.

Michael J. Molloy

The King of Friday's Men. Dublin: James Duffy, 1953.

The Paddy Pedlar. Dublin: James Duffy, 1954.

The Will and the Way. Dublin: P. J. Bourke, n.d.

Old Road. Dublin: Progress House, 1961.

The Wood of the Whispering. Dublin: Progress House, 1961.

Daughter from over the Water. Dublin: Progress House, 1963.

The Bitter Pill in *Prizewinning Plays of 1964.* Dublin: Progress House, 1965.

The Visiting House in *Seven Irish Plays, 1946–1964,* ed. Robert Hogan. Minneapolis: University of Minnesota Press, 1967.

Lane, Temple. "The Dramatic Arrival of M. J. Molloy," *Irish Writing,* No. 11 (May, 1950), 59–65.

New York Theatre Critics Reviews, 1951, ed. Rachel W. Coffin, XII (week of February 26, 1951), 334–336.

John Murphy

The Country Boy. Dublin: Progress House, 1963.

T. C. Murray

Birthright. Dublin: Maunsel, 1911.

Maurice Harte. Dublin: Maunsel, 1912.

Spring and Other Plays. Dublin: The Talbot Press, 1917.

Aftermath. Dublin: The Talbot Press, 1922.

Autumn Fire. London: Allen & Unwin, 1925.

The Pipe in the Fields and Birthright. London: Allen & Unwin, [1928].

Michaelmas Eve. London: Allen & Unwin, [1932].

Maurice Harte and A Stag at Bay. London: Allen & Unwin, 1934.

"George Shiels, Brinsley MacNamara, Etc.," in *The Irish Theatre,* ed. Lennox Robinson. London: Macmillan, 1939, 119–146.

Spring Horizon [novel]. London: [Nelson Novels], 1937.

Connolly, T. L. "T. C. Murray, the Quiet Man," *Catholic World,* CXC (March, 1960), 364–369.

Ó h Aodha, Micheál. "T. C. Murray – Dramatist," *Plays and Places.* Dublin: Progress House, 1961, 18–30.

Sean O'Casey

Selected Plays. New York: George Braziller, 1955.

The Bishop's Bonfire. New York: Macmillan, 1955.

Collected Plays. 4 vols. New York: St. Martin's Press, 1957.

The Drums of Father Ned. New York: St. Martin's Press, 1960.

Nannie's Night Out and *Kathleen Listens In* in *Feathers from the Green Crow* (see listing below).

Behind the Green Curtains. New York: St. Martin's Press, 1961. (Contains also *Figuro in the Night* and *The Moon Shines on Kylenamoe*.)
Windfalls [miscellany]. London: Macmillan, 1934.
The Flying Wasp [dramatic criticism]. London: Macmillan, 1937.
The Green Crow [miscellany]. New York: George Braziller, 1956.
Mirror in My House [autobiography]. 2 vols. New York: Macmillan, 1956.
Feathers from the Green Crow, ed. Robert Hogan. Columbia: University of Missouri Press, 1962; London: Macmillan, 1963.
Under a Coloured Cap [essays]. New York: St. Martin's Press, 1963.
Blasts and Benedictions, ed. Ronald Ayling. London: Macmillan, 1967; New York: St. Martin's Press, 1967.
Ayling, Ronald, ed. *O'Casey: Modern Judgments Series*. London: Macmillan, 1967.
Cowasjee, Saros. *Sean O'Casey, The Man Behind the Plays*. Edinburgh: Oliver & Boyd, 1963; New York: St. Martin's Press, 1964.
Fallon, Gabriel. *Sean O'Casey, The Man I Knew*. London: Routledge & Kegan Paul, 1965.
Hogan, Robert. *The Experiments of Sean O'Casey*. New York: St. Martin's Press, 1960.
Krause, David. *Sean O'Casey; The Man and His Work*. London: MacGibbon & Kee, 1960; New York: Macmillan, 1960.
McCann, Sean, ed. *The World of Sean O'Casey*. London: The New English Library, 1966. (An uneven collection of essays and reminiscence ranging from the splenetic denigration of Anthony Butler to a superb memoir of David Krause.)

Frank O'Connor (Pseudonym of Michael O'Donovan)

In the Train in *The Genius of the Irish Theatre*, ed. Sylvan Barnet *et al*. New York: New American Library, 1960.
The Art of the Theatre. Dublin & London: Maurice Fridberg, 1947.

Joseph O'Conor

The Iron Harp in *Three Irish Plays*, ed. E. Martin Browne. Baltimore: Penguin, 1959.

Harry O'Donovan

O'Dea Laughs. Dublin: P. J. Bourke, n.d.

John O'Donovan

The Shaws of Synge Street, ed. Robert Hogan. Dixon, California: Proscenium Press, 1966.
Copperfaced Jack in *Seven Irish Plays, 1946–1964*, ed. Robert Hogan. Minneapolis: University of Minnesota Press, 1967.
Shaw and the Charlatan Genius [biography]. Dublin: The Dolmen Press, 1965.

Sean O'Faolain

She Had To Do Something. London: Jonathan Cape, 1938.

Seamus O'Neill

The Secret of the Island. Dublin: Progress House, 1965.

Lennox Robinson

The Cross-Roads. Dublin: Maunsel, [1910].
The Clancy Name. Dublin: Maunsel, 1911.

Two Plays: Harvest and The Clancy Name. Dublin: Maunsel, 1911.
Patriots. Dublin: Maunsel, 1912.
The Dreamers. London & Dublin: Maunsel, 1915.
The Lost Leader. Dublin: Thomas Kiersey, 1918; Belfast: Carter, 1954.
Crabbed Youth and Age. London & New York: Putnam's, 1924.
The Round Table. London & New York: Putnam's, 1924.
The Whiteheaded Boy. London & New York: Putnam's, 1925.
The White Blackbird and Portrait. Dublin & Cork: The Talbot Press, [1926].
Plays. London: Macmillan, 1928.
The Big House. London: Macmillan, 1928.
Give a Dog —. London: Macmillan, 1928.
Ever the Twain. London: Macmillan, 1930.
The Far-Off Hills. London: Chatto & Windus, 1931; New York: Samuel French, 1941.
Is Life Worth Living? or Drama at Inish. London: Macmillan, 1933; rev. ed. New York: Samuel French, 1938.
More Plays. London: Macmillan, 1935. (Contains *Church Street* and *All's Over, Then?*)
Killycreggs in Twilight and Other Plays. London: Macmillan, 1939. (Contains also *Is Life Worth Living?* and *Bird's Nest.*)
The Lucky Finger. New York: Samuel French, [1949].
Never the Time and the Place and Crabbed Youth and Age. Belfast: Carter, 1953.
Curtain Up, An Autobiography. London: Michael Joseph, 1942.
O'Neill, Michael J. *Lennox Robinson.* New York: Twayne, 1964.
Starkie, Walter. "Lennox Robinson: 1886–1958," *Theatre Annual*, XV (1958), 7–19.

David Sears

Juggernaut. Birr: The Midland Tribune, 1952.
Hayes, J. J. "A New Irish Playwright," New York *Times*, May 19, 1929, Section 9, p. 3.

George Shiels

Bedmates. Dublin: Gael Co-operative Society, 1922.
Two Irish Plays: Mountain Dew and Cartney and Kevney. London: Macmillan, 1930.
The Rugged Path and the Summit. London: Macmillan, 1942.
Three Plays: Professor Tim, Paul Twyning, The New Gossoon. London: Macmillan, 1945.
Grogan and the Ferret. Dublin: Golden Eagle Books, 1947.
Quin's Secret. Dublin: Golden Eagle Books, 1947.
Give Him a House. Dublin: Golden Eagle Books, 1947.
The Fort Field. Dublin: Golden Eagle Books, 1947.
Tenants at Will. Dublin: Golden Eagle Books, 1947.
The Old Broom. Dublin: Golden Eagle Books, 1947.
The Caretakers. Dublin: Golden Eagle Books, 1948.
Atkinson, Brooks. "The Play — *The New Gossoon*," New York *Times*, October 22, 1932, p. 18.

Joseph Tomelty

Right Again Barnum. Belfast: H. R. Carter, [1950].
Mugs and Money. Belfast: H. R. Carter, 1953.
Is the Priest at Home? Belfast: H. R. Carter, 1954.
All Souls' Night. Belfast: H. R. Carter, 1955.

BIBLIOGRAPHY

The End House. Dublin: James Duffy, 1962.
Red Is the Port Light [novel]. London: Jonathan Cape, 1948.
The Apprentice: The Story of a Nonentity [novel]. London: Jonathan Cape, 1953.

Jack B. Yeats

La La Noo in *The Genius of the Irish Theatre*, ed. Sylvan Barnet *et al.* New York: New American Library, 1960, pp. 212–244.
In Sand. Dublin: The Dolmen Press, 1964.

W. B. Yeats

The Complete Plays of W. B. Yeats. New York: Macmillan, 1953.
The Cutting of an Agate [essays]. London: Macmillan, 1919.
Plays and Controversies [essays]. London: Macmillan, 1923.
Dramatis Personae [essays]. Garden City, New York: Doubleday Anchor Book, 1958.
Bradford, Curtis B. *Yeats at Work.* Carbondale: Southern Illinois Press, 1965.
Clark, David R. *W. B. Yeats and the Theatre of Desolate Reality.* Dublin: The Dolmen Press, 1965.
Gerstenberger, Donna. "Yeats and the Theatre: A Selected Bibliography," *Modern Drama,* VI (May, 1963), 64–71.
Mercier, Vivian, "In Defence of Yeats as a Dramatist," *Modern Drama,* VIII (September, 1965), 161–166.
Modern Drama, ed. A. C. Edwards, VII (December, 1964).
Nathan, Leonard E. *The Tragic Drama of William Butler Yeats.* New York: Columbia University Press, 1965.
Saul, George Brandon. *Prolegomena to the Study of Yeats's Plays.* Philadelphia: University of Pennsylvania Press, 1958.
Ure, Peter. *Yeats the Playwright.* New York: Barnes and Noble, 1963.
Vendler, Helen H. *Yeats's Vision and the Later Plays.* Cambridge, Massachusetts: Harvard University Press, 1963.

Index

INDEX

Date Due

JY 10 75					

PRINTED IN U.S.A.   CAT.NO. 23 231